The Closest Call

A TRUE ACCOUNT OF AN ALASKAN ENCOUNTER WITH SERIAL
KILLER ISRAEL KEYES

TRUE CRIME 49

TRUE CRIME 49

THE ORIGINAL GOTHIC VERITAS

truecrime49.libsyn.com

DEDICATED TO SAMANTHA

"It's not whatcha got, it's what you give.
It ain't the life you choose, it's the life you live"

CONTENTS

AUTHOR'S NOTE

In the late 1970's, a man and a woman, Jeffery and Heidi Keyes sought out the fringes of civilization and obscure church cults in which to flourish and raise their multiplying children. Their eldest son, second born to a sister would go on to become a horrific serial killer. In his own words, "hindsight is 20/20", the ones closest to him after his sudden arrest, "they could put certain things together" he said, but-
"The only person who knows about these things, the things I'm telling you, is me".

Looking in then at it all, one can bewildered wonder, for some sense in it.

When the next of kin for Bill and Lorraine Currier, confessed victim's sister was asked if she wanted to be sheltered from the horrors uncovered of what had happened to them, with her response we can so eloquently agree. She said, "If Bill and Lorraine had to suffer through this, we can suffer through hearing about it. ….. It was important that what had happened to Bill and Lorraine in its entirety would be made public."

HINDSIGHT 20 20

Stale light upon the prison cell. Pale paint, on the beds and rails. The smell in the air, all five senses permeated. The sheet was over him, the report confirmed it. Him lying under the sheets part fetal, jerking once or twice when his skin opened up into the atmosphere. Older images flashing across the screens of his mind. He had once spoken of that wounded deer, from when he was young. It had been part laying on the ground as the boy was approaching it, holding his knife. The creature began to flop frenzy he said, while he had begun in, skinning it alive. Here in the real world the thin Gillette shard which had been peeled from his jail convenience razor, it is finally slitting in across his thick vein. Tilting the hidden cup from under the bed, it making the faintest hissing sound as the quick ribbon of iron blood is twirling down into its own thickness. So very warm rising, toward the heating brim. His smearing finger had painted diligently in the dimness. They had since confiscated his blood works on sheets of paper and they were in evidence somewhere within the compound. Vision alight in the memories he spoke of, the smash swing of his bright headlamp passing scattering over a man bound over, and his woman in terror also made to watch. The scenes that he had kept for himself, they are scratching across the air like static. The papers of his dried blood works were not to be smudged. Each paper transferred by the F B I much later, it was a photo of them all arranged. Each page was a skull of its own. Finger painted in crimson iron ink upon his cell walls. That one girl's eyes still beautiful, even scattered wild and frantic. Of each of the cinnamon skulls on the papers, seven of the 10 are smaller. One skull, its little bone caves are weeping blood.

A type of statement that makes a question.

Across all of their foreheads he has dabbed on each a rust-colored cross. On closer examination the ratios showing so clearly that the crosses are upside down. Finishing then, the 5 outer points on the pentagram with a finer detail. The more precise lines now showing a large upside-down star. The star has 10 points if you count its underarms. It becoming a perimeter, with a place for each skull and in the middle, he drew the Baphomet; The Hermaphro-Goat.

Over the jail bed rail, he had slung the sheet, tying a swinging cradle from up and over in which he slipped in his long hanging leg. The sheet is twisting tighter as the lights are fading from the screen behind his eyes. The neat line of cups under the bunk are now mostly full. Heavy leg, finally beginning to sag. There wet and so close to him, the first paper. The pen ink is still there, but it has become soaked. The sun speckled breeze is there, coming softly through the tree boughs. As it says in that letter,
 "The sun shone through onto highlights of red"
the breeze,   it
felt like forever.

Creaking, pulling up more cinching upon his cooling neck. The largest skull, across its bottom it says in shaking finger swiping,

"We are One"

14

CHAPTER ONE

CAVE PUDDLES

The first time that Israel Keyes approached me, he was in what the F B I would catalog later as a "Cellular Blackout" period. Turning his phone on briefly once having returned home to Anchorage, Alaska to make casual contact, then disabling the signal for days, as he would do.

     We were face to face, when I could finally turn my back to him and walk away, life was appearing in a charade, while I was behind some thick curtain looking out. Ignoring anything else then, feeling honey drunk, driving out of Anchorage and the memory smearing until pulling up into our gravel driveway. My wife coming out and around to the truck, the door was propped open. Her saying that she had seen me through the glass and that she knew something had happened in town. Her eyes starting in with sly humor maybe, however her sentence ending with the outer rings of her eyes flaring and that I had better tell her something! Addressing me by name, "Joe! You are sitting there in full Werewolf Mode?" and I agreed with her. I told her that nothing had happened, but there was this guy and he had appeared out of nowhere.

     Earlier that morning in Anchorage, I had gone to that building, it used to be a conventional 6 plex. The south garage, approaching it when first coming through the tall fence. The inside of this garage had been made into a part common area. The big overhead doors were closed and freshly painted, always appearing readily maintained and smooth but I had been notified from the inside that they had been sealed off from the outside. The various reasons that people would add boards and screws to fasten those big doors in place like that. Now inside the yard, closing the big gate of the tight slat cedar fence, the privacy fence was high enough that you would have needed a ladder to scale it. Along the wall of that garage and I was approaching the man door that was already swung in and open. When I saw it, there was a clang inside me down in the cradle of my guts. It felt as if the door was both welcoming me and warning me from within. Stopping briefly across its open frame as if I was just passing by. The large inside of that garage seemed vacant and I said aloud and flatly "doing some repairs". The sunlight angling, all was still and quiet, in there. Wanting to tread with a light touch, letting only my eye brow and part of my cheek bone dip in, but my shadow was casting halfway across the floor into this darkish setting already and I was all illuminated and glowing out there on the sidewalk, it was the mid-morning sun. The entire time down inside me a warning of such intensity, so faint like the lost spelunker. Deep underground, hollering out down there, foolish ropes and cave gear. But after a few bends, the cries are only coming in as notions. Of not really being sure but that horrible feeling that you probably didn't make it out.

While I continued around the large building Inspecting from the outside, perhaps without having to enter the premises.

While crunching along out there squinting through a snow-cast world bathed white in sunlight, my mind was crafting observations of what I had seen when I had walked by. I had looked into that part utility, part hang-out that was sheltering two laundry machines from a half year of the bitter cold. The door open and left swung into the dimness. The strong morning light was beautiful. In the large, dim and part cluttered area the sliding locks on the big garage doors were still bristling on their edges and they were locked and in the engaged position; but they were nonsensical now and in fact: stranded.

Like Lorraine's .38 caliber pistol was. Little thunder heart, it was laying just over there in the drawer of her nightstand, it might as well had been a hundred miles away.

On one side, trying to craft an answer from something so entrancing and then there was that other thing about the Electrical panel being somewhere, but it wasn't.

Walking all around the long building's sides, all the way to where I was on the backside of that sealed off garage. Just through the wall were the laundry machines that I had seen in there, from the other side now. Then higher up on the wall out there than I would have expected was the chimney pipe for the boiler. Metal pipes blowing poison steam up the wall by code. Knowing that somewhere in there on the other side of that long tall wall was a: submarine type of room with the large clicking hum heater in it and electrical wires converging like air traffic control. A room most people never see.

Coming back now, close along the long walls. From under the roof eave two stories above me I would be seen stepping in my own little rat trail footprints running back and forth now in the shallowest snow for the sake of trying to keep my shoes dry. Coming all the way back around and seeing the commitment approaching and just about to pass that open door again. Preferring to walk right out to my truck and get in and drive off like it was a comedy, but it was just a shadowed narrow alley out there. I had tried a few times already to get out of this favor, but I had said that I would do it. To at least take a look at this one as I had politely declined a few times already. It would be bad business not to come over and give an estimate for a solution at least, how could I not.

There was nothing evident why I should feel this way. Making the decision feeling I was ready and stepping in directly mid stride, down into it expecting a rodeo chute, but when I went in it was like I went in under water. Floating there in the blinding light, it felt so reckless. I slid out of the light lens as fast as I had slid in and I tucked just off to the side of that brilliant portal. Standing part there behind part of its halo of light. The dim interior seemed to ebb as my eyes glowed down into the room. Over there emerging from the fog of the sun glare were the laundry machine's shoulders. The sunlight was casting in blazing empty across the floor. I couldn't put my finger on it but it felt so immediate and that my presence was an intrusion into something, something that would be called by something like: Intrusion.

Less than 3 feet into that room, doing a favor for someone.

Having stopped in, outside of everyone's routine. Expecting emptiness at this hour and it appeared to be so. It felt like a car wreck in molasses, was crashing. My eyes scanning the outer walls. Passing over the maintenance shelves. There was a snapshot of this 55-gallon cardboard drum in the far corner, once used for shipping dry laundry detergent. It has been sitting stuffed with cross country skis and ski poles. The sunlight over the world becoming silver-Kodachrome edged; I was catching freeze frames. The dormant stuff and the forgotten shelving were leering at me. I was realizing there was something and it was somewhere behind me. Turning away from the outside wall. The electrical panel should be here somewhere on "the party wall" a snapshot across the room, there was a very odd window that was high on the wall near the ceiling just beyond the laundry machines. It was up there very short and very wide.

We are all endowed with diversities in our complex. Israel sure was.

Cable wires emanating from everywhere behind the last shelving but finally, no panel. So, I stood there. My knees were almost at the back of the couch. There was such a strange vibe in the room. Staring through it all I was now free to go, but I held on there for a while.

When you are in the presence of something that you know you've never seen before. The mind observing rings appearing on a wine glass as the small plum pool is evaporating in increments. Soaking in this darkening irony that I had been looking for something, here in the real world.

Hidden in the shadow from the light wash of that glowing door, at that exact moment if I had looked straight down the back of the couch, there on the cushions in front of my knees was his backpack, it was open and part undone.

Instantly the silence was broken by a tumble thudding down the stairs? His shoes came into view at my eyeball height, he was running down the treads as fast as you can without pounding them. Appearing all at once, revealing that there is a set of blind stairs on the other side of the washer and dryer. One lady had reported that when he had worked on her home, she remarked at Israel's incredible physical strength. That it was graceful and surprising. The crown of his skull is

18

passing in front of me. Looking through this startled homeowner or renter he was moving towards me and concerning the look on his face approaching? Was there a blip in the transmission? I had moved already, leaning over, and looking up to where he had just come down from. The rising treads came out hidden on the other side of the laundry machines. They were still barely noticeable and so clearly now remembering the flat window high on the wall above them and just out there in the bright sunlight there was the boiler chimney higher off the ground than I would've expected. There was a short dead-end landing up those steps and a door back there and it felt so desolate.

It was a freeze frame of the top of the short stairs.

There were no other ankles up there.

He was passing before me on the concrete slab. But there had been no lead up of footsteps in the small hidden hallway up there. The startling sound had tumbled down onto the first wooden step from the start. I didn't acknowledge his physical space and he was a blur. When I turned back from the tip toe angle, he was standing on the other side of the couch across from me already. He must've snatched up the bag with one hand while I had side stepped over to examine up at those stairs and what was up there. I'd never known either were there until now and he was clutching the satchel with his one hand. The other hand was down into the bag up to his wrist and they were so still in there, in front of the flat part of his upper belly.

I brought my eyes onto his chest at panel height. With a disdain and annoyance, he said "I'd better get my bag!" hands already there though. It sounded rash and barely out of place. There was an energy in the air. It was so pressing. When I came up his chest and slowly up his neck, stopping at the flat plateau just beneath his eyes. He was making some strange expression. A look, gritting and menacing it might've been, the inside of my torso was blooming up and opening and the eyes feel like they are becoming exotic blade metal. I went up to just before the brim of his eyes and held it there.

Grease smearing on the lenses of the background,
Hearing the breaths, after seeing their chest move.
A slit razor of emotion coming up from within me.
The mind is residing in the eyes now.
Becoming purer and more unhindered.
Becoming clear and free of all of the monkey rules for the people.

He would have heard me announce myself from the glowing doorway.

He would have been waiting at the top of the stairs then, while I was turning.

I saw what felt like soft edged holes sunk into his cheekbones and looking in I felt instantly draped in the cold skin. Continuing back down in one movement in the peripheral I saw his neck and it was there larger on his chest too. I saw by feel something part transparent, an overlay complexion of what could be described as Cave Rot.

CHAPTER TWO

6/7 TALL GRASSES FLASHING

Just like on the sky maps, the Google Earth had shown the intended route upon a Thruway, running across the whole of the state of New York. It would pass on eventually to some colloquial road up into Maine, heading East.

He is there with everyone else, him in his rental car. There on the gliding lanes twisting like a slow ribbon. The angle of every curve of these massive road systems have long been penciled onto large sheets of paper and onto obsessive sets of drawings, dictated by some Federal D O T engineering code or mandate. Opening the rolled sets of plans, everywhere little frantic notes as some reminder of some nuance not to be missed later. The carrying away of anything worthwhile of the landscape. Some set of little hills, shaved off! Just to be thrown into the voids. Those little hills used to squint at the dawn together. Their shadows slowly sweeping around themselves. Sometimes the forms would overlap in the dimness. They would have been one at times. They are still part of the landscape though; they are there underneath it. He is gliding over the flattening lands formed contoured by epochs of moving water. Becoming more excited now, hearing it for yourself in his own voice there in the tapes. Israel recalled it for the F B I there at the table under the fluorescent lighting. They had the power to grant the Death Penalty and he wanted it completed in one year's time. Then he would give them all the "gory details" is what he had said and we had a taste of it while he told us what he had almost said to Bill, when coming down the stairs in that old abandoned farmhouse. To finding him standing in the basement in the dark. When Bill was trying to reason with him squinting up at the headlamp. That he wanted to tell Bill that
"You don't realize how much planning I've put into this"

The last part being a blurting out of nervous laughter on the tapes.

It would've overtaken him on the freeway in an emotion that would've had to scratch itself all the way up through the constructs he has built to compartmentalize everything in there. The various caverns on the way up. Filling these haunts from the outside and he is triggering now. The glands are at least, and the hormones and the complex proteins are raining down onto the receptors in his mind, in the vivid memory they are alight in a wash of cascading lights. A recognized and familiar state of being, it is one that could be considered rare, and reckless with passion and of course very private.

Blurry visions, like passing and recognizing an opportunity out there on the miles and miles of the highways. Looking back in the rearview for the reflection though it is distorted and moving. He had described of when he knew he was "losing control" he had said. Like when all of the flashing warnings that: he should have gotten rid of her weeks ago. These things are fighting up through the makeup. It wasn't working any more, he said. He knew that from the smell he had to get rid of her but the heaters had been so quiet and "she was so warm". He trailed off, very matter of factly. Up through the things that even if he ever needed a type of justification it came up through those too. He said,

"The only people who know anything about these things that I'm telling you is me".

When he said it, it sounded nasally, but as it sinks in, it sounds heavier and deeper each time.

However far back the counting down of the exits had begun for him, the countdown was now approaching zero. The first sign is approaching.

It would be assumed, driving on and on crossing through the rural state border an hour and some later. Coming over into the sleepy watersheds of Vermont. The waters collecting larger and larger, eventually becoming the Winooski River. The grasses are tall and natural, it appears that in the past the county road crew would have driven by with a tractor mower once every 4 months or so. This "financial crisis" settling in, rippling in the delay of services even. The clicking bugs momentarily blurred out by a breeze moving across the tops of the tall wild grasses, June 7, 2011.

A cloud sliding across the heavens, underneath it is a spot on the earth that is made up of darkness. It is moving over the trees and the farm scapes. Just across from the big bend in the river, there is a neighborhood.

There is that large blue stand-up pool in the backyard of, that one. The one of the many, the blue pool is glowing in sunlight. The dark line of shade is creeping across the turquoise, then now cooling across it. The bugs begin the rattle clicking, chanting for an abundance louder now as the light dimming. The river is there. Part in the sun moving back and forth in soft switch backs that shimmer twinkle. There is a road between the two, reducing the endless curves of the river into one sweeping arc. The shadow enveloping the river park now. The darkness falls on the Woodside Natural Area. There on the old bend of what used to be the old river. The trail leading down through it and on further there, is the edge of the new river. The cloud's shadow departs and dissolves away in the sun, squinting and drying everything it had cast upon. The breeze and the clouds reminding again, that everything is alone down by the river. There is a small rental car all the way out here parked off to the side hidden, in a hidden lane. The car's mirrors are in the soft tall grasses. Wisps of off gasses, measured in flow rate, are pressing out from the new rental carpets and interiors, all of those insulators of the glimmering wires. They knew from the start the ingredients going in would be exotic and expensive. The most slippery and elusive of them wafting up now in the new car smell, low enough to not make your eyes water on the dealership floor, but almost.

The trunk must've been opened swiftly and something having been tossed in quickly, the trunk lid clunking closed. The tall weeds already rocking as the car door must've opened and then slipped closed again, there is that backpack. It is held low down by the legs as it swings in landing gently on the passenger floorboard.

There is a mustiness, there is a staleness, creeping up into those pristine gasses. It was atmosphere that had been suffocated in darkness, as seasons had passed. Moistures trapped in the exchange of hissing pressures balancing so very slowly and absolutely persistent. Them pushing up into everywhere and anywhere. The lid of the buried kill kit gasps popping open, shining in the blinding light now. Eventually everything inside was dry but musty he said. Finally looking down into his collection of guns and the other contents of a Kill Cache, we saw him put his finger on only a photo of one of them, the photo was taken just after it had been opened. In his last expose', at the end of the interrogation he had asked to see that photo paper again and he went into his mind and there was such a strange passion in his eyes. Looking down into all of those Steal, Rape and Kill pieces stacked tightly waiting for him. Re-digging up the kill kit here from how long before, it is at his feet and he would've felt flooded with emotion.

The Satchel is now breathing out the gasping dank from its contents, like a bagpipe it is off key for now. It will acclimate. This one would later be cataloged as the Winooski River Kill Cache.

In the notes for the next day's interrogation, would have been written down every way to try and pin down the location or regions or how many of these things are there? All of the slick ways to inquire and he summed the answer up so glib that,
Israel Keyes said when he was a kid, he always wanted to find buried treasure, but it was basically impossible. He had waited for the timing in the delivery looking side to side

"So, I decided to make my own" and he cackles on the tape.

"The idea is to have something everywhere you go", shrugging his shoulders and all of the lead up just lingered in the air.

The motor starts with the sureness of any new airport 2011 rental. This kit retrieved having heard muffled from under the hidden earth the rattling hum of the county mower passing by along the shoulder at least 6 times or more since he had buried it there in 2009.

Driving away, pulling out of the tall grass alley, immediately appearing again to be some gray hair, turned around out here in the fringe. What is he doing? He is supposed to be enroute to Maine to help his brothers.

Appearing suddenly, waiting to pull out from the side of and directly onto a bustling highway. The highway arcs around the curving river; the little car is loaded like a bow and arrow. The traffic slows and the little rental slips out across the big lanes. Inside the car nearly microscopic black mold spores are spiraling up soft and recklessly. Before being zipped out the rush of the window, the air smearing them wagging ragged and gone in an instant.

THE CLOSEST CALL

CHAPTER THREE

369

He sounds sleepy then coming to life that he may have driven their car back to his hotel then driven it and parked it in the big store parking lot, it was a pharmacy back then. Then he said he walked back to his hotel. After he packed up all of his stuff he calmly checked out. He then drove his car to the Home Depot parking lot, leaving "that Bag" in his rental. On the tapes there is a building of momentum that suddenly falls from the air and it finishes in the room with nothing.

GIVE US ANOTHER BODY, ISRAEL

The one man at the table is bending the rules. He wants to be so close to this thing. His frothy mouth wanting to stammer so bad he has clutched his power pen. Little yard dog is smelling the estrus, it is coming from something, somewhere in this interrogation room. On the tapes you can almost see him with your ears every time he must be seeing himself in the future in his own eyes. His little pelvis beginning to bump. It starts sure as a creaking, just wanting to get up in there a little, wherever it is. The thing is slapping on his belly and the leg of the table then his eyes coming out of it a diminishing bloodshot in the sudden realization and gathering his composure again because.

Alaska Airlines Flight (Anchorage Alaska to Chicago, Illinois) June 2, 2011. The Engines are running up vibrating over the concrete. They are quietly humming and they are already so warm on the long end of the runway. The 737 is glistening in light off of its flat shiny surfaces and the intruder is nestling into his seat.

On the bend of the old river where is the Woodside Natural Area, it is a River Park. If there out the taxiing window, looking over and down into the dry brush you could see the Intruder, peering around as he had said
"It was about 500 yards from my hotel"

Him acting as if he was fishing for a while, he had on his possession a two-day fishing license for this area it was crisp and new. When he was arrested later it was still there in his wallet (279 days expired) moving haplessly through the tall grasses but then looking around and once he felt he was "comfortable" he said, swiftly kneeling to retrieve the Kill Kit. As his knees touching down to the damp earth, the Pilot then pushing all those levers forward.

The engines would rage inward sucking the air from within themselves, the seat cupping your weight and soon the Indicated airspeed in knots is approaching 80. Feeling those tires wobble as they pass by it. Roaring through it recklessly.

Seeing periodically in the snap blinking lights that are flashing on the massive wheels, realizing that they are spitting water, in a mist mohawk.

The big bend of the river going backward now in the first second. The river Park was just below this boulevard, looking like a crossbow the plane accelerating across it. Over the intersection down the road 2.5 seconds looking out the portside window, it is the Home Depot, that is the side to the left. 4 seconds in and out of the right side passing, it was the old Rite-Aid store back then. A bit farther back in the neighborhood is the Handy Suites. They will go out of business in the next few years. The turbines accelerating, the aircraft begins to stiffen. The wings were hanging down but now they are rooting themselves into the airframe down in there. The tips pointing up firm. Zooming mathematically directly over Susie Wilson Rd. They were close enough to almost see their house, for the trees. It becomes instantly a country corridor. Moving directly through massive sections of forest. At roughly 1.2 miles and there is a very unassuming intersection down there with the Vermont 2A: heading North and South. Further then into more nothingness, becoming a blur and as the snap blinking lights on the wheel's in Indicated airspeed is approaching 145. On this aircraft it is V1: Decision Velocity. Blasting by the last chance to turn back at 146. It is just a notion really, the

release from gravity and lifting into the air. Moments then and they would be clearing the intersection where it connects to the 15. It becomes wilderness up past there, looking back you could see the exit ramp that he took heading back toward town. There is the putt-putt down there and then a long stretch of nothing but trees really.
This is the spot where you are dead if anything goes wrong.

At 150 knots indicated airspeed the pilot rotates the nose upward and it is lifting and moving away. The glide up is pushing you down. It is over you so completely. The hand rest is shaking into the clouds rattling. A flashing light coming through a few times before it is gone. The sound of the roar though is somewhere and it is everywhere.

He came back into town passing the Starbucks in front of the new Lowes and he wasn't quite sure but then he sounds certain that he had loaded everything back into the car at that point. That bag with the "stuff" he says. The empty jugs of Drano and that "somehow I got that back over to the Hotel"

CHAPTER FOUR

COLDMAN STOVE

The F B I's bright searchlights scanning in the darkness across the gathering line of the high tides, sifting through all the archived registries and scanning all the old logs. Shining down into the oblique waters, their light cone scanning as a blurry spotlight of midday. Down into the ocean trying to peer through swaying sea grasses for his movements, purchases, plane tickets, departing ANC on 6/2 landing in O'Hare in Chicago the baggage sticker knowing it as ORD. When you leave really early on a Thursday it is also basically really late Wednesday night too. Receipts, like the one from the store after getting his rental there in Illinois, the searchlight clanging back that it was in Des Plaines. Driving East by Southeast, this leg of the trip terminating in Harlan, Indiana some 176.6 miles away. Pulling into a rural setting a slick anxiousness growing in the car. Rock bumping as he put it in park, arriving at his Mother's house. The timeline and the interviews relaying that Mother took him to a store and set him up with some things for the long travel. Heading to be seen of his brothers, waiting for him at the old Maple Farm all the way over in Maine. She had bought him some camping supplies at a local store and she also told them that while her son was there for a short visit with her that he had to leave a few times to "visit a friend" he had told her. The searchlight diligently banging upon even the smallest of any sardine flashes in the darkness until finding nothing more. Eventually zooming out then on the satellite imagery you see there are "Multiple Road Toll Transactions" that he had made coming across the top of Indiana in a relative straight line. The thing is that on that line, Israel only paid for about 60% of the expected toll charges? She said that he departed and as any dust was settling from his road car, he was headed up on the long sojourn to help his brothers up near Grandma's old place. More than halfway there 753 miles from Mother now and still yet 391 miles short of his brothers and the invisible beeping across the maps slows. This part Amish kid who had part fed his family for a time with endless venison that he had been made to poach from off of some federal reserve or something wherever they had lived where the Canadian border moves with the fog in the cold trees. The part Amish kid sent out to feed the brood, in the moonlight. Eventually sensing the devil's cities out there on the wind from a distance. Their skyline's towers are washing the horizon in brilliant "signal" light. And he goes right to the outer edge of them. Out here, the rural up and downs in the lay of the land shows tower fatigue. It makes sunshade in what must be ink black depressions in the "coverage". Some hills stretching black from the distant crackling light. It shows shadows over lapping in a double "dead spot". Then he pops up on the grid and makes sure to purchase a 2-day Fishing license for the immediate area and then it all goes black down in there.

CHAPTER FIVE

6/8

June 8, 2011   The hum of the bedroom fan running in the darkness.

He had cut the phone lines in the dark even before he had nestled in. Leaning against their above ground pool in the backyard 2 hours ago. The pool makes this really weird giant model of an eardrum. The crisp ticking of a blade in the neighbor's AC unit on the other side of the house ricocheting out from behind and over the bushes. Moving around grunt slowly, allowing blood to flow through every large set of muscles in turn. If there were going to be any flashing lights or security call outs, he said, "they never came". The pool out there deleting him acoustically. The neighbor's dog was unsettled that night though, it said in the report.
It was very hot out and humid that night, he insists. Did he take it too far?

He remembered it for them at the table per the latest security protocols. He was in "manacles" and you can hear him rubbing the chains and those heavy bracelets over and over as he is seeing it again in his mind. The wood was becoming smooth on the chair. It had made it into the report, the chains had worn the wood down and it was noticeably more parabolic.
He knows that he did.

The scent of linens in the dark, of some random older couple's bedrooms. Everything is warm and what must be wood furniture and closet rods, heavy like curtains. Beneath the clothes, bulky leather clodding and various rubber treads. The air is drifting slowly, the faint smell of her husband's cologne bottle. Pulled out clinking once or twice a year. Hers in there also as the air would've been drifting towards the fan motor. They are sleeping, having settled into their routine over the years. The husband and wife dancing a slow, slow square dance. She rolls to her side and then she is even more asleep and after a while, he slumps moving after her. Their movements are like cards being played in slow motion.

The FBI playing back his voice in the interrogation. He said that he had sat out there from midnight. Nearly 2 hours behind their pool in the yard. Listening for all the neighbors to go to sleep and listening to the bedroom fan in the darkness. Revealing exactly where they must be sleeping in the layout of the unknown floor plan. He said how he had moved in and out of their garage over the evening. Looking through the glass of their security doors from in the dark of their garage he must've loved it. When he broke the glass and he was into their kitchen like it was the front door, it was 5 or 6 seconds before he was in the room with them and the fan, he said.

"A blitz attack" he calls it. The chains from the handcuffs can be heard rattling on the tape, as Lorraine's eyes are gasping open.

Her husband's name is hissing over her lips! The bedroom door in the darkness is gaping. A blinding light wobbling violently up the hallway, becoming slow motion. She would've started for the pistol. There had been some sound in the kitchen! Her arm snatching over and down to wake a landing hand on her husband. The headlamp was already upon her "yanking everything off the bed" he recalled. Her face was frantic in the blinding light suddenly. It showed the older age in the woman's skin. Her and Bill squinting blindness in the headlamp's brilliance becoming black and flashing in their eyes.
"I told them right away what was going on" "and what their roles were and that there was no talking unless" he spoke to them.

"Were they cooperative, at least, at first?"
"Yeah" He laughs and thinks for a moment and on the tape, he says" they were pretty shocked" his inflection almost with sad clown eyebrows in his voice. He blurted laugh through the next sentence "People never expect this type of stuff to happen to them" He commanded them that "there was no moving unless he said to and to put their hands behind their backs"

Then he began zip-tying their wrists. Different realities swirl pounding in their minds, as their shoulders jostle zipping click as the coming down that life is still going on for everyone else but for them.

The fear crying out, gushing up from catacombs deep inside them where they might have stored old pictures of roadkill, or snapshots of the aftermath from a Bombing at a daycare, maybe even clicking frames of Hardcore Porn where one of the poor women is made out of a man. The giant storage facility down inside of them for all the horrible things, is overloading.

Their thoughts then interrupted by the tugging as he began doing their feet also. However, in the chain of custody in the second telling after coming to certain conclusions, fixing any little glitches. He said later that he did not.

Nonchalantly watching their expressions as they crossed over each plateau, he refers to it later as "making deep the pools in your eyes with which to fill them" he rummaged the house quickly, stopping into the doorframe frequently and unexpectedly bombarding them with the same questions over and over again. Do you have an alarm system? Do you have a safe?

He says that he cycled down through the list peppering them again: where are the guns, the Jewelry, the cash, the cell phones, atm cards. When he threw it in on them a little more rash demanding about their: prescription pills? It would have then washed by them seeming some relief. Finally laying down their anticipations. He's one of those? " Methers", or whatever.

Rummaging in the house he stopped in the hallway tilted his ear. He says he heard her speaking to Bill in the dark. The lower frequencies absorbed into the mattress; the feverish plans noted to put them face down. Bound it is safer for everyone that way. The hispers clicking in the dark signaling urgency in her air voice. Having bounced ticking ricochet off the shiny flat surface of her nightstand. It would be her patience in the undertow however, that would have been frightening to him.

He says that he leapt from the doorway onto her. His weight coming down, the gaunt endless for the husband no doubt as he had landed grabbing her throat. Her head, he says, went down into the pillows. The intruder was on top of her at an upward angle over his wife on their bed right in front of him. These same elements always re-surfacing in this thing of, when it happens. Pulling from something in the deep, in the morse code in the wind chime. Something out there making these great gravities, becoming massive oscillations across the star charts of his developmental years way down in there, by the time he was the age that Christ perished at, it would have been always just below the surface for him. Among all of the others that voice over time, long ago having become the closest.

He told them that he was always watching them and nothing that they did would have any effect on what was happening to them and if they did? It would "really piss him off". The flat part of his upper belly is over the man's wife's chest and neck area. Her throat gag clucking two or three times, in the emphasis of the sentence structure. She could have been his mother.

They were in shock and in awe he said. "They were really quiet for a long time". At this point he would have been in the house roughly 10 minutes, he said. After some last preparations rummaging the rooms he came back into the frame, he had something for them. It was their own casuals for their feet, slippers, and house shoes. He had begun to move them through the kitchen. The collapsing no doubt washing in, overwhelming them when they saw the new safety door and the big double pane of tempered "safety" glass, all broken in! The tiny salt blocks of glass can still be seen scattered on the floor in the evidence photos. It crackles under foot, as Bill and Lorraine are walking now over them swiftly. The three of them are only dark flashes out of the kitchen door and into the garage. When he had grabbed their shoes for them, he had seen Bill's crowbar laying there. He had used it from the tool rack earlier in the garage. Scanning every inch later the Law enforcement had found a single thumb print of his, on its length. It was hanging back on the peg board at Bill's neat homeowner's tool bench. Lorraine is up front in the passenger side of their own car. The abductor reaches over across down at her hips. His hands go down by her lower back, down by her seat but he finally comes up having secured them with zip-ties onto their seat buckles. The forensics combing over the carpet hairs later, came across one tiny glistening block of the broken glass there on her floorboard. When he gets into their driver seat the dome light was on, they got their first look at him he says and they asked him why they were leaving the house? He says that he was bullshitting them. Telling them this was a kidnapping for ransom. That there were other people involved.

"Did you take the laundry and clothing to make it look like they went on a trip?"
the tape rolling during the investigation.

With the cut phone line and the broken door, he says
"The main reason I took the suitcases was I only had a small backpack with me. I wanted to keep their stuff separate from my stuff, I had a lot of stuff in the backpack with me. I wanted to keep their stuff separate so I could go through it later"

   "What kind of stuff did you have in your backpack?"

Israel laughs a long "Heh" it seems to glare "Nice try" then he slips away in thought. Saying quietly "I don't know……. (He seems to come to some conclusion)   I don't know if I wanna go into all that today"

CHAPTER SIX

DRANO

Being driven away from their home at 2 o'clock in the morning in their car and she is aghast. The world no doubt would have been surreal for them appearing in charade, while they were suddenly behind some thick curtain looking out. "Street lights push back the black neat rows" out there in the witching hours endless darkness but then him pulling out almost immediately and into a little hotel parking lot? It was within walking distance from their house!?

He is back there shuffling a few things from his rental car into their trunk and then thud closing it. Reciting the license plate over and over. It would have been terrifying for them in the dim glow of the trunk lid if they had seen what he had hefted in. The bundle of the large black contractor's trash bags and two one-gallon jugs of Drano. Pulling out now, the release of his foot from the brake. Feeling her body jostle against the car door out onto the road in a dip bump. The body's inertia bounce jiggles and a long sway with the rotation of the wheel under his hands. Sliding to the back of her seat it cupped her weight and stiffening her neck almost enough to keep the back of her head from bumping the headrest. She swears that she felt him gas it a little more, right before that he bumped it and he is driving again. The nagging statement of why are you holding so many cards close to the table, but showing a different one over here.

Out of their neighborhood looking for a police vehicle. Looking then for anyone. Not even in the Rite Aid parking lot. Bill had been made to lie down in the backseat zip tied down to the seat buckles. When the intruder had jumped on her chest and choked her neck in the bedroom, he said later that he had heard her talking to Bill and she was trying to put a plan together. If she had been trying to convince her husband "not to try anything stupid, and do what the man says" he could have played so many different angles. She is a fighter or at least a thinker. So, when she would have seen from the passenger side as he turned the car onto where they had made that new bypass,

From the sky maps and from so far above them is the land without lines. You can see that there is a Major Highway coming up from the South. Up from New York and it hits this massive lake on its way to the state line into Canada's Montreal. There was a different Highway, out there coming toward a pulsing in the dark. Up over where the waters collecting to eventually become the river. This littler highway increasing across Vermont like a tendril wobbling out blindly towards a population mass. Finally peering over the mountain and seeing that massive Lake Champlain down there, reflecting in platinum and then seeing for the first time bent against its shoreline squinting is the I-89. Having come close enough that it zapped connections like lightning. Zapping onto some old backroad recently brought up to Federal specifications. Coming easily across massive sections of trees and nothingness now. You pop up passing through the empty back corners of some distant town's forests. He might have initially honed in on this location to bury his kill kit because of its name alone. Most towns have one road going in and the same one heading out the other side, the compass driving by acts like a sundial. Then in Essex Junction, the compass reads on almost every point. So, when they passed under and into the long corridor of leaves, the ones that he had seen numerous times on the street views. As they went down into the other part of Susie Wilson Road, they were close enough to maybe see their house for the naked trees. Tires passing over some larger culvert. Appearing as a weed bramble, it is a dry bed passing under the road, Little Indian Brook there on the maps. Bumping bounce when the tires passing over its transitions. She would have felt clanging despair and the floor dropping away heading into the blackness, disappearing from their neighborhood's street lights. They had lived there for just more than 3 years by then. The rush of air coming back up finally and it is in dead bloom and of black mildews and fur molds.

Zapping through the country corridors, moving through massive sections so swiftly. A whistle hush in the dark building to a whoosh passing swiftly, a very unassuming intersection out in the lonesome. From the halo of the telephone pole light up there, the shadows look like the dangling feet of a shadow man. The Intruder had been here before, when Bill and Lorraine were first moving in, the first of six months and he was here then passing back past them on the highway, heading down to the old river's edge back then to bury that gun he has next to him now. It looks like a military assault rifle with a huge silencer on the barrel. The Vermont 2A heading North and South and then there is nothingness. Lights up ahead it is the 15 but he took a right on red.

That has them heading back in towards town again, thank God. Collecting their thoughts in only blackness, underlit in the leer light of the dash. Bill and Lorraine carpool together every day. In the dark on a major way between population centers it makes a black hole down in there.

In a few more minutes and they will be under the streetlights again.

It probably stole her breath away as he reached down and turned off the headlights in the blackness. The vehicle is slowing.

They had just passed the putt-putt so that would mean this is that section where there is that one abandoned farmhouse. The one they would both know in passing. Then suddenly he is pulling up and to the right quickly into the blackness. Her mind would be racing in thought, eerie and macabre. She can hear poor Bill breathing and moving around back there on the back seat as the car settled into position and the Intruder kills the motor.

32 Upper Main St.

The fan was still running, cooling over their bed. It was empty in the night. Only 3.5 miles away every move the intruder has made, it develops and their situation becomes increasingly worse and so much more desperate. They are pulling in behind a wall of obscuring weeds and brush. He is getting Bill out of the back seat and into the darkness there is a doorway. It appears and the two of them go down into the lower cellar. She is in the car alone now. Looking around, something is wrong.

Securing them this way for the sake of them trying to escape, he kept telling them. Having Bill reach down while he had Zip-tied his hands to the stool. It would have been uncomfortable, his knees having to find a way to rest. Holding his weight up always part bent. The stool holding his arms together and down. He says he must have lost track of time with Bill once his hands became secure.

It would have been a shot of euphoria knowing that Bill was already locked into the right shape. A guileless observer until the moment of his choosing he could kick him over, face hard into the ground helpless and held instantly fetal. Removing the stool, maybe snipping off the right zip ties and he could take its place back there.

They had been down there in the basement a long time. Then through chance or straining of her legs, moving from cramping maybe. Feeling the Zip-Tie snap off! Feeling the hope of feeling her ankles dropping free. She is twisting to see the one that is holding her down low to the seat buckle. What it must have felt like too, as it clicked off. She was sitting there. A child in the Creation, scrambling for the door latch quietly though. She is out on the dirt. Wanting to scream into the night but it is all empty. She did not know that there was a Sheriff's car parked at a nearby property. There was never any indication that the vehicle ever moved as if it was parked there for some other purpose. He often used napkins as a gag in their mouths. She was trying no doubt to get it out, whatever it was. The running bounce becoming a gag at times. The wet clump touching back there in her throat. As the intruder came up the stairs he saw her ankles at his eye height, lost in disbelief he said. He is running after her, by his account it appears that she never knew that he was coming up pounding from behind her.

Every time your head and heavy chest move one way, the arms can flail and hold the centerline. You sure can't turn your neck to look back. Knowing that he had threatened if one of them ran, he would take it out on the other. She was there in the night running under the stars, thankful the plastic broke, her feet slow pounding and he tackled her to the ground bathed in the starlight. She is 55 years old and he lands on top of her. He said that he roughed her up a bit. Maybe like knee kicking her in the side caving in her lower butter ribs. Something that would steal her breath away instantly and take so much fight out of her. Allowing her though to still be able to hobble herself up the stairs to the room up on the corner. Missing from the hinges, he said all the old doors were leaned against walls and he put some in front of the windows in that room upstairs. He said he wanted to be able to see if anyone pulled up off of the highway. There was some debris around the floor, he said. In her hesitant shuffling up the stairs, she would have jolted back a bit when she came entering the room through the opening and saw the doubled-up mattresses that he had staged there. Bill is right there in the basement workshop down below them somewhere.

So once at the top of the stairs with her hobbling and limping now, he would have had her stand there just outside the door. He had set a nylon rope between the two queen mattresses. One end making a long tail hanging out. You would never know they were there. When she saw the bed in the room it would have sounded like someone was rustling a small calf in the room up there in an abandoned farmhouse. From down in the stairs the echoing erratic muffled coming from above, down through the hole in the ceiling. It would have been horrifying and suspicious up there.

Having her only sit down on the bed as he played along. He said taping her hands more securely. That would allow him to do other things, like retrieving the propane camping stove from his backpack and a pan. Mostly filling the pan with water, the flame glowing in the dark. It was right at that time that Bill from downstairs would have heard some commotion erupting again this one more earnest. It was when Israel tactically completing his tasks, began cutting the clothes from off of her. He speaks about this, in a tone that you would use or hear neighbors talking trash about some other neighbor on the committee board. That was his inflection as he said that "she really started fighting once she knew that "he "was going to rape her" Trying to yell, growling the same garbled line over and over, flailing. He wanted them not to worry and that, it's not like that. Each step becoming so much worse and their situation more dire. Telling her to be quiet, trying to keep a knee on her calf. He says her arms and legs were rocking he said she fought the entire time. He said that he hadn't even really touched her yet. The blue low rush of the flame was hushing. A grunt shrilling from her. She would have had a hope somewhere that she would be able to kick him off of her, trying to roll away from him quickly and running. The terror and the cruelty she must have felt as the hidden nylon rope coming out the side of the bed was slashing across her from above. She is already at such a disadvantage, mostly bound. She is trying to fight him off and she is so valiant that she is hurting herself now.

The other side of the rope coming up and grabbing it with the other end. She would have felt his knees change when the end of the one went through the loop of the other. Shifting his weight. Hearing him pulling it zipping unknowing until it cinching tight across her collar bones. Finally slipping free of any slack across her shoulder and now resting in. Stretching tighter across only her neck, he said. He tells her to stop fighting and that if he pulls anymore it is going to kill her, her eyes were bulging out. The dry tears, over the wet ones. Then he pulled out these 1-inch-wide harness straps. One for each ankle he had made them himself from mountaineering webbing or old dog harnesses. He says that he cut the rest of the rope free from the "Truckers Hitch" that was running over her throat and "hooks up" her one ankle. He gloated in his ingenuity on the tapes that the missing bedroom door still had its hinges and the cruel pin. He pulled it out and let the rope slip in behind it. Then he says he dropped the pin back in. It helping make the pulley. The rope then zipping along over the old hardware. It suddenly becomes tight. This in the past apparently was good enough but she would not stop. He had to run down into the lower room. There was a piece of heavy pipe and some nails that he knew the exact location of. He ran back upstairs. She is open before him but he must leave her there under threat and go off into the night again.

He could hear Bill down there in the darkness trying to move around. Israel quickly and quietly trying to drive the nails into the old wood trim enough to claw the pipe across the corner of some closet door for her other ankle. The line is zipping in the pulley now. Every other Kill Cache they have seen had screws in them from then on, this was an older model Kill Kit.

Her countenance is changing.
Mechanical advantage is the noise the joints make, as the tight line wrenches the soft popping hips, open. He is almost drawing this thing out. It could have been done by now.

Pulling her arms above her head, her breasts would be supported by nothing. His headlamp swings over the room in the dark to the camp stove. The black water in the pan becomes illuminated, the water is still in there and there aren't any bubbles or any steam yet. Perhaps the ambience of the rush flame was more perfect. The blacks of her eyes coming wide, stunned and gasped open still from the suffocation of that brilliant head light. Her eyes are searching in the flashing purple, expecting the crashing wave of hands or his mouth or the clunking bones of his hips. Terrified in the dark, looking through plum spot blinking she sees a cast glow. It is the small rush flame of the camping stove heater. It is throwing out such a subtle blue halo. Leaving her there breathing recklessly like some Witch's Sabbath so suddenly. The flat table in the Interrogation room appearing there in the farmhouse. Snapped out of it by a beeper going off or it was something else. There were some there that were so inept, there should be charges filed against them. Slipping back then into the vapors rising. He is there again for them at the table but it is no longer there. The slat shingles of the house are black blue and Lorraine can see the bottom side of some of them through slats long missing. She is under the bare timbers of the abandoned farmhouse, she breathes in hard through her nose, nothing is happening at the moment though. The mind is in her eye now, it catches freeze frames of this still shadow hunkered over. It appears to be leering down at her in the dark or is it looking away at something in its hands? On the edge of the bed, he must have temporarily clicked off the light. He starts in, speaking calmly and so cold as matter of fact. He is also gauging the warmth of the water, finding the heat acceptable. He is holding the long sloping glass neck of an empty Perrier bottle. It was in the backpack with the propane camping stove and some other stuff he said. The bottle goes from slender to bulbous. The flashing across her panting field of vision is deep purple increasingly, starting to see through it in violet, that he is wearing something on his hands. Latex gloves like the ones a nurse wears.

As he wrote in his letter:
Now that I have you held tight, I will tell you a story, speak soft in your ear so you know that it's true. You're my love at first sight and though you're scared to be near me, my words penetrate your thoughts now in an intimate prelude.

Caught in the death snare, with no redeemer to help her. It would have really been something for Lorraine to hear her Bill erupting in a racket down there. Neither of them were alone yet and he was breaking free. For her, the double heartbreak then. He broke the stool he was connected to and when he did, his hands were still tied but he stood free. The stool still there was crushed, it was now a linked cluster in the absolute blackness still linked at his ankles or his calf. Bill was feeling around. "Trying to put a plan together" is how he described it on the tapes. The dark shadow scrambling from hunched over, appearing kneeling by the bed with the water pan or something. Wobbling, the blinding light snaps on and jostles to life the Intruder saying how he had scuffled quickly out of the room. Her groggy choked eyes looking up from her hospital bed she would have seen him moving out and down the stairs holding the knife in one hand and strangely the water bottle in the other. He says he had "Her pistol" tucked in his pants which is kind of a relief in some regards. Maybe holding the warm bottle upside down and the big air bubble was now waiting at the top trapped and hanging over all of that gravity in the water. He went down stairs with them swinging at the end of his arms and him moving them back and forth and more up and down keeping a centerline in a tumble thud down the treads. He said he was annoyed with it coming to a crescendo of the moment that absurdly once again "he had her all set up, up there and he was having to deal with this now?" He found Bill in the dark trying to get a plan together. The interrogation says that somewhere around this time is when Bill, with his neck yanked to the side, Israel slamming him against the wall! Pressing the knife against his skin. His ankles are clustered in broken off wood, exposing rusty pin nails dragging into anything in the dark. What it did to his spatial awareness it was so unfair. The word "most **meticulous**" was attached to Israel in some Federal memo later. The word laying there on the paper, so ambiguous. But when you see it here in the real world, it is an utter devastation. Utter devastation setting in upstairs, her skin is cooling in the dark. She is trying to listen, trying to break free but the duct tape and all of the other stuff he had done. Israel said He loves to see it in their eyes.

She was wide open as he stomped up the steps, she could have cared less because she saw the spit flick from the intruder's lower lip FUCK! Both something and nothing had just happened at the bottom of those stairs. He said he knew that it would show them that he was losing control of the situation. He was watching himself breaking his own rules. He was moving as part observer now. When she saw the intruder grabbing the 10-22, the gun with the drum clip and the silencer, she would have begun into a railing trapeze. Kicking her legs and arching her back the rope and the webbing, allowing her to rage. The contraption absorbing almost all of it, really just making a wobbling on the bed for him. Straining her back, probably tearing through down there.

Bill would have been on beck and call for weeks between the couch and the cupboards. She would've been "laid up" and it would have affected her daily lifestyle for quite a while after. Heating pads and Epsom salts? "Doctors orders" Bill is smiling like in the photo, bringing in her favorites. He is walking light foot hurrying in, holding the bag in front of his upper belly and his pinkies are up and out. His eyes are alight in the light of the world and like in the photo the corners of his eyebrows are raised. He almost does a spin on the one-foot thing when he reached back for the napkin. Throughout the day mad at Bill because for one thing the car keeps overheating! Not really though, he fills it every morning while it warms up. Rolling, her eyes seeing him so clearly. Once the thermostat opens you know, that you know. Then why drive around with only a ¼ tank of gas!

The tendons and the silver skin hold the muscle to the bone. So morbid swinging there. Muscle letting go, wanting to contract into a ball on her lower back she went breathless when she would have heard the thudding footsteps stop at the bottom of the stairs. Bill could probably feel and actually almost see; the dawn. Glowing for someone else, drip steaming coffee. Over the dark horizons of trees and over how many chicken eggs? There was always so much time for questions like that. His mind is in his eye now. Seeing the fabric laid out upon this vast Creation. In knowing that you won't be there for it when it comes rising slowly over everyone else in an hour or two. The Intruder wanting Bill to go loose, become calm, and sit down again.

That it is not one of "those" situations and to just let him secure your hands it's best that way but Bill speaking over his shoulder the panic of the night becoming a dry knot in his throat, it is to assume his voice dry cracked or faltered at some point when he spoke to the man with the light on his head. "You hadn't gone too far yet and that He could turn back. and that they hadn't even seen his face yet" The abductor contemplated it. He says that he didn't want to use the knife on Bill, his voice seems sad, that it would've been too messy he says. He lingers in the thought and he mentions later that Bill still had "a part to play" the investigators eyes so slightly bulging then darting at each other around the table. He says he laughed and that how earlier that night he had wanted to attack a different man. Being denied of it. He had taken them instead and he said he had an idea that he had been wanting "to do to a woman, but it required a man" If Bill had been trusting and believing, Israel was sliding these constant assurances to him across the table.

Everything he did was to get the victim into that position, where he had all the control. When he laid the Reveal Card on the table, then he reveled in it, all the frantic notes, this was part of the process where there are Risks, they can be mediated, he is adamant. The flood of chemicals dosing across him in there. When they are frightened and unsure, letting him. Locking them onto some normal object placed so incidentally. They are ready now, every step of the way the constant assurances "not to worry, that this is not as bad as you think, let him tie you up, it's for everyone's safety, nothing is going to happen. If you don't listen to me, I'm going to have to hurt her, looking up at her slowly through the decrepit floorboards the outside of the whites of his eyes becoming milky and like boiled egg maybe. His exact words he used were telling Bill "We can do this the hard way? Or the easy way." It comes across as a question, ending though in a statement. If Bill had had any hope in it, if Bill had any faith in it at all, he would've been still sitting on the stool. Clicked into place, as the first layer of Duct Tape stretched from the roll. The coal breathing to light, cascading over the receptors, as flaming pennies flashing as the tape would have touched Bill's skin in the dark. Lorraine upstairs eyes bulging in mid-assault. Israel says he could tell Bill was done listening. The things Loraine had whispered to Bill as Israel leapt through the air towards her, the last words as he crashed down on her, maybe she had concluded the combat text message and whispered I Love you. It would be things that she had said to him that would be leveraging the blaring warnings to just sit down, not to worry it is not as bad as you think. He had hit Bill with a shovel 3 times or so it didn't stop him. That is when Keyes said he noticed the camping stove still lit, had cluttered down from the upstairs through the hole in the floor. Lorraine must be really flailing around up there. He tends to the stove's fallen blue flame. The bottle gas flaring up orange, before going out amongst the damp debris pile, he said the second time. The plan was falling apart.

He said in the Interrogation that "I have a very specific way I want things done". He wanted to play the man and the woman against each other. It could have been either way or upon either of them. Coming intermittently in, the bond and report phase with Bill. The abductor behind the blind light is beaded in sweat coming in again acting nonchalant. Wanting Bill to be numb and believing up until the moment he kicks him over, breaking the stool loose and straddling him in its place applying "the Lube" he says. The large 240-pound lump on the ground begins to rustle and grunt screaming muffled. After "three or four songs" he says it would be over, there in the lower rear corner of the basement concrete where they would have found Bill's glasses much later. The heavy equipment bucket pouring out the sad relics from under the backfill and soil. Maybe Bill was supposed to be startled at the initiation of it all: Bill trying to look back at him, his eye pulling at the corner, with his neck resisting on its own, pressed to the side trying to look over his shoulder the panic of the night becoming a dry knot in the throat it is to assume his voice would have dry cracked or faltered when he spoke to the man with the light on his head. Standing behind him, Bill's head would have been down and touching the wall at times. "He hadn't gone too far yet and that He could turn back and that They hadn't even seen his face yet." A silence from back there as Israel is doing something. At last, the Intruder moving his thumb from the mouth of that warm Perrier bottle. Pushing the soft lips of that slender bottle just inside. The staring off into the fire later, remembering the warm glow upon Israel's cleft face, showing the bubbles in there swilling up as they were "Neck Sharing a champagne bottle with friends around the campfire". Was it New Years or was it after? The champagne sloshing down the filling neck. For the sake of the gravity, it is gushing in. It could be down the back of large quivering leg muscles.

But instead of that Bill is on his feet and she can hear him wounded bear standing "Where is my Wife!?" he hollers out into the dark, hide rattling "Where is my WIFE??!" Israel pounding thudding down the stairs now, the light wobbling onto Bill in the halo Israel told him to Shut up! He was going to tie his hands better so that Israel could do other tasks and not worry. He saw the outer rings in Bill's Eyes and they slit more than they opened. He knew from the muffled scuttering upstairs, that Bill had probably made out her words. When he had his knee on her. When he slid up her leg cutting the clothes off. She had been gagged but yes it had come loose a little. She had been trying to scream to him over and over the tears glistening in the flash of her face that "Bill He is going to kill us!" "Bill He is going to kill us!" He didn't like the knife he said remembering that he had sat there for a while with Bill. He said they weren't taking him seriously and it started to really piss him off he said. The doors from the furnace began to blow open in there. He had never shot anybody before, he told them. He saw the look in Bill's eye and it blew cold breeze over the lamp-lit oil of, of all the things he did to make himself feel like God. The fear washing in around the intruder's ankles. Seeing himself for a slit through the door: the 240 lb. Currier is standing over a cowering thin figure in black, the headlamp is wobbling up at him having been fallen into some rubbish in the dark. Debris had been piled and tumbled everywhere he said, of when he had snooped through the building in the daylight noting the realtor sign out there in the lonesome. The Currier has something above his head his arms are up stretched his legs squatted a bit, it must be heavy and his belly then more free to cradle down it pushes the pelvis back a little into this gorilla man stance it could be anything and when Bill looking blindly straight into the light, He knew that he was dead to rights and he started to say something and Israel started firing as fast as he could he said and he never stopped pulling the trigger until it was empty. The 10/22 was down there from his hip the entire clip was smoking and empty now. It is the same model of the gun you see in the orange bucket in the photo of his other Kill Cache. Firing pencil top eraser sized bullets, coursing quietly through the spinning light tube of his homemade silencer and as each round popped into the open-air traveling subsonic and nearly silent. Israel said he could actually see the bullets hitting Bill's flesh in rippling hydro shock and stamp blasts. With the last tinkling of the little brass cartridges on the ground. Leering now at Bill, he had ruined it! And he was still there in the dark wobbling as he stood there. It looked like black rust spores spraying from Bill's hairline. The devils' pollen under pressure, wafting a mist mohawk into the basement air and in microdot upon the open timbers of the farmhouse. It was almost "La Sorciere" . He sat there for a long while with Bill. Watching as the wildebeest kneels down slowly to the ground. He said that he had made these strange noises.

He was not sure if Bill was dead but he heard him make another gurgle of air when the intruder had stood up and began to go up the stairs. This is not how he wanted it to go, he said and that he had a few things he had wanted to try out. He said he did all of his regular stuff to Lorraine and he got to do the new stuff also. He was furious that he had wasted his silencer because he had some big plans for that thing and that by the time, he had reached the top of the stairs, inside he had leveled off. These floorboards were where she had dug her heels in when she had first seen the mattresses. He says he entered the room with her open before him, and he was in a rage. He took it out on her and he acknowledged that he had went too far and that it had surprised him even after looking back.

Strangely volunteering some irrelevant piece of information, in a melting caramel hard candy. It becomes slick and then begins to melt into the tongue's bed.
Lorraine on the terrible mattress' he described how by the time he had begun in on her, looking down he said he could see her as she was hearing the earliest of commuters out on the country lane. Him saying it was a lonely car passing. Him watching for the glimmer flash of something in her eyes, the traffic passing right there outside on the road at the end of the driveway of the abandoned farmhouse, so horrible and terrible. These same elements re-created into orchestrated scenes, like in the back seat of a luxury SUV black on black with the AC on high for 2 hours out there. A lady who came out of Nordstroms from shopping has her neck and one ankle Zip-tied to a headrest in the report. The rush of watching her keep quiet with no mouth gag right there in the high-end mall parking lot. Jostling, shooshing, weeping and hushing, wanting to cry out to God. Right there next to her child in

the car seat it started with the gun held against the child's head, cold with no anger, she said. He needs it going on right in front of them while one of them is acting upon his every whim.

Pulling the truckers hitch end of the rope. The whole time Lorraine wanting to breathe in like a campfire's edge quiet whooshing. Sharp reprimand tug gagging throat, breathing only in matchsticks. One of the many of the times her brain losing blood grip on the world, it is fading again to only the dream state, distant hard steady thud bumping, in the darkness.

It almost feels like the first time. Gentle though, you can do it for hours. He says he had worked the cinch on the trucker's hitch. Losing track of the time. Barely saving himself. The first couple of times her coming back out of it her looking around awoke from some terrible nightmare, to sob even. Then seeing him blurry coming clear he has been watching her all new again. Watching it all come to her mind, the telltale sign that it is happening over and over. The sun shade of light, it appearing in a soft glow shining through somehow and shining in on the door pin and across the webbing strap as it is tugging and wavering back and forth. The light seeming to be slowly moving toward her upstretched calve. Her foot has been touch tingle fallen asleep, opening of her eyes again and the world is still there. The light square that was on the wall, it having passed over her in the room. The mind spin twisting realizing that somehow you are also face down somehow. Stretching chin looking over to the other wall in the decrepit, this time the light was peach alpenglow and sherbet. A square of golden illuminated and amber pink. The next time the light in her eyes it was dispersed and was much more bland in the dreary morning. He said that he had lost track of time, he had planned to burn the whole thing but it had gotten too late into the mid-morning already.

There were people out on the road steadily becoming early morning traffic. He said she was like a zombie. He says in the tape and that they had been upstairs for a long time, Him and Lorraine. Wanting now to see her come down onto that last plateau. He said that there was a bench set up down in the cellar directly across from "him". That is where he was going to let it all develop; he would've been set up right there but when he ran inside, he had ruined it. As the wounded bear held thrashing down. The things to do to a woman, that require a man. How horribly terrible just the sounds of it, hearing the ranges of his mind being torn apart, closing eyes upon one and keeping them held open upon the other. If only the vehicle had been reliable and if he had the other guy, he could have awoken to spending all day robbing all 3 banks in a row, up in Johnson. One after the other.

Lorraine's shuffling feet moving so slowly. After it all now, giving her the time to adjust to the ebb of the light down in that dim room, the whole floor having become a black mirror, so much blood he had said. When her red glossed eyes passing across it, watching her recognize,
That is her Bill laying over there.

He said she never made a change in her expression or even in her eyes. That she was basically gone by then. Flattening out, at the bottom of those steps, from behind any light glancing down through would seem to sway off of her cheekbone and a few golden wisps making a wash of tiger light in her hair, barely moving with her slow labored breaths and in the company of the zombie still standing and the sound of it still breathing.

He had reservations and was staying at the Handy Suites, only 3.5 miles from the farmhouse and within walking distance to the Currier's house on Colbert St. He speaks of scoping out the houses down "behind" his hotel just 2 hours before breaking the security glass. Him mentioning with no provoking that he had stayed there at the Handy Suites a couple of times already. The most recent of his travels showing him in Essex was 9 months prior. And while he was there, nearing Hollow's Eve, imagine finding upon a bank robbery photo of him wearing skin tight "commando" clothing, and then stepping a stutter start when your eyes finding upon an arson there a few lines down. The air is brisk on the back solarium of the ferry as instant beads of perspiration there, adjusting the tugging posture in the chair that they have bolted to the deck and then eyes nearly crossing on the third of a strange burglary in the police blotter, in a set of blips in the local Saturday edition of the prints in October of 2010.

From 2009 to 2011, he had stayed at the Hanover Suites on the edge of Colchester at least once and then a "couple of times" at the

Handy Suites before the Currier trip. It summing to being in Essex Junction, Vermont at minimum of 4 times, in less than 3 years.

Remembering how he had said, that before the Currier's his goal had always been to fly under the radar but as he came into town, he was already amped up from something previous, something very hard to discern. Pulsing it with sonar in the dark when he said that if he was going to do something, he was going to go big and do a lot of stuff.

Originally his story in the telling seemed that the world was going on and this dark slinking shadow moved into position, into some random town and he descended upon some poor random fools.

In the photo of Bill and Lorraine's little white house, it is partially hidden from the urban trees in the front lawn. A walk way goes up to the front door but, that's not the real door. There in the evidence photos now gaunt, is their empty house on Colbert Street, waiting there is the extra garage door opener. Right there near the broken security doors he had come through the night before.

He becomes very guarded about the particulars of the story. He is continually evasive and downright digs his heels in every time the questioning has him cornered where his answer would give indications to the frequency of "needing to take someone" or if the question would reveal how many people he had killed.

He told them that he loves talking to people while them never being aware at the things that he has done. Some element of something horrible going on right there in the room. Casual conversations of him knowing what really happened. Saying that for years that is how he "gets his kicks". He planned these missions, placing himself inside his very tight timeline. Arriving to the family gatherings from within a day or even within hours of having taken someone, raped, and murdered them. Walking in to the family reception, looking them in the eye as they go on and on and him knowing that he will soon return to the body again.

Even the horrible shed that was in the short driveway of Kim's house, he was very clear that he loves doing it right in front of everyone.

He told them that it was always something with him that he was always doing something to keep from becoming bored. How long could he go without doing something? He responded "It depends on what you consider: Doing Something". The planning phase was intricate and so vast.

He told them, that particular night in Essex that he was looking for a Man, but that it hadn't worked out. He had told them moments earlier that he was looking for a Church,
and old houses. When the man in the Volkswagen Bug had gotten away Israel said that he went back to his hotel and waited before walking out back and looking at the houses there.

He says at another time that he was pretty sure he had found it. A place with a car inside of an attached garage. Once he was in there hanging out, the young woman at the table asking him about Lorraine's "Looks" and did they have anything to do with it and there was a long pause.
Did he know them?   "No" he said.
"It wasn't random" he said in long pauses, the young woman trying to remember all of the rules. When she asked him if he had seen "her" before, He says "there was a picture in there…." he trailed off.

The car had issues, that is why he never went up North to hit the banks the morning after the farmhouse, as had been the plan.

At every turn he is very cautious and guarded as he answers questions from before or bringing up unrelated answers out of order and he chooses particular words "terribly horrible" interchangeably with "horribly terrible". The cemetery in Texas was it a place to "take someone?" as an abduction site? He said "No" that, that was a place to "Take someone". They always have remote sheds or some outbuilding to take someone into there hidden. Not used to "Take someone". The eyes around the table sort of relieved but then searching around in the cat's cradle of string about their feet and hands and sticking to their tongue.

He was very clear that he didn't want his daughter to read about these things later. If they could keep it out of public record and if he would be executed in less than a year, he would give them all the "gory details" he said. Also, that he wanted them to give the Silver Xterra back to Kim. A month is a long time to go without your car he said.

Taking these things into account, there is a clarity that comes into view when you put the cards back into order. He will often do the big fake yawn, or drag out the skeptical "Welllllllllll" to tell them that they are off the trail, or the loud nasally laugh "HAHHHH" when they are too close. Seemingly every time that he has lost the pre-set word tracts and gerbil trails of the way he wants it said. He has a very specific way that he wants things done.

He had been to Essex Junction which he will only call Burlington, at least 4 times. He was becoming familiar with the area. They said that they think that he had not lied to them most of the time. He addressed it himself that there were questions that they had asked and that how he had answered them, it was easy for them to make assumptions that he didn't correct. A few questions were so personal or the details of which he wasn't ready to have spoken into open air yet, he never would've dreamed that he would utter them in front of law enforcement, he says that he responded in those ways out of the pressure of the questioning. Out of his pride of vanity perhaps he didn't need to stoop himself to lying to these rubes. When asked about his first day there in Burlington? Starting on the fresh start, coming clean about the Currier's he starts in with this disclosure and disclaimer:

I will tell you that story… to a point he says.

I was fishing. I wanted a Church he says, and an old house. I spent the first day there driving around and I bought a fishing license for the 8th "it was my Alibi I guess", speaking of the 7th. Then he drove down into the Woodside Natural Area, parking the rental car he says, that he fished around, walking around the tall grasses, watching. Then he says that when he finally "felt comfortable" he retrieved the Kill Kit and shuttled it back to his hotel where he spent a day working on the guns, he said getting them in working order, speaking of the 8th. At 8:00 in the evening, he scoped out the apartment building not far from where he would drop their Saturn later. He said that,

"He wanted someone <u>alone</u>, with a <u>decent</u> running car" indicating that he may have already known
that Bill and Lorraine's car had mechanical issues.

He wanted to surprise the man in the "Yellow V W Bug" and as he was approaching the door handle to take him, he said that it had been raining, an evening thunderstorm he insists. Only seconds from the car door handle. Eyes so cold and black. Maybe part crouched by a truck in the parking lot. He said the man opened the door so quickly, putting the paper over his head, running inside, heels thudding into the glowing door and it closing behind him. As if out there beneath the clouds moving in front of the crinkling stars that the intruder's feet were held by some heavy molasses gravity there to the ground. It strong enough to silence his own breath cinching his own throat. Not to be able to call out so friendly, speaking from the other side, like Ted did. When the pretty girls vanished in plain sight of everyone, they had seen them talking to a guy in a cute little V W bug. The sling over his shoulder as he had shuffled with is little arm in a fake cast, something about helping them or them helping him "can you lift that one side there?" as their beautiful young complexions looking up with twinkle stars in their eyes so instantly soured to bilge water and the soft vellum of their lips becoming crackled in brown and blood and sizzled violet cast forever and instantly to mushroom paper. But how many times can you use the same story around the table, until they will abruptly dig their heels in when they see the mattresses that you have staged in the scripting? Remembering the phase of the moon from the charts of that night nearly seeing the stars through the Jail ceiling. In the next telling he knew he would need a new car. Something that means something to only him as their eyes are filling with guile in his deceit. Almost slippery on his seat like the Butcher Baker was when they snatched down on him at the Fred Meyer store in Anchorage for shoplifting a chainsaw, he had money. He said he was stealing it as a gift for his father, making him complicit in the crime and in the interrogation, it comes out that he had came in his pants as they were jostling him out the glass doors there in front of everyone, but that was back in 1976.
Moving flawlessly through those flood of thoughts saying that and if he had been 5 or 6 seconds slower getting into his apartment that "He almost got it that night" he gloats. By putting the newspaper

over his head and running in he saved himself from "Getting Wet" he says very eerily. The young lady at the table asked him immediately, what was the configuration of his backpack at that time?

He thinks about her inquiry she had come off very down home and country bumpkin when she had asked it. For years her working on the State of Alaska Task Force for Child Sex Crimes and Sex Trafficking and he answers her with an appearance of having his guard down. That it was a light bag with really only zip-ties, duct tape, and some blindfolds? The air in the room seemed to stiffen as maybe he was realizing that he had accidentally went off of his script. As he was sinking deeper within himself again, she tried to throw a little more butter in the pan, anything from letting the egg start to stick again. "Did you bring that stuff with you from Alaska? What a strange question, he answered too quickly "yes" but then just as he said about misleading them, he thinks about it awhile, then his eyes snap back and he corrects that those things are incidental and they might as well had been in the kit. Him acknowledging in huff of air and intonation that he had gotten flustered there for a moment and then they got back on track with the questioning. He had never mentioned anything regarding frustration or wanting to keep looking for not finding the church. He never brings it up and it appearing only as a footnote really, saying it once at the beginning of the story, and once at the end. After being denied of his desired victim at the apartment with the decent car, he went back to the hotel instead. Waiting for a different person who fit the bill but no one was out on the street because of the rain he said again. If the "man" had went to plan we know that he would have had a new small car that was able to make the 125 miles or so route along the 15 as he specified, to rob 3 rural banks along the way. In the bag during that phase of the trip he would have had road flares he said, letting the dimensions sink in. The cops so familiar with these things. In your grip this stiff chemical sausage when it is burning slowly approaching the soft grip of your plush hand you will do anything to get it out of there as the sputtering flame approaches ever closer to your flesh. His original plan was to later bring the car all the way back into Essex Junction and abandon it at some seemingly end of the road. Somewhere off to the side where when they found it, they would know the driver was long gone and the car being in the middle of nowhere, far from any logical evidence and he would have torched it off with the flares he said. Us then seeing the tow truck under contract passing the crime scene tape, jostling out heavy with the dark green Saturn burned to rust rocking up on the bed. Out from the tall grasses of The Woodside Natural Area, or was it the previous kill kit in New York? It still isn't clear but the plan had only gone off part way. Either leaving the car at its own kill cache site, or it is leaving it at the kill cache site of the previous one "New York" he specified.

He told them he had an idea that he wanted to do to a woman but it required a man. He went nearly directly to the Curriers house at midnight saying he was pretty sure that he had found it. He never clarified and they never asked which visit did he "find it". His particular requirements he starts with the secluded confines of the access to the house from inside that little garage with the car in there and of course never addressing Lorraine's "looks" he went on and on instead about no kids, no kid's toys and much like the Otero's first issue, no dog. He cut the phone line with his side-snips that he brought this time in his backpack. Cutting the phone lines is an archaic precaution and the law enforcement even asking why? It was overtly there and done for some purpose and that being perhaps only to give the impression and the incorrect assumption that he had never been there before. He knew her age, he said snooping in the car glove box while he waited for them to go to sleep. He said he knew the exact room they were eventually sleeping in. Moving directly through the foreign hallways in seconds into their bedroom, because of the fan of course. It was hot that night he reiterates. On the night/early morning that they were killed, though the temperature had been 90 degrees at noontime, by midnight when Israel left his apartment to supposedly find the Currier's house, at midnight it was only 66 degrees

He might've gone later, late at night the first whiskey and ice and looking at the archived weather data for that night. They have little cartoon icons of the phase of the moon these are behind clouds by the hour he could no doubt relive it from the weather chart, him remembering the silver edged cloud of the moon gaze. There is one amongst all the many that does show a light drizzle before midnight. 90% of the websites never having received a report of any rain, he insists upon it.

The experience played back so many times before, eventually telling it in the open air to the law enforcement at the table. His experience part supposed even, describing recurring traits, revealing lines spreading in the blue print. He always brings everything with him however upon entering the garage and he looks over and sees the brand-new Security Screen door, it was locked. Behind that, there is a new Security Glass Entry door into their kitchen with the deadbolt and it too was locked. The light screen door he jimmied he said, but when he broke the glass of the main door there was another reason, he needed to get into their bedroom as soon as possible.

When he said later that he had jumped into the room from the doorway of their bedroom and grabbed her by the neck and had slammed her back down he said that she was trying to put a plan together. Her scrambling in slow motion as the walls inside of her dream cave, scratching slow zipping fingers across her bed sheets as she is reaching like lightning, memories flashing in her mind, perhaps: remembering trying to tell Bill again that someone has been in the house while they were at work! Seeing maybe that Bill's car seat had been pushed all the way forward again. Knowing how hard it is for him to reach down there every time, with his "condition" making it difficult. Bill no doubt reassuring her saying that none of his tools are missing, the air compressor alone is worth $200 at a pawn shop, the hose alone is worth $50! Scratching towards "her gun" the law enforcement stating from the first that the pistol had been under her mattress. In the tapes he says casually that it was unloaded and in the nightstand. They asked him in the interrogation if he had moved the seat in Lorraine's Saturn and he acknowledged that he had. It was the length of the legroom that was all wrong and they had caught it with tape measures. Little things found, put out of place when they return home on their very set little schedule and the creepy feeling or some object placed incidentally out of place again.

And then that one guy? She had told her friend that she knew a guy was stalking her, or something. The report saying that Lorraine had told her neighbor that she had looked out and caught a tall thin man, gaunt looking in at her. Later her few bar friends recalled that they all knew that she had seen this "guy" and the story goes, it was more than once. The light security door and the new entry door in the evidence photos of the inside of the attached garage going in like it was the front door, the ones with the tempered safety glass. So she could see in there. Imagining Bill after it was all done telling her she had nothing to worry about. The large birds looking over at papa as he tapped his knuckle on the glass to reassure her "It's so you know, that you know". Even still, she bought the pistol. It had been last fall in October.

All of these as she is frantically beginning to move across the moonscape, lead heavy across her bed sheets as a horrible wobbling headlamp is running blinding speed across the hallway walls. It is through the bedroom door and it crashes into her collar bones. She would have been reaching for it in the dark but instead he laughed as he said that

"It wouldn't have done much good; it was unloaded anyway" and you can hear him that he almost can't sit still he is so giddy and slippery in his seat there.

Nine months since October, his itinerary showing him there with opportunity.

These obscure scenes, garbled across large lenses. As the twinkling thick glass are approaching each other's lenses, the light ring in there flips inside out and then it all comes into view and then the seeing goes so much farther. On one side, you can see to across the heavens through any, consolation:

the 2 new security doors and the recent purchase of her pistol.

On the other side the lenses zooming in now, down, down and then suddenly appearing in focus:

Bill and Lorraine only had $100 dollars in their account when all activity stopped.

With Bill's condition changing the oil would have been a real pain and his medication was there in the house when the welfare check broke the door in to crashing bird cages and squawking. If they had more cash available, they could have got the overheating coolant leak fixed at the mini-lube but it was the new doors and possibly the little pistol laying there in her nightstand that made his eyes flash when he first saw it there. Lifting her mattress for a big tacky hidden toy maybe, there on some weekday mid-morning, possibly. Settling into his little "Pigs trove" He could have been looking at their photos and medications soaking it all in when he opening the drawer or lifting the mattress and he would've locked to ice. Seeing that they had been spooked? Knowing that she is thinking about it often and unsettled at only suspicion. Probably cutting the old phone lines just to be safe, she must be thinking about it unawares occasionally in her day to day and he would've felt euphoric as the glass shattered and knowing the fear was washing up in her as he was wobbling so swiftly and directly through the strange hallways and the supposed unknown floor plan.

He chose a site less than 5 miles from their house on an old backroad in the dark. The Currier's would have been couriered over to the farmhouse. He said he wanted a man alone in a decent car. The man in the VW bug would have been set up already if it had gone to plan apparently. Zip-ties, roll of tape and Blind folds, plural? Frantic duct tape rocking his head from side to side. Maybe Israel had months to plan out how to get the most out of the pools in their eyes and when it was revealed as the blindfolds coming off. The cruel medication on the counter back on Colbert St.

The people of the church, the earliest ones shuffling in unlocking the doors to find it just as he had said they would. He was so upset at Bill for ruining the silencer he had "big plans for that one" citing it was made for the big show at the church everyone in the state responding while he would be robbing three banks in a row on the long quiet 15. Dropping the car less than a mile or two from Bill's or Lorraine's now broken home. Her story coming out later in waves. The older couple with the perfect floorplan, then later how close she had almost escaped. How hard she had fought him off "the whole time" he said. Winding down, he seems deep in thought or having come to some quiet conclusion that he really did go overboard with the tying and the hardware. Long pauses and then Jolene asked him nodding that,

"The ropes had become a big part of it,

hadn't they?"

Thinking about it for a long while, then in downcast, him freely giving up new information suddenly that
"I guess I had spent a lot of time on the webbing straps for her feet and stuff".

He tried to make it not "uncomfortable for her, for that part," thinking again he goes on pause for a moment, a rapid abacus clicking, suddenly then to a stop.

Black slithering in his eyes when he said drifting off in thought "Not to lose circulation"

After he was arrested, thinking about the next trip planned? He told them that he had been going to stop by and see what was left of the Curriers he said.

When he would have been passing back through town returning from his brother's up in Maine. If the local police had already been there on the site at the farmhouse! Hands on hips and hand kerchief over noses and mouths up near to that one door to that lower room. If there, the forensics examiner would have been able to note that although yes, she had ligature marks on her hands and feet, her swollen calves were not plum black, like having been dipped into the devil's ink. Answering the Detective's questions negotiating the Murtie-operandi that yes, much like his silencer that worked, the intruder had used very "Unique Features in the manner of the restraints". Amazingly yes, she could have still walked down those steps on her own.

Looking off in a daze Israel Keyes had reminisced "that was going to be a good trip"

Those same large lenses, fastened into some contraption. Moving them by degrees, they bring forth a convergence of images, both of them smearing and the images interlapping over each other:
On the one macabre screen, it is of the floor made into black mirror. In it there is the light coming down through the hole in the ceiling of the old farmhouse. With her standing down in the cellar on the slick floor, Puffy face from so much: suffocation.
Then the other smearing scene, the FBI interview. They were there with Heidi Keyes at her home in Texas and she said that, she had bought him some camping gear there when she was still up in Indiana, in Harlan.

The FBI agents watching her facial expressions as the brown and blood mylar recording it, something in the way of "It is the camping stove that is going to make all the difference.

He put on soft leather baseball batting gloves and then he strangled her from behind with a rope. Frizzy hair jostling on half of his face and pressing against his clenched jaw.

He said later very distinctly volunteering that he had used 2 condoms out of the rape kit while he was in the Farmhouse.

Lorraine Simone Currier (The Charley Project)

Lorraine is missing with her husband, William, from Essex, Vermont. They were last seen by their respective co-workers when they left work at 5:00 p.m. on June 8, 2011. Both of them apparently made it to their home on Colbert Street, but neither of them showed up for work the next day, which is uncharacteristic of them. They have never been heard from again.

When police went to the residence, they found all the doors locked. However, a window in an interior door connecting the house to the garage was newly broken and the home's phone line had been cut.

The Curriers' dark green 1996 Saturn SL2 sedan with the Vermont license plate number ABF-818 was missing, as was a snub-nosed Ruger .38 handgun Lorraine had recently purchased. A photo of the sedan is posted with this case summary. Lorraine's two pairs of eyeglasses and her contact lenses were left behind, but her purse and wallet were missing.

William has ankylosing spondylitis, also known as Bekhterev's Disease, an incurable disorder which causes inflammation of the joints. As a result, his neck vertebrae are fused and cannot turn his head from side to side. He also suffers from diabetes and requires insulin daily; he does not have insulin with him.

Lorraine has cardiomyopathy and requires daily medication, which she didn't take with her.

Two days after the Curriers went missing, their car was found abandoned at a parking lot in the 200 block of Pearl Street in Essex Junction, next to a dumpster between two apartment buildings. This is less than a mile from William and Lorraine's home, and a short walk from the bus stop.
Investigators released a sketch of an unidentified man whom a witness may have seen driving the car; the drawing is posted with this case summary.

William worked as an animal care technician for the University of Vermont at the time of his disappearance, and Lorraine worked in the financial services department at Fletcher Allen Health Care, the university's health care center. They have siblings living in Vermont, but no children.

The Curriers haven't used their cellular phones or bank accounts since they went missing, and all their medication was left behind at home. Their bodies have not been located, but foul play is suspected in their cases due to the circumstances involved.

CHAPTER SEVEN

FRIDAY IN DISGUISE

While Israel Keyes was moving the stuff around from one car to the other again, this being the morning after. He says something very peculiar there in the tape. He says:

"I didn't really have the disguise on at that point"

Saying how he had jogged back across the street then checking out of the Handy Suites. Crossing in daylight the dip bump out onto the road and shortly after pulling into some random parking lot of convenience and backing in next to some random parking spot. Coming out of the rental it is next to a dark green Saturn. The bag with the clunky bottles of empty Drano and all of the dirty clothes in it? Such strong evidence to pass from one car to the other, into his rental again and leaving it all there less than 4 miles from the murder scene and within walking distance to the abduction site. He tries to remember it for them and says that he is also pretty sure he disposed of almost everything in the dumpster at the Handy Suites where he had stayed, later he would burn the rest out in the rurals of New Hampshire just after leaving his brothers up in Maine.

He continued on in the recording on the tapes sleepily that he had driven their Saturn up north to use it to hit these 3 small banks. He had described, scoping out the logistics on the sky maps over and over. Him imagining his plans playing out, as they are unfolding across the terrain. It would equate to about 17 some odd miles north out of Essex Junction where it would be that he said the car had begun to act kinda funny and the temperature light came on. The car is overheating. Israel

67

scanning the dash remembering now so clearly. Moving the luggage around last night, mistakenly grabbing a jug of the Drano in the dimness looking at it strangely, the two jugs said Antifreeze coolant. This Friday morning in disguise, he said he had been up all night.

When the all-nighter becomes the day after, it starts becoming pallid and bleak. Even the moving sky up there and all of its moving textures, the light truly is coming down through them once again for you. After so many hours the mind begins to kaleidoscope. Over and across the windshield the wide reflection glancing is streaked to its horizons. Is there movement in the background? Hollow eyes snapping over.

The vibe in the car would have been off of the charts. Deep in the gaze of its Intensity and pulled to wire all along the edge. Then suddenly one of their cell phones shattering pinging with an alert notification! and he appeared there again, instantly eyes opening already locking on the phone.

His mind no doubt uploading the chain of custody of the whole thing he called, when

"It happened"

The memories passing so swiftly, only a few spots are almost still real. Recollections of back in their house walking by, registering something of old pillow clay and oyster shell, there was fluttering under the sheet draped over, was it a dove house. It would have been that crackling of the glass on the floor that should've clicked him away from the memory snapshots it having now become later. Visions so exact in the flashing of what all had transpired through the night and up until that moment in the car.

The sun was over the cattle and the yard-arm by now. Getting grip here in the real world. There was this thing that he had really wanted to do, but as he rolled the smooth options, the phone was in his hand. There were rules written in next to this detail on the plans though. It was frustrating inner conflict at the time. However, in his own voice later in chains it comes off as contempt when he says,

"It didn't even have text"
in a scoffing.

He had wanted to do a ransom but he didn't want to have to talk to anybody. This time he was still following his own rules but later, "back when I was still smart" he says on the tapes. Bill and Lorraine having had been made to answer these questions all tied up. Shrugging their shoulders that yes, there are 2 of them but, in these trying times. That, that particular phone's payments weren't current and it could only dial 9 1 1 for emergencies. They tell him this openly and it hung in the room, their words pulling to wire passing through the blades in the intruder's mind and he was cold as stone, the wind bitter on their face. The Kaleidoscope light is so bright and glaring through the windows of their car now, it is late into Friday morning. The interior of the car is all illuminated and the upholstery is made up of fibers. You can see them glowing and part translucent in the sunlight. All of it cast across the blink of his eyeball there and upon its glassy screen. Was it a contact name? Typed in the first night when Lorraine would've gotten the new phone. Sitting up in bed, it was fun saving the nick names into the Contacts. Some of them maybe were from childhood. What should she put in for: work? Or was it caller ID that said it was the animal testing labs at the "University of Vermont" wondering if Bill is okay? Or if it was "Fletcher Allen Health Care" he would know which. Adjusting the frumpy sweater, it was like rattled tinfoil coming out of the big suitcase but maybe it was slowly unfolding. The creases would've been obvious but they are softening. The hat is perfect. It casts with its brow a half shadow across his face. The sunglasses are back in there. The object then is to be obscured by the time of day and the type of car, and the position of your hands on the wheel.

Looking down at the cheap little phone screen, it is saying one of a number of different things, but it did have voicemail. The oncoming traffic is sporadic going up north he said, halfway to Johnson. They had it set up so all you had to do was push the little button if you had a little envelope in the corner of the screen. He used to have one like this back in Neah Bay. In the voicemail alone he could tell they were concerned because if you know Bill then you know Lorraine and between the two of them, they said they always called in. Hearing the threads of it tightening across the coworkers' voices in the voicemails. Tossing the phone down on the seat he said. The plans were meant to be rolled out in sheets, to be poured over and pencil erasing out in the middle of some semantic.

How real are those moments allowed briefly?
Pouring over in the hidden obsession.

Bill & Lorraine's coworkers at their respective places of work, they must've hurried over perking up into the phones them ringing, only to realize that they were speaking to each other. The coworkers sensing it at as a tickling in their throats. However, they would've become horrified after the police had gone out for the welfare check.

There just so happen to be an immediate service record for their Saturn and it had been completed at a little shop just before they had went missing. There is a report of a liquor store employee seeing Lorraine stop in there at 4:30 that last stop for the afternoon.

There was roughly 40 miles on the odometer that the law enforcement couldn't account for. He said he was heading north out of town towards Johnson, 17 miles almost halfway there and he said he was just short of it when the car began to overheat and he doesn't want to pull over and pop the hood to add the coolant. There are only enough miles to go half that far.

In the 40 some odd miles from the mini-lube to 8 Colbert St. Israel driving 3.5 miles to the decrepit farm house on 32 Upper Main St. in the absolute black. Driving back the 3.5 miles this time to his hotel at the Handy Suites once more. He says that he drove north toward Johnson the next morning but he turned back. He said halfway? Up that highway only 9.7 miles, 16 minutes each way by sky maps. Is a quaint little church in a quaint little town with no police of its own, in no other than a place called "Underhill". There you see the little steepled building The United Church of Underhill.

He says that he had been up all night and he was thinking about the 3 banks that he had lined up. He said he wasn't sure that he trusted himself. His hands were shaky and he hadn't slept he said. No doubt thinking of the logistics of any roadside car trouble out here. Anxiously tossing his hair back from his neck; it is hanging out from the hat; it is not quite perfect.

Last night when the man with the Volkswagen Bug had run into his corner apartment, out from his car in the rain and almost "got it", it had ruined the Church plan. A place to "take them" and do stuff he said and maybe leave them there for the people to eventually find them on Sunday Morning. Here he is bumping along in the problem car that was supposed to be able to at least make it on the desolate road to the farmhouse. Accounting for 7 miles, half of it one way and the other half on the way back. The thing that had really burned him up is that he knew he would have to destroy both the silencer and the barrel now for sake of the concussion baffles in the one and the slow spiral scraped into the lead of the bullets from the other. All of those bullets passing through the darkness stamp clicking the wall and Bill when he had "lost control"

Bill still had a "part to play" but that had been ruined as well and he had said as much. He looked at the fuel gauge and his eyes bulged; the car is running low on gas! He said he was finally frustrated and turned back the wheel. The shadow under the turning car now heading south, frustrated the 17 some miles supposedly and he pulled back into the Home Depot parking lot again backing in next to his rental car. He moved the last of the stuff and he pulled out and parked it back at the CVS or the Walgreens, it used to be a Rite Aid. He swiftly wiped it down and walked away. He had calculated the angles of the cameras correctly there in the blind of the dumpsters and the apartments. Backing out one of the times that morning most likely right after he had checked out of the Handy Suites, he had almost backed out into an ex-peace officer from Oklahoma. The ex-law enforcement witness had seen this guy through the glass. It was the dark Green Saturn from the news broadcast and the posters later. He said he could tell something was wrong or that something had just happened to the guy in the car. Later the artist, sketching the nose and the curly hair. It was a pencil drawing without a doubt it captured the Intruder. He said that he was "amped up" and needing to "do something".

Wiping down the edges of the Saturn, off to the side of the cameras walking back to his rental car and driving away he said he would come back by to maybe torch the Currier's car where some other Kill Cache had been dug up before. Now having returned back to Essex and readying his rental car to leave, there was a great amount of the plan with the church and the banks if it had went right still undone. Loading the car expecting heavy loot, at that point he had either gotten out of the disguise or was still in it.

Roughly ½ of a year later in Texas they would have him on bank surveillance videos on a plan that he had got to pull off the bank robbery and he was wearing a construction worker disguise. In this case it was a bulky black coat and a paper dust mask. He had on a hard hat that casted a shadow upon his face, he always called it a helmet though. He also had on the dark safety glasses. From under the hard hat his hair was coming out, it was not quite perfect. When they had eventually asked him to put his hands behind his back there off the highway in Texas, it was from that bank robbery that he still had all the old small bills with ink on them. The ones that were moldy in the report from being buried under that tree as trash. The canister had later lit up the small bills under the lights. They knew it was him on the video and they came right out and asked him about the "thing" that they had found in the buried bucket. The thing was this strap of doubled up duct tape. It was in there with the gun pieces and stuff. It had black hair attached to the tape sporadically and it had been used for something. However, the one in the video in Texas was much more golden in nature. Some people call it Dirty Dishwater Blonde, unfortunately it truly does describe the color. The locks of hair in the bank robbery were down to the construction worker's clavicle in curving strands like Jesus. They asked him if it was "real hair" and it was of course. Where do you buy real hair? He laughed "You don't have to buy something if you just take it".

The cards were showing in patterns of fans and they were all related he said they are all relevant. So amped up, on his way up to the 3 banks on the 15 starting in Johnson. An arterial vein branching off to each main highways once again passing those same transitions in the highway again in daylight but taking a left on the 15 and heading out of town, leaving Susie Wilson Road in the rearview window. If he had pulled over on the side of the road any trace of steam rising from the hood, passing periodically there a handful of country folk that would have assuredly pulled up to help this older gal's car; her radiator would be boiling hot! Them imagining her skin scalded puffing down on her face in their hurried minds slowing down and putting their arm on the back of the truck seat, looking out the window, a cocked eye seeing it up close he might have stared at the wrinkled sweater. They would have reviled at his face coming around. What if he giggled at them? Back in the flow of the pre-planned parts of the story and there were some things that he had to do for that other life. His compass is hitting on some Northeast heading and here he is pointing south again and returning to back to Essex Junction, possibly at the exact moment that the Police were pulling up to an 8 Colbert St. for a Lorraine and Bill Currier.

THE CLOSEST CALL

CHAPTER EIGHT

WELFARE CHECK

10-23 apparently meaning that they have arrived on the scene and that they are going to start looking around. The house seemed fine. Everything was locked up and tidy. There was a box type shop fan built into one of the windows in the garage. It looked like a major liability for break ins to the cop but he is looking through the glass on the back man door into the garage he can see their car, is not there. There is a little air compressor under the plug. It will be captured in the flash and the shutter in less than an hour or so. The place is as they left it, the birds are in there under the sheets in their cages. The sun has been up for hours and for a bird? Bill and Lorraine would've been on beck and call for a week talking the birds down. Sing Song, not to worry, everything is ok and that no one forgot about you. Perhaps the moment the one bird finally would've nudged its massive beak on Bill's bent knuckle. Maybe then he would've looked up to Lorraine with that raised eyebrow and her? The bird's losing feathers the other one had practically thrashed and smothering flown to Papa's arms from the cage.

The officer is free to go now but he lingers a moment or two. He sees the neat homeowners tool bench in there through the glass. Coming across something eerie as he looked into that dim door. Almost turning to go, his due diligence satisfied already. In a flood rage of blood rush, the responding officer's hand is moving like a rattlesnake made of molasses, reaching for the mic-button, racing eyes. How to convey in combat text that he could barely make it out earlier but that you are certain that you see through part of the garage that there is broken glass in tiny blocks appearing to have bloomed where it fell. Under the door into the kitchen! And he has been out here looking around for at least a minute or two! The intruder could still be here and I'm all alone and that I am believing that you love me or someone there does enough that someone is coming for me. It is such a relief to know that, but when it goes the other way, it is like being left outside, the things that the Currier's had went through, a Kaleidoscope to the eyes.

They set up these number codes so that in these types of situations, his other hand is now rattle snaking towards the hip belt where is his service pistol. He is maybe seeing an image of his daughter in his mind in an instant. Rattling a fluid staccato of numbers. The smell of his wife the one time in that old cabin on the lake, within a shutter flash. "! 10-62 sometime late last night,10-33…requesting …. backup…"

Perhaps at the exact moment that Israel Keyes was pulling away, north out of Essex Junction again now in his own rental car.

CHAPTER NINE

RIM-KIT

From inside the tall, scrawny Parks and Rec Maintenance Guy's jail cell he wrote his death letter. Only until looking back on it all from a distance, removing the spaces between things that might have been said very far apart, even divining them back into order from entirely different interviews. The Courier's car was very dark and low to the ground. In the darkness of the farmhouse the Saturn would have been nearly invisible. Existing there, only in glances of light across its glossy edges and waiting there for them, in the absolute darkness.

Numerical date 11-29-2012: the second to that last day of the month, in the second to the last month of the year, essentially the eleventh hour. Him knowing, that this would be the last time he would be able to walk into this room with the table. In the last of the last tape, he nonchalantly makes a long eye lock with the young woman who has done a very good job trying to apply the methods. Looking into her eyes she doesn't look away, after a while he does. He sheepishly smiles and seems to accept the way things are. She smiles and nods politely, her too appearing to be at the will of the fates it seems. When unexpectedly and out of tempo he asks to take one last look at that picture, the one of many that they brought in for him to pour over. Of all of the other people that came to the table, she had formed a pretty effective relationship with him. This time he wants to give it an honest attempt for them and she slides the copy paper over in front of him.

Under the fluorescent, the Lady officer within his reach, has done an excellent job. They did her hair up and she played coy, the first lady, the second lady, on lenses overlapping even telling Israel that she wouldn't expect to know the data or something on this one thing and that, he could bring her up to speed, if it was alright with him. He melted in her hand and he was giddy but he had to have thought later about those first interviews and now looking over at this other distraction. The one guy is shaking his foot under the table. He is catching something in the wind and it is starting to drive him crazy. Seeing himself so clearly in his mind the water in the drinking glass rippled from the table leg. Early on she was there with her big hips and she was still there and now she is wearing jeans. The ones she'd have on under the Ferris Wheel in Palmer. Her husband eyeing suspiciously from the vanity mirror, pulling out her

"State Fair Jeans?! " But he trusts her.

He has seen her work photos. The dark gauntness at least once creeping across her cheekbones over an extended weekend sometime. As she took a shower maybe he would have peeked in at the file there. The photo slipping into the open air it would seem to be sizzling like an acid apple. The eyes becoming boiled egg staring into its textures they are so real. The first lady officer at the table Officer Doll, her husband would eventually go on to be the Chief of Police for the A P D.

Her earnest intern routine in the room with the table has been working and Israel is there and he is almost ready to answer these questions that they have been gently footing around. Because he had taunted them with his playing cards. Stroking one of them over and over. He'll maybe tell you what it looks like. Looking for places to taunt them using the name of something so very obvious but only to him. He told them outright that he loves it. He has cards out on the table now, almost greasy on his seat. She is moving closer to the corner of the table in the mean of averages. The letters coming into shape and this was when he was still just some guy and he looks at her, the first girl cop at the table. She is nodding and his eyes looked like wet thick candle pools he bestows on her the prestige that

"Well...you've got your monster" it took everyone by surprise and even the one guy across from the interrogation. He's got the Royal Seals clutched in his hand and he has his own stationary with his name in the Letterhead and he has his own little business cards.

The copy paper sitting there on the interrogation table had two photos printed on it. These are of his Kill Cache in Blake Reservoir, New York. He had given them it's location and they had retrieved it. The bucket had been buried under large boulders that are standing like a Teepee. Them making a tight cave, not quite as large as a porta-john or an outhouse. There in the floor of that rock closet, under a few head size stones was the bucket. Buried with only 2 inches popping out of the ground? The mummy shit and the weight of the sealed bucket appearing to be an old field latrine. The Bucket seeming to have been filled to the rim, once closed tightly at least one more visitor squatting in there onto the bucket lid. It smearing onto the rocks, working its way down to the warm orange lid. Recalling the Eagle River mini-kill kit. It consisted of only a shovel, black trash bags and 2-gallon jugs of Drano. Also, when asked about the moldy money he had secreted in the plastic bag under a tree in Texas, wasn't he worried someone would find it? He had said the same thing, laughing that "No one wants to pick up trash?!"

His finger is on the lid of the orange five-gallon bucket in the photo. His eyes appear to go deep inside the paper. On the lid it appears that there is dry and smeared mummy shit. Looking down into that bucket from here in the fluorescent. His eyes begin to change and she is listening intently leaning in, he is about to say something or is deeply in thought remembering the fragments he has said to them during this thing.

On the FBI video the grainy white timestamp in the upper left-hand corner says,

29Nov2012
11:19:36

And he says "Can I see that, top picture?

Arranging the words and the cards on the table it takes different shapes. The wood breath becoming silvering and pickled. Oldest son standing wobbling in the river current. The ideas in his young mind then not grounded in nor bound to the laws of this real world. In its fermentation it wobbles out atypical and pointing out into the unknown.
When it is splashed for a few difficult and exciting years in the yeast slurry of the Puberty Sequence.

The chains can be heard quickening and rattling on the tapes as the pickled word is made up of letters coming into shape from down in the void of the "Mutual Delight" that Dr. Anthony Stevens speaks of so eloquently.

CHAPTER TEN

IT'S STRANGE YOU NEVER KNEW

Mother was standing with her right arm down straight along her side: Defiance. Older now the other arm is bent at the elbow coming across her lumbar and it is grabbing her other forearm, cuff or wrist it is all of them at once. It looks like a painting on a tarot card when she does that. There is so much poetry in the body language it is part *servant* part **Master**. It is **Feminine** crossing holding *masculine* both playing both roles at once, Gods' son and daughter spinning in verted helix, chromosome silvery titanium. In every pulse of your heart splashing gush up to your brain. Out to the ends of the warm strands of red silk. They are so thin and the last of the drunk oxygen and powder dust iron steps off of the ride up there. Suddenly then, they are coursing down the cold blue violet again. Drawn hissing as a poison dioxide of carbon.

The optic nerve on which we see, it goes in and connects into your mind back there and you will believe the things you saw as the magician poofs his wand and what was so, becomes not so.

The big top of the brain is actually two parts, laying so close together they appear as one. They are not. One side logical, categorized, void of even the concept of emotion. The Otherside, illiterate and fluid, it cannot even count, but it sees everything for what it is, the name of it; oblivious. Deep at the bottom of the brain where they come together the two sides shaped, make a cave down in there.

Half of this little cave is the one side; the other half is the other side and the ceiling and the walls of the cave are made of eyeball material. It is not pointed outward like what we're used to, it is pointing downward and into the cave. Below the clear floor your subconscious is looking up at you and the ceiling of the cave is looking down on you,

Memories, seasons, flashing on the walls and the ceiling, the second pump of the wings. Lifetimes flashing right before your eyes, in The Dream cave.

The cross section of it in a cave man then, laughing as the wildebeest kneels down slowly to the ground, dragging meat home to old mother. She had kept him hidden under fur and he had clung to her paps as an infant.

After they had all eaten, the bones are still in hand, relaxed and gnawing with greasy lips and waved around, the rib bone in storytelling around the fire.

The young maiden sitting across from the fire everyone knows they are basically together. I'm not sure how it translates in caveman, but keep your Hands off! In fact, don't even get caught looking at her.

This one though is somehow cross wired, malformed, abnormal or dysfunctional.
This is the place where you lived every time you ever dreamed.
And every time that you were lost,
in the fantasy:

"Where will you go, you clever little worm"
Serial victims found and unfound, the detectives are finding just the scattered pieces of the killer rebuilding his fantasy, here in the real world. Evidence arranged in order, travel receipts to hidden buckets, the click of the propane camp stove fire, it is so close now to put a hand on your shoulder, almost there, gulps so loudly thirsty throat, alas, the steaming water bottle. The thing that obsesses you, you can never touch it. The trail ahead is pallid and bleak, even if made real for just a short moment, now temporary in the real world. Trying to make a turn back in the river of Creation, wobbling against the river. The fanning cards slipping in his hands show the patterns recycling. Arranging them on the table it begins to show the form lines that are

radiating from the center. Panting in the strain of the current, staring at the thing that must be,
Mother.

In the family photo he is around 14 years old and his father is there. This photo is in the wake of a recent wedding, it is his first sister's. Mother's daughter the curly auburn hair.

Mother, a Proverbs 32 woman? More like Proverbs 35! I guess there is always collateral damage,

In the fringes of the church, mother moved like rumor, having to move for the sake of them. Trying to ever be invisible, to government interference. Public schools were of the devil, their institutional blueprints, resulting in the exact same smell and of course the exact same indoctrine. Saturating nearly all of the devil nation. If this play in the dirt kid was there instantly inside the cool institution, of any third-grade homeroom. The uniform classroom atmosphere would be balancing now impregnated, having exchanged this globe of part fresh air having just been blowing through the firs out on the fringe, it is mostly of nature. The air around him wafting from being transported there.

and modern medicine? Ha ha Haaaaaa! The little boy was a toddler when they had uprooted and moved again, God's blessed will. And this time, he really meant it. Some infraction from without, someone in leadership who has become a swine treading upon a bed of pearls. Someone in the family taking the brunt of it at times, if they hadn't done, whatever it was. Stopping the Spirit and blessings of the Lord!? Snapping out of it. Back into the moment state.

This woman, seeing her son's face when he was a toddler. Seeing him as he had experienced his first touches with the world's things. What emotions they do evoke, to be contemplated later the questions of what had he seen in those one things, the things that bounced back a return from the child that was out of place.

The little boy lived in the woods, the hum of the towns and the devil's cities out there in the night, the smell of the foods on the wind. The moon played like an accomplice; he loved to watch. In the daylight though he saw a boy like him drinking a green concoction, it had bubbles coming up the straw and it looked, Mother hissed! when he approached the subject only once.

The sun starch of tent canvas, dry stiff parts up high and the damp rumple down at the bottom and corners hidden in stagnant air. The diet of lentils and beans and the other: God's real food.
The endless quadrants of elementary desks, a life free of all of that. Free of all of those poisonous hygiene products that people slather all over themselves, even their teeth! The young boy eventually sensing a comparison, there.
Without the hum of electricity, the hauling of water buckets looking up. The reflection of those airliners they are endless and there are people in those chairs up there. Isolated from the worlds he began to hunt the creatures in the bible, the rifle cold as the wind. It is still in the blind;
and it fires. The steam rolls up belching from the stomach as the young man is doing chores to drag meat home for mother and she praises him; part splashed in micro dot blood. For a while it shined on him like a hundred years of sunshine. Out on the fringes of their existence the range of the game trails and he began to come out on the edge of the town's folk. Coming out of the woods:
as he wrote in his letter
" Streetlights push back the black neat rows. Off to the right a graveyard appears, lines of stones, bodies molder below"

He is walking out slowly soaking it in: cemeteries, a landfill, the abandoned farm houses. His family could live like royalty in any one of them. The young man creeping through the rooms, in the decrepit. Imagining breakfast with the spread out of ransack, clothed in cob web and dust. Walking into the family room the shadows of father and mother nearly stained on the back wall. All the years of the farm radio then eventually the television. Burning their eyeballs, they cannot see the world for what it is.

What would you then gauge as normal? The child's eyes, seemed to random flash like camera shot upon certain textures in the world. Reminding her that her son there is also part "numb nuts" who rattled loose on the train and her understanding for a moment that her son must at times see the world through the lent eyes of his father. His

Father's rights, they can never be denied. Silk coding forever there inside of the helix, her being able to remember him making the slapping transaction of that privilege.

Snapping back to the moment state, the child's eyes are flashing upon the tent walls, camera flashing slowly at the cups lined on the open board. Flashing then upon all of the handmade laundry. Then now his eyes flashing strobe nearing on the walls behind her. The child's mind flashing and she was there when he would've unexpectedly turned toward her, locking gaze looking through plum spot blinking.

Snapping out of it, back into the moment state. The faith to believe in something so hard,
their life has always been! In the Lord's Likeness!

In the photo of them there, it was mother. She is wearing what appears to be a home-made dress. It is proper and timeless and it makes it look like she wears the pants in the family, at least at times. Brother and the oldest of one of the sisters tending to the littler ones. It is cast upon them, this while feeding the babies fixing mis-buttoned little shirts. When the little one was teething his younger sister, no doubt would have been in the dark room with the baby for an hour by now, red hot and howling. The fit rage of gnashing gums periodically shattering her unprotected eardrum. Where were Mother and Father? They had said they were going to the woods to pray? Iz too was frustrated at his father, they were living out of tents and off of cup boards. The "house" is in disrepair there are new materials on the site that are turning grey and sun-stroked. There are too many children it seems already. Her older brother would've eventually popped into the doorframe for her with a cool rag for the hot little rascal to gnaw on and took the old one anew. He would have brought her a drink maybe and rubbed her shoulder. Wouldn't she then look up at him? Maybe he had interrupted her deep in some gaze, she was becoming overwhelmed but the smile in her eye now, the natural emotion flooding in at each other.

In his developmental years he had poured over photos, finding them in libraries and bookstores looking at them his eyes flaring and his cheeks flushing with the artworks of **Maurice François Alfred**

Martin van Miële. You can see the desperation in their eyes in there. Clawing out in ecstasy and wrongness there are eyes watching from the shadows in the background. At times the meat in the larder would be running low. Older brother is strapping his rifle on and his backpack, he is packing light. He would've known the terrain he had been set to hunting for years to feed this brood. Buckets and buckets of gut pile smearing in the dark. Living out of tents, without even *laying a roof,* sometimes it's best to just walk out in the wilderness and wasn't it -Henry David Thoreau who said "The world is but a canvas to our imagination."

The canvas was tight in the wind, flapping at times in a suspicion that perhaps them kids were being used as rubes. As he went out across the acre little mother watching him walk into the trees at dusk, he is fearless, she prays for her brother. He is such a blessing to the family and to her.

Into the woods inside, he would have circled back at least once. To come up quietly and maybe to get to hear one of these constant assurances from the Lord for himself. Something to quell this coal gut fire that his father isn't really a louse and squandering their lives like from in the Bible, A sluggard they called it. The path was obvious to him he would've known the lay of the land and as he approached the opening in the woods where he knew they would be, this woman held so much and coveted in her husband's hands always randy.

The son creeping up for some nourishment, some flaring reprimand sharp and deliberate.

As he then edging his eye past the leaves hanging there, eyes flaring wider, then slowly squinting.

He always had an excellent attitude, his family said. Normal instances, playing incidental,

He mentioned in passing once, you have to go back and catch it. It is in a fragmented section, trying to get momentum again in the interrogation room but one of the contraption's swinging arms knocked over a drink onto the papers of the story that he was trying to tell. Replaying it over and over, there it is hidden in the passing.

He says that when he was young and just starting out, that it was an armed robbery, and you hear what must've been a micro squirt of dopamine puff spore mist smearing into the dark mirror of the Intruder's mind, because his voice becoming dripped of honey and lucid.

The voice cracks on the tape.

" Was it a Bank Back Then?

Was it a Bank that we can reference,

back at that time, Israel?

"No, "he sleepily tells them, exhaling lazily inflection.
"It was a small store"

Snatching back up and away the limb of low hanging fruit, quickly up out of reach from the guy sitting across from the interrogation. The dream state's anesthesia, soak spilling quickly across the table cloth of his mind,
 a fading grin glistened through before. He started to tell again how this one time.
The woman who was at the till, and he was just a kid really. He said as he had scanned back again over the floor plan in the middle of the robbery, it was a car crashing in molasses. He says that as he swung the tip of the pistol back towards the lady. The swing stop clearing from blurry and then it was as if the building and then the outside too was at the bottom of an abyss trench or something. Everywhere the dead's silence. "she" was looking frantic across the deathscape and coming suddenly to his eyes locked onto hers already,

"Had you "done" anything to her?"

"No, I hadn't really done anything" he said,
except robbing the place with a gun.

The lady would've seen him stunning through images racing back behind his eyes just then.

A beat of time too long, her fear maybe becoming puzzled.

The strongest realizations blooming across his mind there two things so familiar, crossing and overlapping instantly there before him like a vision.

"That she looked like my Mother"
And that she was terrified, he said and that he pondered it for a long time,
  before that he did it.

As he wrote in his Letter:

I looked in your eyes, they were so dark, warm and trusting, as though you had not a worry or care. The more guileless the game the better potential to fill up those pools with your fear.

Behold Mother's arm is down across her lumbar walking Guru raised eyebrow, a gesture in an honor to the old woman in the medieval woodcuttings, carrying the bundle of dry sticks on her hunched back. All there, here in the real world.

The hot tub is steaming, this generations' wealthy. Coming out on the edge of Resort towns, out here on the fringe. Just through the trees from the Keyes Children. Looking back with tilted head the boy is watching you and yourn.

They had inquired quite briskly and with some duration my brother. What were you doing in Vermont all of that time?
Heidi Keyes later sitting in appointment with Federal Agents disclosing statements as they required them of her. She said that she had questioned her son regarding the trip when he never really went up to see his brothers. They had terried there for him at the Maple Farm in Maine, let it prosper Lord, By your Grace. When his reason was that he had taken some time off to do some fishing in the sleepy watersheds of Vermont, she would've nearly hissed inside knowing that he had been these last years pioneering his way in the norths of Alaska! The "Last Frontier?" Peering down into the waters of Five

Annual Runs of Wild Salmon. The kelp bed's surface for us is a slithering Medusa rooftop.

Fortunately, the F B I having subpoenaed and analyzed the matrix's old connections, looking for all of his Cell Phone Data over the years. They found many defined patterns where his cellphone service would "Blackout". Which would be the completely turning off of the phone, removing the battery and the Sim Card. Thus, the towers would still be sending out that strong signal light but them pinging on nothing, back then. State of the art clanging search light, scanning the archives and dissecting the obsolete older code. Forever still is the data, caught passing in massive swaying forests.

A shockwave across the darkness in a flash, eyes the size of tennis balls and black. Sea lion molars are set and then snapping a Silver Salmon's pistachio shell spine. The back half of him quivering as pink slime came up around the long ivory fang. Mouth opened to oblong OH! The front end only has one move left and fighting more it feels so foolish, terrified and wobbling as if someone had commanded them to. Wobbling frantically making it easier as he is gulped. To be reduced to thick milk for the seal babies they are so cute and soft and by this time the Killer whales have all changed their clicking whale language they are in here close with everyone else, moving among the dilapidated reefs, sliding through the projects with a ghost revolver down low by their knees as they glit into position.

Information shooting in quick bursts the biologists listening bent at the sonar ear phone on some boat, they press the ear in with one hand, the other is a finger raised in the room. To describe the things that they hear when the Killers have the young mother, she is becoming isolated: **Tactical.**

The little pups, she will redirect, she will look back for you, she will do anything that you ask her to.

In an article printed in a larger urban area newspaper, for Palm Beach County: Israel would've been 29 years... at the time.

~ **BOCA RATON, Fla.** – *Almost 10 years after a mother and daughter were found dead in the parking lot of a Boca Raton mall, police have released new images in hopes of finding their killer.*

The Boca Raton Police Department posted an eight-minute video on its Facebook page Tuesday to bring attention to the open investigation into the deaths of Nancy and Joey Bochicchio. The video includes new photographs from the crime scene.

The bodies of Nancy Bochicchio, 47, and her 7-year-old daughter, Joey Bochicchio, were found in their still-running sport utility vehicle in the parking lot of the Town Center at Boca Raton on Dec. 12, 2007. Both had been bound and fatally shot.

No one has been arrested, but Boca Raton police believe the killings are linked to an August 2007 carjacking in which the victim survived.

"She indicated that she had been abducted, as she left the mall, at gunpoint, driven to a bank in the area, forced to withdraw money, taken to a secondary location, where she was tied up again in a different manner with some unique features to the way she was restrained," Capt. Matthew Duggan said in the video.

The victim provided information that led to a sketch of the man believed to be responsible.

Duggan said there were "definitive links" between the two incidents. He said the abductor placed goggles over the women's eyes.

~Jane Doe said it all began as a normal shopping trip. She drove to the mall with her young son and parked her black Lincoln Navigator in a parking lot near Nordstrom department store.

After about two hours of shopping, she walked back to the vehicle and placed her son in his car seat in the rear passenger side. Then, she said, after putting some shopping bags in the front passenger seat and the stroller in the back, she walked around the SUV to the driver's seat.

Only then, she said, did she hear her son cry out for her. That's when, she said, she looked back into the car and was shocked to see a man seated there next to her boy holding a gun to his head.

"I was shaking, and I was just in disbelief that this was happening," she said. "He said 'Get in the car now.'"
She described the man as about 6 feet tall, white or Hispanic, with a medium build. He had a ponytail and was wearing a floppy hat and sunglasses. She said she begged him not to hurt them and just take what he wanted, but what he wanted was for her to start driving.
"He just said drive to the bank,' she said. "He didn't raise his voice, he wasn't angry, wasn't yelling, wasn't frantic."
She said he seemed to know what he was doing. She didn't want to try to yell for help because her son was strapped in the car seat and the man was pointing his gun at him.
After being ordered to an ATM, Jane Doe withdrew all the money she could -- $600 -- and hoped the man would let them go, she said. Instead, he told her to drive to a remote spot where he ordered her out of the car. He then handcuffed her wrists and used plastic zip ties to bind her feet and her neck to the headrest in the rear seat next to her child, she said.
He then pulled out onto the highway, in what Jane Doe said was the worst part of the ordeal.
"I remember seeing people in cars passing me and just wondering how no one knows, you know, that this is happening to us," she said. "No one knows that there is this horror going on inside this car. No one knows that I'm going to die today."
But in the hour or so they were together, driving and briefly conversing, Jane Doe said she somehow sensed a change in her abductor. Once cold and calculating, he slowly warmed to her. Eventually, she said, he turned the SUV around and returned to the parking lot. Leaving the engine running, he got out and took her driver's license.

When the big ivory molars were set, the Killer whale never pausing for the prestige, crunching down and cracked her pool ball vertebrae severing the toothpaste fluid and her bottom half then instantly having forgotten who it was, her identity forgotten in a heavy dull click, the top of her is thrashing out a deep red cast of arc in the sun back dropped glistening across the water. In Iron splashing out free again. The red simply absorbed by the rocking water in the backseat of the Luxury SUV with the AC running.

All of that and he is standing there, her son now aged 33 years. Looking her in the face when she asked him, "Son where hast thou been?"

And he needed so bad just to explore the back ass crack of the Winooski River watershed?! Their fish and game regulations read like this:

Vermont
-**Rainbow Trout** ,**Brown Trout**: minimum length 10"; daily limit, 2 trout

Every creek, slough, river or brook in the Index saying nearly the same thing

She did the math, from the time that he had left her place in Indiana, it was both that night and also the early morning too, that the one college girl went missing down in Bloomington and she was beautiful. She said that she figures that her son must've been out there for up to three or four days?! Plying the wilds of that bullshit forest? They say that back in the day Johnny Appleseed came through there too. Eventually leaving when he started to get the trout shits.

CHAPTER ELEVEN

MAPLE SERVICE

At one-point years ago Israel had connected suddenly with Grandma up in Maine. He kept her service diligently and stayed up there a long while. Pulsing along the road paths of the Adirondack. A creature contemplating the moon, while cast only in its moonlight. He had used her birthday in particular as a reason to touch down far too early and then out of the necessity of some random thing or flimsy excuse, making him having to buckle down and rack up a thousand miles or more on some rental car.

The fantasies had started as a matter of fact. The thing getting stronger every time he lets it catch a big breath. Lately it has started sucking in so strong he has to fight the hatch closed. He was living in atmospheres which he would compound greatly onto himself. A creature changed now from the unseen pressures. It has changed the form of his energy, being no doubt like the Adirondack forests, mimicking and abiding at the edge of that invisible line of cold air above them it has changed them.   Each year he would be forced to drive the breadth of that whole area teasing in and out of those trees, them acting as a high tide line. Marked out under the front, becoming a cloud forest, becoming a different creature all together. Altered by living amongst that environment for that long. Becoming familiar with all of those abandoned resorts from back before the railroad had connected us much faster. These had been the posh retreats out on the fringe then and he would cluster these little sinister missions around the excuse that he is just passing through for the likes of Grandma's Birthday or any convenience of occasion.

It makes you wonder what if Heidi had been understanding of her son and his paraphilia for trans porn. What if she had let him experiment safely with how to describe feelings at a younger age of the things that would crystalize into things that would ferment into the joy and the nut pulse as he closes his eyes. Instead, the daydreams and the books on: "people that do the things I do" he said.
Reading of Ted Bundy, Golden State Killer, Ocala, Robert Hansen, BTK, even the Zodiac. He said he read them all.

It was when he started finally breaking into living person's houses. That's when he knew he was different. The vase of stems and buds on the end table he recognized them. He had walked in with the refrigerator buzzing on in the night. Later as he was climbing back out of the window with a few guns and some other bullshit the vase caught his eye again. It was a death flower and it had opened while he had peered through the door slit at the couple sleeping. The death flower had bloomed, it was beautiful and chanting and he stopped and he stared,
and it felt like forever.
Then in a swift of fabric or something else and he was gone. Instantly into the neat black rows and into the darkness.

Once upon a time there was a VHS tape rolling as a Matriarch of the Church of Wells was standing pointing finger a vengeance curse telling parents of a shamed adult child of theirs for some infraction, "You will be judged by your fruits!" she sneered over and over, standing as an accuser with arm stretched out of God's wrath. The little girl, Heidi's last child, looking up snapping eyes to where she thought Mother was, but she was farther away. The little girl's expression is flat. Knowing that there is a lesson to be learned in there somewhere, but the lords' way is above our ways and they are elusive. The answer is around far too many corners in this maze that he has made for her: the architect of such things. The little girl slips off the stool and tut-tut, follows along behind mother like the good calf do.

Any dust from his road tires had maybe been settling down to the dirt over the hours, back there at Mother's driveway as he had dropped completely off of the grid and he has been down in there somewhere for days.

Having to go through the transition soon, so that he can pop back out of it and up on the grid again.

A conservative 6 or 7 o'clock arrival should yield fellowship and an understandable early evening to bed. He is nearing the end of any miles left to contemplate and remember freely all of these things,

Tonight, at around 9:00 he will be pulling into Smyrna Mills, Maine.

Old memories of time with Grandma.

If he had driven straight through, he would have been there by 3 o'clock that afternoon.

Coming in directly from the Currier's, in his rental again. He said that he had pulled over and it would've been assumed to sleep but he said he was still "amped up" and really wanting to do something. A frantic anticipation now scratching wildly from on the inside of the painted glass. A frightening clawing, almost anything will do. He had been driving while scanning for opportunities. There was this one place and as the counting down of landmarks now approaching zero, pulling into this rural turn-off he probably would've went from a junkie right before your eyes. Erratically playing the parts, pushing calm and in control, is the shaky wrist.

The trees overhanging the gravel road, this is a spot that glowed on the horizon for him. A place out in the lonesome with a feature that assures you with near certainty that someone will arrive sooner or later. Him never slipping a line of when he had actually found it. This spot having a collection of things about it that made it better than so many of the other pull offs,

At no doubt numerous times out here by the river, overhead coming in the clouds in a rigid perfect glide, a giant roller-pen lens, scrolling mathematically over the creation. The blinking eye stopping overhead, looking down on this place from screen view, he would often take screenshots and print them up from the likes of Mapquest.com on Kim's computer. When he was arrested on his phone there still was a photo of the exact computer screen. The part Amish kid was attempting to cut the line with the other side when he had jumped over the dead-air space, leaping from the computer screen where the software could know everything, into a static image of it, still and

glowing only on his phone as a photo file, basically the same face right there distorted on the screen but the coordinates, the I P address, server bank, time of day, location lock, all lost, it could've been a picture of anything to the scanning hardware back then. He had arranged it, then he had clicked it. Pretty sure that he is taking all the precautions, he knew by then that he was being followed by something like doom from the other world. This warm glowing image on his phone acting as a tiny window of a little bird's eye amulet, a blinking distorted globe view on his person, but here finally and safely viewing the websites and photos of Samantha Koenig: on the screens in an abandoned house with power and WIFI, even hunkered down in a pig's trove of a dirty little human nest by the old landline. The light from the screen is glowing on his now horrible cave rotten cheekbones as he is losing grip, the first soft waves of peach sherbet life light from the screen, it shivers on his face, so horrible, what if he licked his mummy licorice lips.
He said that she had gagged when he applied the lube.

Eventually, he is suddenly up from the greasy edged little human nest over by the old landline and is moving quickly. Oddly stacking fur hides by the door and they were still laying there all arranged as he came from in the flames and passing by them, he went through the opening swiftly and they would be black glass dust splinter by the time of the changing angles of the sun tonight. He would be watching the structures burn from some small elevation nearby, he said. The reports showing that while the red lights were flashing there across the grass at the scene of the crime and the inferno that some guy pulled up. Roaring whoosh having to talk more loudly trapped in the house it sounds to be in fury and he pulls up and asked for directions. Maybe when they said how many miles that way, he might've gasped a soft Uhn sigh, at the distance.

The air in the house had been starting from a small whooshing on towards its unknown greatness, something was coming up after him swiftly in the light tunnels of the computer. Something like from in the bible. In it, it says "They will run their race". On the one side, washed in light their ancient athlete is pounding fiercely. It's skin, flashing the colors of our swift sunset, flashing every one of them, from every angle. Somewhere in the dark one though, is the sound of piped thunder and you can only hear it with your eyes. A contest of the champions, even of one of Heaven's own most beautiful Angels and one of Hell's finest of Rangers.

"It's nice to have something everywhere you go" he said. Hearing his teeth click with your eyes, when he said it.

It should've been devastating to him when he came in and there off to the side was a Ranger's truck! Maybe it was just parked there as a ploy. He distinctly says that he had envisioned the Park Ranger walking out of the brush and stumbling upon him "wrangling the young couple" there is an old saying something about ~ a bird in hand

he still pulled further into the position though. That is how good this spot was.

There had been that Sherriff's car after all, parked across from the old farmhouse, he had said. In the black emptiness perhaps, Lorraine had maybe seen it there in the ghastly shadow world. He had told Bill and Lorraine that "there are other people involved, when we get to the farmhouse". As they are arriving and she saw no one.

Her heart little hummingbird,
    so sad at the frightening flutter.

as her wild feet were running in pounding. Small stones no doubt flinging up slowly for a moment behind her, the second footstep coming down, tearing between two worlds, one short one here in this, place. Maybe the Angels up there were trying to supercharge her spirit, cranking up the star's pin brilliant strike across the whole heaven, a daughter of man, like in the bible, instantly and so very unbelievably washed in a scape of God's starlight. running from the part open door of the Saturn. The Sherriff's car in the darkness was cast in dim moonlight.

The last of her sure footings coming down now to the white blind flashing in her eyes heart thrash pounding your vision in each slow jiving foot stomp, in the dark she sees no lit-up laptop screen in the sheriff's dim car, seeing it empty, if she ever did. It would've been devastating as he pummeled her. Remembering then a woman that

could be his mother, onto and across the ground. To feel her ribs
wracking in nightmare breaths heaving.

The record showing that even though the moon had been
waxing stronger the last few days, however numerically it was only
shining at 43% illumination. There were clouds passing over in the
night but it wouldn't be until right about now at mid-day on the day
after, back at the farmhouse standing frightening grim, obscured from
the road from weed and bramble it is the Little Indian Brook, the same
one that runs up and along the end of Colbert Street. From the
Currier's little driveway and stopping by the tree in the front yard that
will be draped in Yellow Ribbons and the photo of them. Standing at
the mail box looking left at the end of their street instead of houses it
is a wall of weed bramble and brush. At its edge there is a small
depression in there dry most of the year. The same one in the back
yard of the farmhouse, now bathed in the crying out from the night
before.

He so many miles away already nearing Maine and he said that
he was going through Lorraine's "Belongings" he said. Pulled off to
the side, any moment the heavens could part the roof up there. No
doubt warm pollens on thermals wafting up from her draped fabrics.
They are glowing, caressing them, he is lavished in pulses of the
waves of the charged particles they are flashing across the plasma in
his mind. The screenplay of the dark farmhouse increasing all around
him suddenly.

Still compiling the images, but now only being able to hold them for
less and less each time before it crashes to a blank screen again, here
in the real world. There the day after, watching this spot on some rural
river. Stroking the fabrics in the rental and handling the hair in his
hands as if they were acting as an anchor line into the dreamworld. He
is holding on to them and he can stay in there longer for now. The
sound of the river lapping at its edges, the background fading to blur.

It must've been 1997 when his mother and father were trying
again, all the way up there by the Canadian Border and then still out of
town even more too. Looking out from the trees past the road where
they dump trash and old appliances. Back there looking out upon

them, an their'n. The cross section of his silencer years later, the Law enforcement had heard back from the guys who actually wear the gear and they were all impressed with the design and blown away at his craftsmanship but back then when they lived in Colville, Washington, he was just a kid really. Old eyes blinking at this new world. About to inherit it in sun stroked suspenders and the random smell of damp cloth. To champion over what, as he comes to age. The tent fabric is hanging soft in the background around her smiling face, eyebrows raised, talking for hours like kids under a bed sheet's make shift tent, eyes alight. At times one of them opening up,
dropping off into an intense whispered voice in the quiet deep hours, hearing periodically about someone whom are adolescent, having recently committed suicide. The acquaintance laying cooling as someone would find them quizzical, with shaking hands, lower lip upside down turning inside out, knowing that sizzling gag tear, that it burned them instantly and forever there.
Imagining the young kid still,
their peach soft jaw, it steels to a grit
from weeping,
and then some normal object, placed so incidentally,
it seems to sizzle out chanting into the air of the room. The other people in the day to day never seeing when it is right there in front of everyone. So deep now in the smearing, never knowing that thundering heart silence with it just at the edge, it is howling and so beautiful and calm. Ready to depart this shitty carnal form in one sharp thunderclap in your mouth and coming to strength between your ears, eyes 14 years', old already. Only staying here for the sake of younger sibling maybe, that they won't be left alone walking in to ask about a snack and finding there a different him, thrown back collapsed onto a home's broken bed and the wall behind it and the top of his shoulders splattered in shell shock beneath a fine rust colored spreckle of tiny rust crimson stars across the low ceiling in the blowback. Eyes opening and then instantly he appeared there again, or part of him still did.

Drifting through the days mostly hollow, like drifting through chain link. Learning each tiny curve in the pen strokes. Eventually each performance, a masterpiece matching the print lines exact, off of the face printed on the dollars, the art of counterfeiting all of those mimicked monkey rules and all of the gestures for all of the people. The entire time feeling it all dead broken inside.

voice breaking so unexpectedly, to rattle ribbon. Then the sob and then the come down. Coming to terms as the sun is creeping towards the blue-black horizon, eyes alight, washed in glistening stars twinkle across the dew on the tent fly wall in the deep morning hours, with the only friend that you got, in this shitty fucking …world…………

How easily having let slip the lamplight of life from the flesh of the hidden dead hands and face, right there under the surface, here in the real world. Letting slip the typical happiness's, the zombie inside numb clutching at anything that throws off the most noise and the most sting, barely hearing for the maddening static. At that time and in that town, there was this little girl who had two prosthetic feet, but she had won awards and she was so full of pepper, that she folded her little sweater over her arm and nodded pleasantries and clackety, stepped out onto that warm walk to her Sunday school. Learning to live in atmospheres compounded, 1 becoming 3. A little creature that if you saw her with the ever eyes, walking by through the limbs ticking along the road up there. Sending out shockwaves of Dignity. They said she was a celebrity in that town.

So powerful through the trees, scattering beams of Defiant. The trail passed by that one spot through the leaves, it tumbles playfully down to the river's edge.

His older sister is there in the middle of the family photo. She is wearing a white wedding veil that is pulled back showing her smiling. She has pulled her hair in dark auburn up and over her shoulder on the open side, it comes down out over her tight neckline, over her wedding dress front, the last of the tips of her hair are pressed between her bosom and a brown church suit and tie of some sawed off runt little rooster. He is looking at the camera, the look in his eyes says, this is the biggest thing that has ever happened to him. On the backdrop of wide pleat church curtain there is evergreen boughs in wreath showing the top of a heart that they must've made thereon the back wall. Surrounding the young groom are seven siblings the one at the top of the heart is in his arms. At the bottom 7 o'clock position is their father. He appears perfect and plastic, like a fundamentalist's Kenneth and Barbara doll from a Missionary Play House.

Next to the bride in the photo is the cherub, the latest baby held there by Mother of course and clumped on to the side even more back is her next eldest, her son Israel and directly behind her on flat ground is the next younger sister. Only his head and a moon slit of his neck are visible. The light source off and to the left. His whole body and part of his chin are in the darkness. She is there with one hand laying cupped on Mother's shoulder. Her lips are flat and firm and her expression seems to change like the sea from afar. Something migrating through anxious then piercing, settling finally she looks scared or very concerned. The next in line.

THE CLOSEST CALL

CHAPTER TWELVE

RIVER WED

He was down by that river in rural Maine dragging his hands through Lorraine's suitcase. Numbing in the blurry fabrics and there rumpled in all the rest of their stuff was their "9 1 1 only phone" and it had been on in there the whole time! He said that he had quickly disabled it.

Calming into enjoying the rush of it all again and he said that he was running her silkies over his hands, in the windshield there is a white blur and it is moving. He says he looked and saw this car that had pulled up and the young girl is getting out and she is giddy and ready it seems. The young man is getting out and they are so happy and vibrant and turned on. The intruder was in there; chanting. In the glare of the windshield the markings all over the young kid's car was of crepe paper and soap bar.

Down here by the river he was scathing himself in parentheses and font it said "Just Married". He was tortured for want of them. He wanted to already be out of the car. Approaching them in a tone and gesture that indicates that you are realizing you are floating recklessly somehow. The zip-tie back there jostling the young man's shoulders. He described it as "they never expect something like this to happen to them". He is watching them through the glass intently.

The river shimmer golds, that twinkle through the fabric. Soft clothing becoming translucent and where the aura at its brightest, where other than the honey glow, the clothes actually become invisible.

There is her nude form in warm plump light. Would the small smooth stone be so farfetched, if she threw one at the water? Often very anticlimactic and she made a little bouncing pouty face she was so cute and funny, but then that rump little rooster would come over and in the friscalating light this groom he is so young look at the back of his neck. This is the one who gets to saunter over and show her how to skip a stone? and he lets one fly. Coming out of his hand it is spinning flat and low to the water it is traveling around some center within itself. The balance in the counterplay of the heavy lobe passing by, then the smaller sides they are farther away but it moves in there, it has found itself. Maybe the kid had already gotten lucky, because it appeared by the intended flight path that it was text book and it was perfect. The stone coming down about to splash that first critical touch it is expecting it, glistening in light, over the sheen of golden glass.

When Israel's Mother Heidi was interviewed by the Agents, it came up regarding the Currier trip, she had said casually that while her son was to be stopping by on his way up to the old property in Maine where her other sons were there waiting and he is going in to help them. He is their oldest son. Remembering how Israel had increased the wealth of the family property many years before in Maupin, when they lived in Oregon, by God's good blessings. There was something that took place though back then and everyone deserves their privacy. It summarizes down to that at some point her young son wasn't living at home any longer. The Keyes trying again out in Oregon country. He actually had returned there to Maupin with a friend near his age, to help the family complete renovations on the house that they had endeavored.

It had an excellent location; looking down on the river from some small nearby elevation. In the year of our Lord 1997 it must've been. During the renovations the son, a young man now. His father the aloof appliance repair man there watching the swift and sure carpentry skills Israel has picked up along the way or had been learned somewhere. The young man, wiping sweat from his brow with his wrist he came out as an atheist looking over his shoulder tilting a bit as he said it, as a first step he said; and the Father disowned him there in front of everyone. Bittered the slit eyes become. Alone now sanding the new handrails, they were essentially perfect. There are so many angles and surfaces to touch with grit sand paper. It needing to be meticulous in hours kneeling and of touching up into every crease and crevice continually repositioning.

In the room with the table, he told them that he had read about all of the serial killers. Robert Hansen had lived in Anchorage, Alaska himself, but that was back in the 70's. Robert was a Baker, they often find jobs that would place them there at a time of day when all of the big swinging bulls would be out in the fields and where the softer, more un-alarming man has her undivided attention to spool his little yarns and to relentlessly gain proximity with his authority, or his warm services. After rush hour the office girl is tip-toeing to look down into the doughnuts. They are so fresh and so soft, right there for the taking. He is staring down into hers. Dennis was an inspector made code enforcer with his uniform he had appeared in the window at mid-morning peeked in the curtains and the lady was incensed with anger at the intrusion, or how many hens come in fluttering about the old stove and how she needs a new one but her husband says they can't afford one and could he come by and take a peek at it for her, the poor little town's long tall and smiling, appliance repair man. The one who never wants anyone to get a good look at his many children. Seeing him coming down the lane, he had a walking gate. Back in Anchorage the Butcher Baker on the prowl the baker driving through down town at 3:30 in the morning. Beth had disappeared from the road or the parking lot of the old Buy-Low store on Northern Lights Boulevard 3 days after the first girl of the pair had come back alive. Robert Hansen had started an assault on a type of girl that wasn't what he loved to hate. The first girl was just trying out a little prostitution, but she had had the worst of luck. He drove her just out of town first to McHugh Creek, just as he possibly had with Beth a few days later. 15.4 miles on the old paper maps that he had obsessed over. He told her with gritting jaw, she said unbelievably later, that he was anxious and desperate in the car there. He came to a conclusion about something and glanced over vulnerable. Her hands were wrapped in punishing electric wire from the spool in the back of Robert Hansen's truck or the one from the house, violent "sex growl" when he told her that he wanted her to let him pull up her shirt. He will cut off her bra with his big knife, no doubt a gulping after he said it, then they can drive on and he doesn't have to "do", anything else here on the roadside and she lets him. Her breaths must've stilled as the knife went up under the strap. Holding her pumping heart, as he jerked the knife she would've saw him there above her, "the Butcher Baker".

His eyes are coming down from it afterward. Dimming they had pulsed when her breasts meant to be hidden away and only peeked at, as they had splashed out free form when the blade had slid up the ribbon, and it was good. It appearing as his eyes coming down from it, dimming from the pulse. He later drove on and on 100 miles and did eventually assault her but he never "finished" she said.

She was beautiful. The poor girl that he had abducted a few days later had started fighting him as soon as he started in on her, she hadn't made it past the first stop. Freezing to death part slashed and wounded having run and fell into the ravine off the park parking lot at McHugh Creek.

The Butcher Baker's daydreams starting most likely from when he was in the Boy Scouts. Tying knots with twine and lashings with his scout knife. Out in the tents under moon clouds, thinking about the girls at his school back in town. Ridiculed of them, is the consensus of his peers. But little bobby could still see an angle. A few scenarios that it could still go down with the girls and still be feasible. Quickly the good one becomes the only one, beginning to be replayed over and over as a young boy. Always hidden. Never letting anyone know. Even after all these years, eventually it has become part of his Signature.

That this was the part of the scene,
    right before the sex in his little fantasy.

So, then this boy from Cove, Utah, what was the scenario? He would've known every nuance. There is a very specific way that he likes things done, he said.

In a house full of sisters, adults now speaking of Maupin, Oregon in their own interview with the agents, she remembered it fondly at times they would all go to the river shore and the girls would change into some linen dress and swim in the river together. Climbing out of the water dripping down the fabrics becoming translucent the oldest sisters, there is hair down there and the white river dress is clinging. He was at times helping to raise the younger kids, there was a time in particular when their parents were busy with obligations more frequently and the two oldest ran the house as little mom and dad. He always braided their hair they said.

Sitting with their backs nestled against him he is running his hands through the fire strands glowing in lamplight before bedtime, maybe wearing their flimsies.

These places that we know that he chose, they begin to make the cipher.

Whitewaterguidebook.com /oregon /deschutes-river

> "The Deschutes River in Oregon runs hundreds of miles and is runnable for its entire length. The most popular section of the Deschutes for meandering rapids, great fishing, and overnight trip options is from Harpham to Sandy Flat and runs through the small town of Maupin, Oregon."

Being called back home from out on his own for the first time to finish the family house, he was 18 now. He was able to make amazing progress. Once Israel realized that the building schedule, that it really had none. Israel had so very much equity in the proceeds. A little here, a little there, nothing had been getting done and so much that when they eventually sold the property, they transferred some of the wealth into a place back in Amish country again and eventually it into Israel's name later. It was still there when the investigators keyed it up on the computer it came back glaring and so eerie. Back then finishing the house off of the river and from that porch he had built, now the good son sanding the post railings.

Sanding there alone now, the various slats of wood and vertical miter work, dissolving in peach light as the background is coming up between the railings. Shimmer twinkling golden and glimmering off of the wet surfaces of another group of innertubers floating by and in them is a girl wearing her bikini. He can see creases of the thin slick fabric folding and opening as she kicks her legs at the boy next to her. The boy grabs her foot and with a rascal's eyebrows he pushes it away. She is spinning on the tube. She fans her arms and legs the supposed g forces and squeals it is her brother maybe.

In the Interviews with the Keyes family later they had recalled there was a trip where the whole family had gone caravan style, still praying before each meal. Wherever the Lord saw fit for them to set up a bit of comforts on the sojourn down to California. To never forsake the fellowship of the brethren, in this case they actually were blood kin. When you live a life separate from the devil cities and all those little towns separate from a nation of the unsaved, an apology is in order. Be prepared to "give answer" is what it said. These are the in laws. They were confident that they had left Israel there with his friend Eric to work on the house, pray finish the house and that they would return in 3 and a half weeks, how much of it spent in the arduous travel.

For years he said that he contemplated if he truly did believe in Devil Worship?
He told them about the knives and the sacrifice that he had wanted to perform,
while talking about this girl by the river in Maupin, Oregon. Moving in exchanges around the table. The video crew in the other room watching from the upper corner they should have sat up straight and radioed into the slim line earphones telling them frantically that after all of the stalling and maneuvering that finally "he is there! He is in the room with you now" looking up from the paper photo there at the table telling a story as the images are racing across his eyes and some hit like a heavy drug and there at the table now: the Intruder.

In the vapors of the sewage tank story, he is standing up, naked knees bare in the world for them again. Until the brustle rush of canvas calling him back to reality. Reality coming back to him as he was over top of her there in the outhouse structure, both places at once. The stench of the black swarthing below them in the tank, disappearing in the blood rush of his ears he is there again looking down into those vat pools of wine sloshing in her eyes she wants to close them so bad. He is controlling everything and it becomes maddening. The young intruder in the story slowly looking over, as the one guy in the room with the table speaks shattering the projection on flowing canvas "Israel did you have "the" knives with you at the time?" Israel looks over with clear T-top lenses and acknowledges and then says "yes". Looking back down at the girl's little deer frame, heaving lungs he realized that he didn't want to do it to honor satan or for some greater purpose but that he wanted it for himself, he said. She was pretty young. He said her name was Leah or Julia or something

Some wants becoming needs, some needs becoming the obsession.

His younger sister, young mother to the little ones, in those next few years that he was out in the world she sent pleas to him, that he would come "rescue" her too. Those plans however never materialized for her. During that time, he says that he was often over the border into Canada.   That was when it was later nearing the Year 2000 in Montreal. Seeing it there as it says in the bible, a City of Man. It must've seemed to flash of platinum across his eyes. Approaching its wicked skyline and the lady boys there. Like a recurring dream, popping up unexpectedly over and over, over time. He wants to be doing it with people just over there. He takes the mouth gag off and wants you to hold your own gasps.

It is something about the part that comes right before the end of the sex,
in his fantasy.

He spoke of it later: it wasn't until 2002 creaking on a train, across open terrain, that his Father died. The old man was still believing in God's assured healing, but they had both expired on the way somewhere apparently. The reports are very clear that the procedure that he needed was common and it would have saved his life. "They refused modern medical assistance" looking bitterly at the word "Day Surgery". The program for his Service would be printed as Arizona. Taking the southern route, the warm dry air good for the ailing. Jeffery Keyes in only moments, the old appliance repair man will be whisked away to the next world, and as his eyes will soon glow down into their new eternity? It will be leveraged from the things of his own mouth and by his own life that he had lived. That first wave of septic vapor,

his father clawing wildly at the painted sheet glass from the inside. All of the things that he had clutched at fading from this world to the sound of clacking rails. Mouth going into oblong Oh and body pumping morbid as it overtook him.

The endmost heart, weighed against the things that are wobbling there, in his hand slowly opening.

Eventually then on the tapes speaking again of the old cabin in Constable he stops resolute and he puts the cards away and says "that stuff, is all ancient history stuff".

Almost into rural Maine again, down by that river, watching the "newlyweds". The skipping stone glazed into the surface tension of the golden glittering, it bellied down throwing a spin of skid water and it was flying again it appears to have lost no speed at all. At the table he describes the park restroom building where he had taken the girl with the inner tube as the ones with a concrete floor with a big tank down under it. A tiny little building with a hollow plastic or metal bucket type potty toilet in there close to the back wall. He was always so methodical and so meticulous. He snatched down upon her she is wet in the air as she was scuttling and maybe squinting to go #1 or # 2, most likely both. He says allegedly that he puts her face down over the nasty toilet thing tying her neck to the handicap rail and moved directly into the sexual assault, but it went wrong as soon as she looking into his eyes, speaking calmly even though she was so scared he said.

The girl from the Deschutes, finding balance from the tube. It offers resistance so you can push yourself up, however as you lift away, the tube becomes equally more deflated. Negating the straining of your wrist but then she is up on her feet now. Feeling so heavy on the land and she is tip toeing up to the Recreational Rest Rooms. Balance hurrying her little arms out, her fingertips ticking, is she counting or just flashing them, blinking every other second. Out here it is rural only, river traffic lazily flowing by. She told him that she wouldn't tell anybody and that he didn't have to hurt her, or kill her. The silence weighing in sheet tons.

Him sounding these parts as if kind of dumbfounded, sliding on the chair seat, a grin swarthing just behind lips laying there so glib.

She said that he was good looking and that if he had asked her in a normal setting she would have wanted to. He later outlining very clearly that he had watched her party float by and grabbed her from the river and when they finally asked "what did he do with her?" he said so casually that he put her back in the river, to rejoin her family or her friends. The FBI has no paper on this poor girl. All calls have sounded empty to even vapor or rumor.

Israel was anxious and angry watching the new married couple right there by the river, he said. As the story framing towards something, it would be wise to consider any other circumstances where he is waiting, watching and "them" then thwarted slipping through his hands. Particularly when the story appears to present nothing valuable at all. Day yawn, there in the sleepy interrogation room. They were asking about his activity while living in Anchorage. On the boards was only 1 known victim in over 8 years.
"I'm only going to give you what you already have" he said

However, in the doldrums of the procedural waiting he is speaking so freely appearing to have lowered his guards, using vulnerability to help stave off the boredom or something. Settling into the chairs, the program tucked neatly away as the house lights have gone to black, a soft glow from in the proscenium. He is speaking of that other life and of slinking into some position into one of the multitudes of small secluded parking areas all within a much more expansive park under one name. Having learned to meter the reality that his life was over now in jail, but also being excited to finally be able to tell the story, or something. Taking care not to get overcome in the fulness while bringing the truths right up to just below the surface of the water of the conversations, or an interrogation even.

It was really cool; he had been working on this silencer in his shed. He laughed, "hup", when the guy across from the interrogation made some foolish and almost childlike assumption. Israel Keyes enjoyed telling him that it actually is possible. That he had fired every brand of sub-sonic bullet that he could find, off the shelf and even from obscure old guys at the gun shows through the Ruger through the silencer, down into a bucket filled with water in the shed, right out there in front of everyone. He said that is how he gets his kicks and he had perfected it. The silencer was there attached to a duplicate of the same model that he buried just south of his creepy cabin in Constable, NY.

The Ruger 10/22 semi-Automatic hunting gun made tactical by removing the old wooden sportsman's stock and the click locking sound as the sexy composite, black, synthetic thing, comes out from under the coat of the guy who was just standing by the truck. The stars crinkle against blackness in the cold air the heavens becoming frightenly clear. Just like outer space at those hours out there watching waiting in the endless.

The strap sling on his "Number 1 gun" was homemade, making this deadly little vixen, "hands free". It develops out of nowhere and as it is coming up, on the furthest back of the stock there is a tiny release that having come silently free is snapping out a military style thing made of steel rods and a place for under, over or in the shoulder of your gun eye. Watching it unfolding the jaw might now slowly be dropping as it already having swung out like a switchblade, getting really deep, real fast, and it having already stopped like a slapping proclamation. Then there is the sharp end of the gun and strangely it is huge, nearly laughable it was one of those black tube arms from a ShopVac Hose extension like at Home Depot, he said it blinking both being a reptile and also "the nicest guy you would ever want to meet, an amaaaazing father, one hell of a handyman" and even after everything "they can't believe it is him". To them there must've been one really great one in there somewhere, or something.

That black tube has things inside of it that he had ground and sanded the edges of circles into over and over. There are things that are perfect to slip down into it now acting as tube ribs, stiffening the baffling silencer while baffling all of that sonic from those little brass Tylenols rocking one after another from the drum magazine pushing its loading gun metal tongue up into those crunching metal blocks crashing yet sliding by, back and forth at blind speed glistening in of the finest of thin lubricants. Explosions down the light tube its kaleidoscopes twisting in rifling through a world suddenly poked of holes. Constellation drill bit letting the hornet holes of little fires and brimstone and sulfur G S R blow out whoever dare and it is pouring out of the one right next to it and all down the helixes of eardrum blow lights being easily dispersed and that pop crack of each round is now quietly phlaumphf-ing out of the shopvac tube arm made silencer. He had his earpiece in, he made a point to say it there even out of tempo and he said he kept pulling the trigger as fast as he could until it was empty. Eyelid still quivering at the brass having tinkled down. That is what they would see in their mind when it would be developing out of nowhere right in front of them. This couple that was there alone and they were right on the other side of the door. Ice steam breathes up into lit blackness. The most preferred aspect of the gun is at its sight alone possibly getting "them" to "lock up" when they saw it coming out: the breakdown stock and the silencer. The shopvac tube arm possibly is like any one of every other one across the nation at Home Depot. One is on the end of his squirrel gun, as it would have just stomped down hard, in black stiletto.

However, he said that "they" were not ideal victims and when they inquired around the table if it was because one of a short list of assumptions, the needle was weighing his words and it stopped on the question "were they overweight?". It was a comic relief from the guy across the table making some vaudeville quip about Israel liking "300 pounders"? Eventually his preference he said "light weight" these were heavies, or one of them in there was. He said that he was just about to go for it, body rocking in the momentum stilled when a police cruiser had pulled in. Can you imagine? and he said he was edging himself out in the dark and into the steam cold. He was going to go for it. Apparently, that is how good this spot was too. This time another cop car also responded into the vicinity of him calling it good for the night. That guy pulling in there, he had ruined it. He never got to use his "#1 gun" he said. Never using it in that really cool part of the plan whatever it must've been.

From the metal bracelets it sounded like he wanted to bite his knuckle at the missed opportunity. If the vehicle had only been reliable: debit cards, Identification, zip-ties, duct tape, blindfolds, plural. In an "oh well" kind of way he said that he packed it in for the night. Almost seeing for themselves the washing tiger stripes of amber light rippling slowly over his face and his eyelids. Cutting short the warm come down, some garbled voice was inquiring for a deeper understanding maybe moving instantly on their own instinct alone asking what kind of car was it, back then? that they could reference. Bringing him back from somewhere more real, a blinking…what. He couldn't believe the drinks and then of course the candy was nice almost something like a dream state responding in the expose'. What kind of a car?

This beautiful arrangement of Stars, faithful and bright glittering in the heavens they are all named by names long forgotten. The Greeks they called these stars, the Pleiades. Something about a man's daughters cast into those stars forever there. Held tight, cast only in moonlight. For the glitter lights up there, they see us moving in and out of shadow. Blinded of the blueness in the light of the day, as it darkens the eyes seeing them down there looking up making such an impression
and as they are passing over the rolling horizon a different people pointing up and naming them new. The Japanese manufacture a car with it still there on every grill, there as their logo, they were perfect but there was that Park Ranger's truck nearby and he said he kept waiting for him to leave. He couldn't afford to be rustling the newlyweds if the Ranger came out of the woods.

He was frustrated while setting his car in order, because of obligations leaving the spot, passing by them there. Looking back, it would've burned inside, they were so perfect. They never knew how close of a call it had been or how lucky they were. He seemed so glib there though, almost giddy on his seat. He mentions timing things like this around the Bear Paw Festival and more importantly the Fur Rondy, because the cops in Anchorage would be mostly downtown, he said.

Later when he would eventually arrive to his brothers, he says that he had been up for like, 36 hours. Maybe late that night the little new wife her eyes in fright gasping open, just a Dark Dream though. Or were they from long before? Only him watching the "young newlyweds" warm beautiful skin soured and corrupting. Their more innocent eyes staring off through dark bilge as he is describing them to the agents and the detectives and the attorneys. Hidden in plain sight in some incorrect scenario. The newlywed wanting to cry out across the table, right there in front of their faces.
Down by the river, talking about the young girl and he said he returned to the outhouse building off the Deschutes the next day because he was sure that he had dropped something he said.

Apr 29th, 1997

COLVILLE (AP) -- Skeletal remains found in a wooded area outside town are those of a 12-year-old girl who has been missing for more than a year, Stevens County Sheriff Craig Thayer said Monday.

A homicide investigation was under way in the death of **Julie** Harris, Thayer said. No suspects have been identified.

Children playing along a rural road found the unburied remains Saturday, Thayer said. A check of dental records confirmed the identification.

The cause of death was under investigation, he said.

Harris disappeared March 2, 1996, from her Colville home and was reported as a runaway the following day. The girl, a double-amputee, was able to get around on her own with prosthetic feet.

Those feet were found last April near the confluence of the Colville and Columbia rivers.
No other signs of the girl had turned up until Saturday.

CHAPTER THIRTEEN

"THAT IS HOW HARD IT'S GOING TO BE FOR YOU, WITHOUT ME"

Awaking on the plane for a moment,

                          coming back from somewhere
more real.

He said he quit drinking around his army buddies back then because he couldn't trust himself that he would start talking about "stuff", he had to.
Opening the eyes, they are slitting and frantic, jealous in that first flash of light. Microbeads of amber milk appearing between the repteye-lids. Having to constantly gauge what the paper man would do and then trying to grin like he would and doing the monkey routine again, waking at cruising altitude.

He said it so plainly that he had studied all of the maniacs. So very excited, his eyes jabbing over and through the book racks for any other passing bodies. Darting eyes then falling into the pages he slips, into the fantasy.
        Libraries, obscure bookstores, then years later on the television set. It was the privacy and accesses to those computers though, with which he spoke in such confidence to them on the subject
now. Reading he parts about where they become, hazy minded, and sloppy, struck a cord with him apparently.

In the room with the table, huffing out a breath of air he resets his chips to play puzzle again. They asked him, who were his favorite ones?
He gave them a disclaimer how he didn't consider himself like any of them as a whole. The stagnancy of the empty beats of silence again. The reports saying that he was at least a lot like the others while he was always trying to snatch the control of the rules for the interrogation, it continually becoming more of an Expose'. After all he is the one who is so comfortable with a stale mate. He sempt to be rolling something under his tongue while his hands blindly stroking along the edges of his deck of cards and his favorite ones he said?

"haven't been caught yet"

The eleventh hour falling on some Thursday. The wallpapers and the textures of the afterworld would have bloomed and the ink spilled across the screen of the eternal for the Intruder by that Sunday evening.

The Golden State Killer on the other hand wouldn't have been arrested for another 6 years or so, but if he had to choose one?

Ted Bundy, he said,
or at least certain aspects of him.
It was the ones who could hold together

shock waking! with the haze of red bloodshot in the eyes of their mind as it came crashing down for them. To keep separated the two different lives he said. The ability to keep them both going. He said it casually, relaxed and speaking freely. The jaw dropping subtly, looking upon brother, who is opening himself to you. All of the day dreams, it was always another thing with me he said. Building canoes, old rough trucks with a soft tire hanging down in front of a push guard. The push guard occupying the entire front of the truck. Much like the big black and green one that Israel had in Anchorage for a short while. Back when they lived at one of their first places, the one that they received mail at for his new:

Keyes' Construction.
 It was the place at an angle, crossing over C Street within hollering
distance of my parents' place. He mentions a big truck in his letter.
They had exclusive access to him.
Making small talk around the common table.

The Currier's bodies were so far over the horizon for the Law
enforcement because, back in Essex Junction, coming down Upper
Main St. in the cop cars as he had told them of their location. Pulling
in ready to creep with flashlights down into that dank cellar room.
When they passed the dry bramble of Little Indian Brook. There the
adrenaline pooling bitter on the back of the tongue of the detective.
32 Upper Main, where on Streetview standing there grim in the crying
out, just like in the old real estate photos online that he had told them
to look at.
Clearing the brush suddenly turning up and to the right and just like in
the story and with the hours passing in the expose' hours before the
News Break interruption,
the common table had become the doldrums. It seemed he had gum in
his mouth.
when from out of nowhere he had said,
 "B T K is a hack".

The coffee cup held like a glowing crucible in one hand, the lips
passing hot nectar. One could have easily have sat up too late, the gulp
choke from a stutter start making a spit spray of mist. Looking up,
eyes so alight in a surprised wide smile choking in deep coughs. The
kid from Colville looking up in an "awe shucks mister" laughing like
brothers and sisters but they didn't.

February 27, 2005 the budding young Serial Killer was probably still
just learning himself. Where would he have been the first time that he
saw the News Update interrupting over some old television set playing
behind some old counter,
saying that B T K: is in Custody! February 28 and it is confirmed that
it is really him! The plume of emotion, wanting to snatch some papers
and steal away. Shifting eyes just before finally alone to pour down
into the whole thing of,
what was it like?

Israel had composed an email back then. Almost on the exact date.
In the message he remarked about having just returned from visiting
friends in Port Angeles and that it was at 3 o'clock in the morning.
There is no time stamp on the meta data of the email though other than
him making sure to say it was on the 27th, now the day before. A few
days later he was recorded at a camping spot that was accessible only
by boat, back then in 2005.

In the photo of the Otero's little white house, it is partially hidden
from verdant trees in the front lawn. A walkway goes up to the front
door but, that's not the real door. Dennis Rader had crouched there on
their back porch, out in the open air. There was an unattached garage
further in the back. The front door on the back porch swung open and
the young boy is bustling out the family dog. He is wrangled back
inside,
"I came through the back door. I cut the phone lines.
I confronted the family, pulled a pistol to point at Mr. Otero and asked
him to, you know, that I was there to basically -- I wanted -- wanted to
get the car. I was hungry, food. I was wanted. And I asked him to lie
down in the living room. And at that time, I realized that wouldn't be a
really good idea. So, I finally -- the dog was a real problem, so I asked
Mr. Otero, could get the dog out. So, he had one of the kids put it out.
And then I took him back to the bedroom.

"You took who back to the bedroom?"

"The family to the bedroom. The four members."

"Not to worry, he needs cash and the car keys and to let him tie them
up, it is better that way.
When he started to strangle Little Joseph Otero, his mother gasped
back to life and started heaving breaths and
"After that, Mrs. Otero woke back up, and you know, she was pretty
upset, what's going on?
So, I came back and at that point in time I strangled her with a death
strangle at that time."
"She asked me to save her son"

I went ahead and took Junior, I put another bag over his head and took him to the other bedroom at that time."
Wichita, 803 N. Edgemoor

When Jolene at the table had asked him about "Lorraine's looks" he said so readily that he had found the house because of:
No Kids
No Dogs
And an attached garage with a car, all still unresolved. All of this on the table for that trip and it just so happens that maybe it was some horrible accident or just some terrible coincidence but,
when asked by the investigators and agents and attorneys jockeying and fumbling around the table, some talked over each other and they couldn't even keep their own mouths closed while he was divulging information. Frustrated with their arrogance he let it slip this one rare instance. They were asking about this girl that had disappeared in the lower 48. College kids stumbling out of a bar 41 minutes after 1:46 in the morning. Later cctv video showing the young woman and a male friend named later in a civil lawsuit walking towards her apartment. On the way there, her classmates saying they saw her near her apartment walking in alone and then she was gone. Israel there suddenly after, rolling into Mother's place in Indiana the next morning, going shopping with her and she is buying her son some camping supplies, it was the camping stove in particular. On the return trip he had been scathing himself so amped up he had said later they had walked through the trees, like from a bible story. The interview spoiling, the gravelly voiced guy's leg is shaking the table, every time he would reveal that huh, huh, that sure the timeline would've been tight and the schedule would've been rabid and racing but still, Israel would have been passing by that very spot, that very evening, on his itinerary for that trip. The sand paper voice finally quiet, his lips a smirk slipped by but his belly gurgled in his throat. The boy from Cove Utah having been splashed in microdot blood. He looks at these meager scraps and slivers of information in their folders there on the table.
The date: 6-3-11 is 6 days before the Currier's were reported missing and at its earliest it is also 5 days before the night they were abducted.
Missing Poster

Date Missing: 6-3-11 Lauren was a beautiful girl. The previous spring, she had went planting trees in Israel as part of the Jewish National Fund. On her reward poster it looks so similar to Samantha's. It says Reward:
Age 20
5' Tall
90 lbs.
Blond Hair
Blue Eyes
She was a Sophomore at Bloomington, University of Indiana.
One look at her photos, it must have destroyed her loved ones.

Back when he had left Mother's Porch in Indiana, just starting off on the long way, waving bye after a brief stay with her. Within only days from Lauren vanishing forever. It ends up if you were going to sneak off of the main through-way through New York on your way to Maine, the extra miles in the detour of taking Exit 27 up into the rural border of Vermont never happened. He says later that he had went straight up nearly from the start. Up to nearly touching the border of Canada. Nearly identical to how Coleville is situated. The old abandoned farmhouse here though was in his own name after the proceeds of the sale of that property in Maupin. It came out even later that his father had put it in his name to protect it from some creditors coming after Jeff Keyes, some swine of pearls. Passing along the way the Blake Falls Reservoir in New York State. Where he would soon throw the guns that had been ruined in the old farmhouse, throwing them into the water on his way back. No timeline, no narrative, only that when he came back from seeing his brothers in Maine, that on the way he had already burned most of Lorraine's belongings in New Hampshire at a remote area. Then passing by the Saturn's absence draped in police tape where he had left it. Stopping that part of the plan because he was going to maybe burn it at an old Kill Cache Site, he said. He crossed Lake Champlain according to the flashing eye in the swaying sea kelp. It never snatching upon any receipt of the Grand Isle Ferry there. It ends up that nearly all of the facts were found out and written down tirelessly from a local investigator who served Essex Junction. Murtie the real gumshoe, listened while being talked down to by the suits in Alaska and particularly the shiny shoes shuffling under the table during this story. Israel saying, he bought the paper just before he boarded at the dock.

Crossing over the state line out there over the darkness on the old steam punk ferry. They always have the Saturday paper for the sake of the waiting. You can count on it. What a place to be on the last stretch and see if there is any breaking news in the police blotter especially if included are any be on the lookout for these types of things that could easily and quietly slip off the rail of the boat if needed. Later the humming steel deck is slowing up to the landing back in New York state now. Driving straight forward out of the dock and straight back to the old farmhouse in Constable. Throwing her pistol finally into the Blake Falls Reservoir as he had specified, just south of the cabin. If he had never told them, we would've never known. Lakes and their watersheds making these large geographic shapes
and relationships,

they are all relevant.

He is all clean now, nodding along with them, then he breathes in swiftly
You see!?

The gesture brought the gaze into the man's eyes. The man's pink thing looked down squinted a little and went back inside and then he said to shiny shoes,
"That's how hard it's gonna be for you;

Without me"

CHAPTER FOURTEEN

COLD AIR DAMMING

April 7, 2009 Southwest Airlines Flight (Seattle to Manchester, New Hampshire).
More than two years before the Curriers.

On the long end of the Runway the 737 is glistening light off of its flat shiny surfaces. The engines are running up, steady humming and already so warm there vibrating over the concrete and the Intruder is nestling into his seat. The engines rage inward sucking the air from within themselves and the snap blinking lights on the landing gear show that the wheels,
are spitting water in a mist mohawk. The hand rest is shaking, the sound of the roar is somewhere and it is everywhere.

The mountain ranges sliding forward, starting as a thin foam shoreline sizzling across the water at dawn.

Dark clouds slow drifting in the river current of the horizon black. Out the round edged window the portside looking left, the sky goes out over the sheet metal and it goes out of view over the whole of the Northern Hemisphere. There is a horizon of dreary clouds down there. Tilted away from the sun, the air below becoming so very cold and heavy. Beneath those clouds it is so amazing, there is a world down there and it is spinning. The land is sliding so smoothly ramping up taller. These soft Appalachians, wall of mountain coming through the clouds and hedging in along a massive slab of frozen air coming down from the pole over a world of cold ocean and the massive land mass and the sheet of cold air settle in together. Thus:

"Weather in New York State is heavily influenced by two air masses: a warm, humid one from the southwest and a cold, dry one from the northwest.

Much less common is a **cool humid northeast** from the North Atlantic, and it results in a persistent cloud deck and precipitation which linger across the region for prolonged periods of time. Temperature differences between the warmer coast and far northern inland sections,
 can exceed 36 degrees Fahrenheit (20 degrees Celsius)

with rain near the coast.
but frozen precipitation, such as sleet and freezing rain, falling inland. Two-thirds of such events occur between November and **April**"

His eyes would be open then, in the dark of the other side. Delighting in the dreamy memoirs they linger on and on,

shock waking up! to a bristling world as brilliant as the sun. Pupils constricting and scatter looking through pinholes. The cabin walls and the hairs on the upholstery are golden and translucent. Crackling across the Stratos, having nearly crossed the entire breadth of the country only finally 120 to 110 miles away from the distant airport: Boston Regional Airport Manchester. Pisces eyes and fish throat tacky and foul, the airframe then descending. Down through the frosty air, down through the bristling crystals. All the way to where the water was wet again, down on the concrete in the parking garage when he would've stood eyeballing the rental car. They called it a Hyundai Sonata.
        The Hyundai Sonata is passing through the capillaries of the sprawling airport and from the sky maps its grand footprint looks like some capsule in the structure of a cell or something. Down near the warmer coast. The Sonata is a miniscule and it is pulsing along with all the rest. Pumping forward in the beat of the stoplights but it is now curving into a larger vein and then immediately it is into an artery. There is a Walmart SuperCenter 2.9 miles away: 7 minutes.

Afterward going back down on the Number 3 passing again the large runways but they are on the other side of the Sonata now and far off behind all of those fences segregating the cytoplast. Flowing down the mainline to Boston. 242 miles: 4 hours 4 min.

Wherever the counting down of exits had begun, clearing through on the major interstate connections, then at once a signal change and you are crossing over a river.

Instantly off into a little place nearing the waypoint, off onto some Main Street of some nowhere section of Bumfuck, New Jersey. It is only 15.4 miles from Richard Kuklinski's old "Hunting Grounds"

Richard had recalled some of the stories from his youth, back from when the "IceMan" was just trying to figure it all out, this thing. Living in New Jersey as a young man he would go down into Manhattan's Hell's Kitchen neighborhood and kill bums and hobos but, never any women, he said. He was adamant. They have no idea how many people that he had killed, it appears to be a lot though. Perfecting his different methods eventually making a small spray bottle of Arsenic. He described walking onto a pounding dance floor in the 70's. The lead up would've been exhilarating. Walking right up to "them" in a crowded room, it probably would've all went lucid. Looking through the eyes of a werewolf as it is creeping up all around you. Waiting for it to fully bloom inside and then looking into their eyes. Shoulders moving all around in the light strobe he walked right up and misted the guy in the face like it was a sneeze. Large gold chain racking on open chest quivering on the dancefloor it must've been a coke overdose. He described wanting to see it in there in their eyes. Richard Kuklinski was a very large man and he almost always wore dark shades over his eyes and he had a large beard and a moustache. On him it looked perfect but on a smaller Ichabod Crane it would have a tendency to look absurd.

The last 1000ft to the algorithmic center of the destination and oddly the road's name changes. Arriving at your destination it is a long arcing road with heavy commercial properties on one side and on the passenger side it is parks. They seem to go on forever, this dusky little road one side lined with grass, then restrooms, baseball field clusters it goes on and on. It is an economically depressed area in Hackensack. It appears to be made up mostly of snub-nosed little buildings and clandestine Auto Body Shops.

CHAPTER FIFTEEN

SALEM

In the photo of Deborah, the spelling of her name is semantic. Because after a few whiskies late into the night when Israel Keyes said he would "you know" go on the computer and look up of any news, or pictures of "them" that maybe their families had put out. Maybe some plea for answers or maps, news articles, anything he could find. It was super rare because for years he couldn't find anything. On the tape you hear it, the other voices periodically in the room with Keyes are actually: five different guys! There is a noticeable difference in their voices in the tapes but those two, are each a Federal and State Attorney respectively. There is that moment we come to after hours of replay where we the humble citizens finally might realize that maybe they really are, better than all of us. The thumb and the fist, thoughtfully holding the chin; those Nantucket mother fuckers. They probably sat in those First-Class seats just lost out the window. Really dissecting this new case. Everyone has a weakness. Trying to decode the key of how to get to them. The blade began to appear suddenly for a moment as he pondered these things. Forsaking the luncheon at the Federal building walking through the lobby passing the young woman in Jimmy Choo standing on one foot, lifting the other softly behind her. He is staunch walking through, the background blurred. Beginning to understand the deeper waters of this case, becoming driven now. Her legs are long and she is a real ride but he glazed by in a daze, he never knew. It was surreal in the elevator as he started to see the massive knife blade flashing in and out of existence in his hands, or already latched there on his hip waist. By the time he was coming through the door into the Hotel Room the plastic card was cast off onto the bed crossing the threshold it was already in the grip of his palm. The door closing slowly pressing, did it actually click? It was so balanced in his hand his mouth is stretched to oblong. He is envisioning himself coining the terms later for his memoirs maybe.

Tomorrow when he walks into that room armed, with his team mates: Federal, State, Borough, Municipal. All coming in as a lethal organism the leg moving forward, it is so heavy. The torso cam rolls adjusting, and its arms? Stay clear they are swinging as a beautiful counterbalance, coming in Android, greeting and sitting down with this part Amish kid in the manacles he has been sprayed in blood at times. Looking up at them blinking hello through his T-top framed glasses but the frames have clear library lenses in them now. Across him the blood it would have looked like the wet swath from a can of spray paint, red hissing across his chest. Or at another time maybe to drop a cup from the cupboard accidentally, down onto the tip of the large spoon leaning in a bowl of thin waffle batter causing a shocking sag to splatter across his face, slide grin never flinching.

When he displayed that he was disheartened because he could never find anything in the news. The one guy at the table working the angles said "Anything? Israel" it was more monotone and condescending and more importantly it comes off as a question, but it finishes as a statement and Israel's eyes went sharp edged corners, the edges bristled in the razor light when he blinked.
Coming back then with dilating circles in a hard reset.

After his arrest, after the raid on Kim's house on Spurr Lane her computer had been seized on Federal Search Warrants. The laptop laying there on the no expense spared table and the milli-pulses are surging into and coming back out of the hardware. The numerics, smearing the wax away, looking down over fields and fields of the old data storage, labeled as deleted but never cleared. The same stuff still inside the tiny packet, waiting to be called up, ready to be reset if ever needed. The search engines finding upon them in there like ant eggs and so more importantly what had been typed in on the keyboard at times. More than 40 cases that were on that computer documented as keystrokes however most only as screen captures of the website for the National Missing and Unidentified Persons System website. Many of the people would not have been feasible for Israel to even have been able to have involved with at all. There is only one person who pops up as missing and matching perfectly with his travel itinerary for that trip and she was there in the computer. Even in only stutter clicks of a search typed in as it was spelled.

So, when they came into the room they walked with an air of confidence. When in the momentum of the close, when the tempo demanded it the one guy laid her photo on the table. The hag that had disappeared on his "New York trip" and the air becomes still and lower. He says that he is not going to talk about her. They push him and push him, Jolene even making sure to tell him before leaving that next time we can just talk, no high-pressure stuff, it sounds like she pats his little hand there but when the one guy had said "I'm right aren't I" and you can hear Israel becoming agitated.

You can see it is Keyes through the disguise in the bank photo in Tupper Lake that was on the table in the previous Interrogation, however the heavy coats are deceiving making him seem a much heavier man standing there grainy on the bank main floor and he is very specifically wearing dark shades over his eyes and he had a large absurd beard thing and a moustache on his face that he had fabricated from human hair.

the guy at the table confronts him that "she does have some significance to you!?"

"Yes" the intruder says "but not like you,,,,,," he is interrupted before he is encouraged to finish.

Nothing more than a day or two in the newspapers, he said. Nothin more than a blip really,
miffed in the past that in the media it had always been a dry condiment platter. To see "their" faces displayed over a news banner anchor?

There would have been this flood of euphoric in Israel's mind toying with it, he spoke of getting carried away with the Media thing once it started, but they had never really materialized before the Curriers, he said. The Intruder probably feeling unfulfilled and sitting loose on the airplane lost out the window. It would've begun to take shape.

To fly over the little town at early mid-morning?
Imagining the sun touching on his night skin, instantly greasy there on the seat. The praises be upon some excited forensic technician who probably gasped when they would have finally stumbled upon and discovered it. That this part Amish kid had unknowingly clicked into that keyboard that was connected to the tower, it was Kim's computer, having typed into the data complex her name incorrectly, typing it instead as it appears in the Bible.

Eventually typing it in then Debra:
    You see her suddenly before you on the screen. The expression on her face? Her head is cocked to the side so that her eyes are set one lower than the other. Both loose and tense but there is a flatness in there, it comes off as a "go fuck yourself". The snapshot appears to be a mugshot, her skin is puffy and there is a roughness, there are blemishes that could be the healing tissues of a scraped nose from a fight with another girl or a pimp and the photo was in the room again. This time it is poised and just out of site. Because by now their relationship has soured to adversaries.
    Coming in android, after the big fiasco in Vermont where the rules were if they had kept it quiet and out of sight of his daughter seeing her dad's name and face on the news that he would let them have nearly all access.

 Back in Essex Junction, coming down Upper Main St. in the cop cars as he had told them of the old farmhouse's location. Pulling in ready to creep with flashlights down into that dank cellar room. When they passed the dry bramble of Little Indian Brook. There the adrenaline pooling bitter on the back of the tongue of the detective.
32 Upper Main, where on Streetview standing there grim in the crying out, just like in the old real estate photos online that he had told them to look at.

Clearing the brush suddenly turning up and to the right and just like in the story and there was nothing there. Standing over knee high grass in the breeze it seeming to be still crying out in the echo of that one night before. After they had went to the "legal" landfill and identified the area the log books say the dump truck loads of debris would've been dropped and scattered and buried back then and soon thereafter, off behind the wooden stakes the ground was being eased back by equipment and forensics wearing white suits and full face respirators, scavenging the old dump with rakes and magnets and cadaver dogs and the unmarked fluorescent F B I tape marking off the sections, diligently wriggling in the wind blustering up from the embankment of a major highway. It was all there behind the glass, on national news by nightfall there, so it was yet only a lunch hour news break for us. The scene showing in Anchorage and he had lost his cool when he hollered at them finally confronting them that they had "done a major archeological did right next to a major highway!" he had seemed outrightly shocked that they would ruin the good thing that they all had going. So, this time when they shuffled in and glancing pleasantries around the table Israel starts speaking and it is so clear, that he is doing it: he is initiating a preset of "word tracks" that in laying out sequentially contain some stratagem and this one was Top Notch.

He starts in an "oh well" kind of inflection, coming in abruptly with hardly any lead in,
 however, the last part he trails off, lulling you in, un-alarming. Then the Snap Back cringing on a sharp reprimand!
Keyes starting in casually:

"It's inevitable that,,,   this day comes,   you know?....

          "What day?"

"THIS DAY!!
This is the day where you say give us more information or else, right?"

Letting it hang in the air and then he laughs that long cackle on the tape. Then the come down off the laughter and Israel is breathing in and the one guy comes in quickly that,

"No, I think things are going to move on, things are
going to move forward,
        and I'm, We've never been inconsistent with saying…"

And they go politely back and forth that they both feel that the
relationship has broken down and the "Bosses" back in the F B I and
the Upper Ups are giving pressure to just move forward "traditionally"
and you can see it so clearly that the guy at the table is creating a
groove in the mud in the bogged down interrogations and he starts to
slide this little "word track" in the slick groove and you can hear him
catch the scent of it in the wind. The first step is to, from across the
table make complicit their opponent's own mouth and breath throat:

> "Like you said earlier, progression is inevitable on this,
> whether you help us, or not help us" and it starts to lay
> out sequentially that and then calmly that they are all
> here now to make something happen together his words
> still talking, a gravelly voice from the back it sounds
> like he is up on a raised platform or something, maybe
> a large hood pulled over most of his face and the voice
> says to Jolene at the table speaking over them he tells
> her:

> "Why don't you talk about, what New Jersey News is
> doing"
> it registers that when he said the word "about" you can
> hear who would become special Agent Jolene Goeden
> of the F B I nodding an instant and earnest Mm-Hm.

> She starts in professionally and cordially that:
> "One of the things that we've talked about from the
> beginning, we're gonna keep you posted as to "what's
> happenen… "so clearly in the phonetics she had
> softened it with her country twang.
> "So, nothing is a surprise" the last part is crisp and the
> S's sound surgical and emotionless. You can hear the
> paper slitting slash coming out into open air as the

photo of Debra is washed in office light there on the table suddenly as she had said it, a bit of theatrics.

and the vibe dropped off in the room and his countenance is changing there, cross-table.

The setting of the road where Debra would've went missing, it looks like a tarot card: a long arcing road beset on one side by cold industrial overgrowth,

the other side: grass fields divided into: children playing in parks, in some, graves. Sprinkled with the homeless. Each compartmentalized but overlapping at times.

Debra's son was standing in his own kitchen later as an adult when he remembered it back then for them when he had told her:

> *"It's unfair to say that I didn't care whether she lived or died, but it was once the truth. The last thing I said to her (years ago) was, If you're not going to get clean, you have no room in my life."*

When he had said that, he was just a boy. Seeing a swirling briefly down in there, something like pain but then she would've blinked real big before she walked out. Such fallow memories probably pulled out every other decade or so.

To abduct a victim from a place called Hackensack? That's pretty good.
She has a filthy mouth, bitter to her own son. Out on the old street's curb it is littered with little vials of rat lung and black tar and amphetamine.
To snatch her from a road that welcomes you as Salem St.?
Only to then eventually intern her to the earth in Tupper, Where?
He had said to them openly as they were all sitting there trans table in the interview
"Well, you've seen my collection (porn)" and he comes into an airport called "Man-Chester".

Jolene is laying it out how New Jersey F B I is looking into her more and they were bringing it to him first and "that situation" she leaves it open ended and the clock lapses silence for 6 seconds and he says resigning:

"alright"

The guy with the word tracts slips in a:

"Thought maybe that was a place to start"

7 seconds pass by in silence.

"No"
"I mean, not as far as I'm concerned"

The word tract following "What should I tell, what should we, tell New Jersey?" 15 more seconds of silence
"I don't know, whatever, tell them whatever you want" The intruder sounds sad and that he has lost a little wind out of his sails. They hit all the check boxes of ways to ask it, is she the one buried in New York?

buried? New York?
he answers "No"

Does he know her, why would her name be typed into your computer, Kimberly's computer. Are you responsible for her disappearance? All to which a terse "No" but when the guy in sequencing the equations asked no longer about coordinates, or locations or corpses but asked now touching on the heavy hanging fabrics of the Shady tree carpenter's mind waiting for the images to become clear, projected scenes across the wagging curtains when he asked now:
"Does the image have any meaning to you?"

Israel says "Sure, but probably not on.."

4 hours 48 minutes 284 miles from Hackensack, following a state highway up to the North West until it hits this large lake and the 30. It bends back on itself still traveling north at least coming to an old Logging town. Today considered as a village and named for its location: Tupper Lake.

Debra J. Bologna
Slight build 5'1"   112 pounds
Married to Ned Feldman on 11/12/88 and had a son a few months later in 1989. They were married again on June 20, 1998: Missing

Depending on what time they would have pulled in, driving slowly past the Community Bank in town there in little Tupper Lake Village. The flashing sign on the bank would've said at 10 minutes before 1 o'clock in the afternoon, then that the temperature would've been just above freezing for the first time since dinner the night before. The exact numbers being stored into some data complex for us to come back and find them later. Coming back to find them from the future, reading them this time in a higher technology. Once retrieved though we know instantly what the conditions were: The sunlight it had become so diluted down in and through the dreary cloudy air, the state of the water lingering lazily in and out of ice. Waters at 2 o'clock in the afternoon are waking sleepily again for a few hours, to look around at a puzzled face. Locked again suddenly at mid-supper. This front of weather holds true over nearly all of the Adirondack Forest of the north. All the way across into Maine.

Years later his mother in the FBI interview, she had lived a life cursing the Federal them. She said that she recalled her son had told her a few years ago that the highways running along that cold forest, that he was surprised at how many abandoned hotels and resorts were up there in the off roads. A few years later she needed to take that route all the way into Maine as well and as they drove it watching through the glass over the haunted houses up in all of those hallows. She remarked that this must be the exact road that Israel had mentioned. He had gone on and on about all of these old buildings everywhere, in the rolling endless of those dank trees.

On this trip though, midway in Tupper Lake, thinking of the kill kit that he will lay in wait at the end of this trip. It will go in down by that one river in Vermont, in Burlington. For now, though he is entering a forest acted upon by long cold fronts, entering the Adirondack. Wet dew breath in the night, lingering as frost. The endless buildings and manors it is rarer but when finding an old church the plume of euphoric. Frost crystals glistening in the headlamp. The trucker's hitches pulled tight from the old corbels and other seemingly ancient wood lathes. It could've been such an easy stop in Bingham.

It conjures a vision, there would've been room to stretch out and spend some time reflecting on life and death, invoking thoughts from deep within. Maybe broom sweeping a section of the floor around your camping gear in the glow of some impromptu circle of candles. Sending wax soot up into the open roof timbers. In its true form the ambiance turning the sexual intimacy into Necromancy at its purest.

A few sleepy days later in that same hayseed Community Bank in Tupper Lake, the surveillance camera captured a man walking in wearing a large winter coat. The night must've been rather uneventful; he was in good form. His hands weren't really shaking. He admitted later to disposing of "the" body somewhere in Tupper. When they looked up of any missing persons for that trip. The one that he had rented the Hyundai Sonata out of ManChester-Boston Regional Airport, it is there now on their timeline for his travels they would prefer for everyone to look over them and see if you were in the vicinity of his travels, they are looking for anything that could be of interest.

The assumed straight-line Itinerary looks like this.

Returning the Sonata, the rental mileage registered as 1047 miles driven.

Landing in Manchester March 7, there is a reservation for the Highlander Inn in for the next day, if it was needed. But when he travels, he doesn't sleep very much at all he says.

4/8 Manchester to Hackensack NJ   244 miles

Entering Hackensack Main becomes Salem st. Driving south crossing
both Lido and Essex St.

4/9 Hackensack NJ to Tupper Lake NY   284 miles

4/10 Hotel Reservation Hampton Inn   94 miles
  Colchester, Vermont

4/14 **Colchester** to Manchester Airport   175 miles

"No," Israel says there across the table,

"I'm not, No, I'm not going to talk about what is on the computer."
... "I didn't kill her"
..." I just don't want to talk about it"

Imagine being a teenage kid in Jersey. Imagining seeing her floating
along through the hobo trees, the leaves obscuring most of her.
She slowed a bit when she had passed through the chain link.

        What if you showed up with saran twisted around a crunchy
rock of bug killer, or a dab of black tar laced with rat poison. It is hard
to get Lab grade anymore but watching "them" do their thing when it
hits them. Maybe he saw her coming down the lane, with a walking
gate, almost a spirit and image of him from behind without the hair.
That first wave of septic vapor across their mind and they would look
over at you so intently as it began to overtake them. Clawing at
painted glass from the inside, their mouth going into oblong Oh and
body pumping morbid as it would be bottoming out, but he said in

chosen words that he loved to strangle them. Who knows we never will.

From the first time that he had walked up to the Sonata, then after a quick stop at the Walmart Super Center and if then driving to New Jersey and eventually arriving in Tupper Lake, Robbing the bank successfully, disposing of some body? At some point making the 3-hour drive to the last reservation on the itinerary. The "New York Trip" basically complete already. Soon he will be returning the car back at Manchester Airport but that is over the horizon still. Here he is at the last stop,

The Hampton Inn in Colchester, Vermont.

In the parking lot then of the Hampton Inn, there on the street looking downwind along the road, if you allowed your mind to float above the part sidewalk. Coasting along until seeing some signage there, it says it is the Vermont 2A heading North. 7 minutes by car icon, or 36 minutes walking in a straight line. Soon enough there shockingly is this little unassuming intersection with an empty traffic light blinking in the lonesome. After all of these miles and the various lodgings, here only miles from the parking lot back there at the Hampton. Hovering over is the empty blinking traffic lights. If you were their pedestrian turned observer floating at head height watching the little intersection out in the nothingness of trees and stoplights, watching swiftly two years pass by and a few months more before your eyes. Slowing down then to 2:36 in the morning of 6~8~11, you would hear a whistle crackling whisper building to a whoosh of a dark green Saturn passing by swiftly gone out under the haze of those lonely lights and the shadow of his dangling feet. The woman in there, the shadows covered most of her face, obscured on the passenger side. Passing by in the night it appeared as if she could be his mother and she was aghast. Red tail lights into the darkness long sweeping circle the red candle flash over at the intersection of the 15 heading back towards town apparently. The red lights dim again the orb of bright light in the nothingness it is slide passing the big putt-putt in the green glow dot of the trees then it goes black in the night down in there.

The bed at the Hampton Inn was only miles from the back intersection with Susie Wilson Road. He can see it there glowing under the clouds. Driving from the Hampton Inn then turning right on to Susie Wilson Rd. passing Colbert St. you could almost see the younger Currier's house for the trees and coming to the intersection in their neighborhood. They had moved in about a half of a year ago at that point. When they would crackle over the security glass in their kitchen, they would have lived there for over 3 years by then. Driving a little more and just before the river there is a road between the two, it reduces the endless curving of the river into one sweeping arc. The Woodside Natural Area. There on the old bend of what used to be the old river. The trail leading down through to it and to the new river's edge. The Sonata sits in plain view on the freshly shorn grass shoulder and flat embankment. The scatter straw from the big machine left just short clumps of what was straw stalks of the hardy grasses across the ground, they must've been tall and natural. It will be at least 6 months before the mower rumbles by again but he doesn't care. 5 days and 6 nights the temperatures are lingering just near the temperature water crystallizes at. Re-burying the kill kit here from how long before, it is at his feet he would've felt flooded with emotion: actually, being able to see blurring over and through the two years into the future, as if through dark pollen smearing on a black mirror.
Debra J. Feldman

Feldman was last seen at her home in Hackensack, New Jersey on April 8, 2009. She has never been heard from again. Few details are available in her case.

THE CLOSEST CALL

CHAPTER SIXTEEN

ARCADE

As he wrote in his letter~

"It was love at first sight"

When he had held his own daughter unexpectedly for the first time, those hot starch blankets seemed to almost sear his skin. His teeth glinting touching and something happened, he said.

In the hospital, as they had been smearing away with fast raking fingers that chalk slime that had been baby choke covering her little body, he was lost in the gaze.

When they had held her down to the table and she arched her little back up in defiance, wiping frantically the jaundice wax paste from all of her crevices and there in the close background, he was awestruck.

His rectangle pupil eyes glittering at this brave little traveler. Squeeze dropped a tear she is so small. Looking blinking blurry miracle down upon her there, so very precious a tear. Smelling her still wet of Death.

It was a huge moment in his life, he said. The flat part of his upper stomach heaving deep and cautious, while her in the crisp swaddle. The puzzle of it all, gentle goat horns turning slowly as he cocks his head to behold her little hand and blinking returning from clicking hooves on some windy peaks in the dark ever world somewhere. His voice a burbling goat's bleat burping out in a proclamation that Shhhhh! quickly hunching down to hushed breath again that: he will never do any of those ones; ever again.   He said.

Remembering the smell of her birthing and it is catalogued down into the massive storage facility in our brain right behind our nose. In a world of such delicate synapses over distant threads their two-connection appearing as if it were a firm handshake.

The M R I when scanning the head, as it smelling in some test smell, them seeing it blooming in there bursting forth across the screen. As this is the place that accesses memories. Pulling them up, laying them out shockingly and almost in an instant in a vast array sometimes so very truthful. Finding upon things over time in the everyday, the smell of Coffees or Chocolates or the aromantics of his Cigarillo smoke or even still alive almost, the smell in some thick braid of human hair. A normal object, placed so incidentally.

It was during a short phase of the interrogations where we could let hours pass by in there with him. Them having had squandered such a warm bliss in the mid-morning sun of getting to hear him tell all the parts of what it was like for him when he was young and developing.

The camera catches a frame back on film. After a few rains, the hobo door has been hanging there motionless. Breaking the dimension of the still photo, the adolescent boy peers in around it and into the dank dead of some old farmhouse.

Standing with one leg up a bit on the pile of rubbish. There is a sword blade of sunlight coming down through the timbers and the warm roof up there. A band of golden crossing and in his hair, it is illuminated.

The sunlight swaying slowly down through his eyelashes and the peach fuzz and across the paper he is holding. The light in slow drunken pendulum. Waiting for the curator to peel slowly the next page free.

In order to get your back to lift up and peek over yourself like that, it shows in blushing disappearing too abruptly under a line of grease paint, revealed in the lamplight of flesh tone make-up. Showing so clearly there in a straight line across her neck.

Caking at any crater and there is the slightest of mounding making shade texture in the moonscape of her face, but only if you look too closely.

In the spirit world, them hearing the xylophone of 3 or 4 different gasps, sighing from her little deer throat as his eyes moving from one photo to another over and over.

The slow swaying sun, sheening across the paper, over her in the shine back of the slick surface, interrupting his gaze. Squinting momentarily frustrated at the nuisance and moving over as the blinding light now no longer swaying, it is straight as a rule and plunging exact and sure, it glides effortlessly off from him as he slips off into the shadows.

That she was doing everything that he wanted her to, that is how he had described that part.
In the last weeks before he was arrested, in the shed so very close to the end of it for him. Mixing and cross contaminating the cosmetics, afterward bringing them back into the house.

At the end of the run, later remembering these behaviors, damaging and reckless. Increasing now and coming in, in sets. There was that one alcohol binge where blinking blurry into the mid-morning light, the lady had come knocking at the door. Finally inquired of him her contractor, she had felt bad, but when she saw how far he had let himself go into such a disgusting state, it was disturbing. The milk fats of him must've days ago begun to turn. By the time the door had creaked opened squinting in the light, it had by then become clumping in slippery and yellowing viscous. How cruel then would it be, to be in his clutches. Watching him after his own words, he said about those times that he was "losing control"

4 years before the deep morning of that flight to Texas, the weather conditions were aligned and the frigid sub-arctic cold air was breathless. Resting atop those massive crumpled up ranges, but we move too fast to see them moving so slowly.

The ocean lays there barely warm and barely moving, but she holds her heat mathematically.

A rail car comes clicking unassuming out of the Haunt somewhere, unawares and so quizzically these rails? They are still pristine and he wracks to life from it. Gasping in that first sharp breath and cramming his wrists into his temples and on his forehead making a tight, shaking face in an overload of wishing so hard for a moment, that it wasn't so.

CHAPTER SEVENTEEN

GRAVEYARD

I was out late, plowing snow on a 4-wheeler in full cold weather gear with snowboarding goggles over most of my face. Pushing both old and new snow from this walkway & some assigned parking areas. It was an impromptu favor for some reason, helping someone out. Pushing the heavy plow blade into the undisturbed blanket of snow across the ground. Passing by that insulated man door, it was locked and closed now. The memory of that strange morning where, who ends up to be Kim's boyfriend had come tumble thudding down the stairs. Remembering the vibe in the room.

Bristling bear 4-wheeler, grumbling buzzing around, the tires are squeaking for ice grip. Somebody usually takes care of the snow service but something came up this one time. After a few days of freeze thaws the snow becoming hard as stone. Headphones, turned up over the hum of the motor and the machine should be loaded back into the bed of the truck and heading out of Anchorage within a half of an hour or so.

That building is very long and symmetrical and when I was near completing the large walkways, I knew someone was there watching me. It was most likely coming from one of the windows above. Often it is some little old lady or kid looking down. They almost always wave back. However there hadn't been any activity since I had arrived out there in the dark. Arriving outside of everyone's schedule and routines. There had been no smell of hamburger meat frying or pestos, or not even any dinner curries emanating. I looked up into the glass panes they were all so steep and dark. I clunk popped the gear with my foot, the blade grinding along and as I was approaching the corner of the long building it seems that there were these sets of incidences that kept floating up from down below. Remembering by feel the warning of intensity that I had felt that one morning when I had been here before. Things of such as, the strange manner of how many times my sister had asked for me to meet her co-worker's boyfriend back then and here I am again at the Bunkhouse. Peering across the dark blue of the scene, it was like looking out over the surface of the moon. The wallpaper of this world and its clock, slow sagging in honey as I was rolling slowly passing the corner. There was no light on this side of the building. This isolated little parking lot was all dark and 75% empty except one snowed in truck there, in my memory it might have had pipe racks and a cargo bed. At that time his phone number was (907) 301-3412. If I had called it right then it most likely would've went straight to voicemail.

Blood rush then, as a lone car drove by in the slush out on the snow in the street. The driver was looking straight ahead scanning just before crossing the next stoplight there on the corner behind the wall of trees. I was nearly invisible to them in the quickly passing periphery as they were grip sliding toward the changing lights. I stared off, over the handle bars, staring across the commuter lanes and over across the soft hills over there behind the wrought Iron fences, what are the fences for?
The grounds across the way having their own set of lamps in there, casting smaller orange halos onto the snow. The shallow hills are lined with head stones. Only a fragment of them coming out into the light, almost all of the rest of the big Cemetery, being shrouded in darkness.

I turned the key off. The putt-putt motor becoming silent and the brisk air pop-ping the vibrating existence when I took my earphones out. Listening to the city's hum and I knew so clearly that there was something there with me. The lavender sky was night backed with the orange Sodium Vapor lights of that very northern town. The passing car in the dirty orange snow, it was cast in combat light. I felt I was lost to the world.

Stopping in undisturbed snow, behind me a blind open plane.

It was all so very serene and beautiful though, like it always is. The inner energy creeping and fanning out, in deer ear.

Coming together standing now next to the machine. There on the back of the 4-wheeler under a loose bungee cord was my aluminum snow shovel, it is considered more of a grain shovel in the Lower 48. As my eyes went over the wooden handle, I went to reach for it, an inner voice from the lessons learned, reminding that a scared rabbit hand, welcomes evil. Calmness when the handle slid into my hand. I felt as if I wanted to be with no other. I felt numbed and honey drunk. The nearest of the 3 sets of the main stairs, the one near the dark corner, the clean-up required by hand shovel. I let the wide blade come down and I put pressure on it and pulled it. The grinding metal head scraping slowly and firmly. Over and over scraping rhythmically, reckoning again the coincidence that this was that same apartment building. Never having found the inside of the boiler room. Remembering that she had asked me again that she needs this favor and it really would be a great help to her. I could never quite understand what had all happened in the laundry room that one day. Immediately the shovel in my hand was so much more beautiful, than without it. So, I scraped slowly on the one set of stairs at the corner. Signaling my existence for a block in all directions into the darkness over and over. Taking it all in for a long time. Eventually out there, I was alone again. So, in the lit darkness I packed up and drove out of Anchorage.

Later than expected, finally pulling in to the driveway the warm windows glowing in the spruce tips. My wife came out to meet me and asked If I had went to help my father. Her knowing he was working just down on Cordova Street at the halfway house at that time. I told her no. She seemed skeptical; she said that I had been there a really long time so she thought I must've gone to help someone? I told her that it was so familiar to me and I described to her how the emotions had flattened out thinner and thinner inside me as I had dragged the shovel slowly and deliberately. She said I was there a really long time and I probably freaked the people out, but I never saw anyone. I felt down deep like I had just done something amazing.

THE CLOSEST CALL

CHAPTER EIGHTEEN

TRENDSETTER

There was a girl born of this world in a city of man and she was so special that there were shockwaves coming off of her. Her laughter it would,

"Giggle-burst forth into the room and lighting it up" her father said.

Over from Spurr Lane in a straight line passing nearly over the old Salon/school program where anyone could walk in and be a test subject at discount, for some young person who is working on the requirements for their own beautician license. Having them lean over you, the frizzy auburn curls puffing close to your ear. They love tips and you can see it there in the long line of apprentice barber stations. There are different types of girls and a guy now and then, him dissolving into the sorority. Sensing the different ones as your turn approaches. In almost a straight line between the coffee stand and Kim's house.

Not that much later, under the spruce boughs at our house, my sister was helping load up some of her stuff from a wonderful dinner. Out by the cars now laughing about something that had just happened, her being a hapless Samaritan. "Oh yeah!" she says, there was that one thing. "Look Joe, could you please meet my friend, he wants to buy you lunch or something, whatever." also reassuring me that he is really cool
"We sat around the fire at (redacted) place a bunch"

With simple gestures assuring her that I wasn't interested. She looked
as if she was hurt, because why would I roast her for nothing? All I'd
have to do is meet with him? Besides" she said looking after some
supposed adjustment to the cargo
        "I already told him you'd do it"
then looking back.
C'mon you help everyone why won't you do this for me!? The floor
felt to drop away for me for a moment, but then I was clear in my
mind again and such a feeling of confidence building as I asked her
"Why would you do that?"

We had all laughed shots around the firepit earlier, people are cow eye
watching us by the cars, from over the large bed of glowing coals.

 She asked astonished "What am I supposed to tell him!" the last part
ending in breath flutter.
 I raised my finger. Inside my mind was spraying mists of lacquers
into the air. Clouds of graphite powder finding as the feelings, of the
thoughts, were moving by in the dark for me.

        I remembered there the feel of when she had come to me after I
had plowed the apartments and she had asked me how it went and I
remember shaking my head and saying that I had really done
something over there. Her expression was odd and she said "You
never even finished!?" and that there were 4 or 5 parking spaces there
on the far end of the building by the road with the traffic light. That I
had never touched it! I remember hearing what she was saying and I
remember seeing the darkness over the soft edged snow in my mind.
There had been a lone pick-up truck parked there, it might have had a
cargo bed on it. It too was covered in snow 8 inches deep or so. I
remember how it had all felt, becoming more familiar with a sliding
doom and I shook my head again and I had told her then that I wasn't
sure what all had went down over there, but I know that I had done an
amazing job. The feel of these memories flashing as parable and there
is a lesson down in the dark of it somewhere. But for now, there face
to face by our cars I was so very relieved then for some reason, not

knowing the words yet. I started to speak, not knowing then who he even was.

He spoke of the Two Lives, and that he has been two different people for a long time 14 years......
and about his regard for the guys that could hold the two lives together at once and he talked about needing to do something so bad, still being amped up, rubbing his chains on his legs until the edge came smooth on the wood. In the Expose' under the fluorescent lights he said one time that "Over the years," he said, that every once in awhile he runs across someone, that in certain ways that they use distractions to hide the person that they really are. That he is attuned to it because they are the things that he does.
I told my sister there with the car's hatchback up in the air,

"Here is what I want you to tell him and please make sure, that you do."

"Tell him, that I can't see the angles"

and her eyes went deer like in there.
As she popped out of it, she became incensed and her eyes slit at me and it galvanized part of our relationship negatively for a month or two until it came out in the news. Coming in from Texas.

Eventually just before, Kim was paying for almost everything and they weren't even in the same bed anymore. Attentive ear, "could you be a doll?" she had him run up to the store to fetch more wine for her and her group of friends, they were starting in. Him without a doubt at least once, walking away, justifying his own set of dignities, hearing a pause up there and then small genuine and harmless chuckling laughter, of course there is always some Vaudeville Voltaire up there saying some quip or innuendo, the sound: vectors. They cackle and someone's hand lands on another's knee at the apex of the laugh in the room. One of Kim's friends saying candidly about the new Boyfriend, that had a kid? On Spurr Lane, Kim had the note on the house but it had been their abode.

"I thought she was smarter than that" is what the friend had said.

Her and Iz? He is sleeping on a mattress in the other room, Kim is older than him and later he said he was upset because she wanted her freedom and regarding his daughter? Kim rejecting him and her! They were separating at some point soon, him returning to the Lower 48 to start again. That is what he told the investigators.

"Kim was devastated. She would've done almost anything for him." That is what one of her old co-workers said.

They had separated in December, however the tickets for the trip had been purchased back in October, before she had caught him growing weed in his shed and it ends up it was a big deal.

Back when he had arrived in Maine, just before or after he had seen that Park Ranger's truck near the young newlyweds off of the river in New Hampshire, when he had finally arrived his brother's found him in a strange state. He says that they knew that he must've had a rough night or something because he crashed out dead to the world for a long while. Sleeping through watches of the sun. His brothers had tarried there for days, alarm rising as the rural soft mountains must've killed all of his phone coverage or something his service had been all blacked out. It was becoming normal in these scenarios his family members recalled him having fouled clothing on and strong body funk from extended times in the field without showering or hygiene. The long seats of the road trip, the sweats and it's extracts of tensions and stressors in beads of oils and toxins appearing across his skin. The lube stretching out slowly creeping, amped up for days in the wet swamp sheen he is adjusting his clammy genitals in the car ride again.

Robert Kuklinksy was known as the Iceman, because the police had found a missing person that had been gone long enough that they had assumed must be dead, but then the body showed up fresh. When the coroner did the liver test there were the last of ice crystals in there. They knew someone had frozen the body and re-thawed it out later for the sake of the Time of Death. After the IceMan's arrest and final incarceration his wife said that as long as she and his kids were functioning correctly everything could be great, but if they were getting calls from the school about one of the children for once, or

God forbid his wife showed problems? That it would equate to showing signs that it was all falling apart finally and that he was losing control becoming very agitated. Realizing later that they were his semblance that everything was still ok. If they faltered, he would become frantic and alone over the darkness inside as he was trying so desperately to hold it together, these two lives.

As it had gotten closer and closer, there was this thing that Israel had really wanted to do and he was at that part of the planning stage where finally everything was in place. Thinking all week about the departure on Wednesday morning. Knowing every detail programmed in, ready to float down over some unexpecting burg.
"How long can you go without doing something Israel?"
"It depends on what you call, doing something"
Driving around at night, for hours on end. The week had consisted of him going through the scenarios over and over now getting so excited with it in the apprehension, The closer it gets, it makes the heart gallop.

Putting his daughter to bed with sprite giggle that when they wake up and open their eyes that they will be getting on a plane for the vacation!

He noted that South Anchorage had a few spots picked out that were alone and real quiet around closing time and that out there the little coffee stands were open later than most.
Also Wednesday morning at its earliest, is actually still Tuesday Night.
He would walk up to the little window as a customer and make an order. Then afterward, he will pull out the pistol and rob them as they would be wrapping up their till.
Israel acknowledging that he was starting to lose control. That he "couldn't keep them separated anymore" those two lives.
There he is in his own white truck; part of the robbery plan was him removing the heavy ladder racks and cargo boxes.
The clock has now ticked down to zero.

Him describing these parts while holding the paper cup in his shackled hands. Within the cup is a crafted coffee, an Americano, now in the interrogation room even. Who was the chocolate bar for?

Marvel at the falling ashes. They almost float, but not quite. His eyes so cold and wild and black. There beyond the thick soft snow falling in clusters. His sweaty plans are casting over the world lit in the alpenglow street lamps. Just before closing time.

Across the parking lot there and he was scathing himself inside for want of them. A scene playing out was recorded in digital and stored far away by some security system. The video files would have to be requested by the business owner with the section of time being: what happened last night? It was still wrought in the unknown. The section of time of the file is isolated along the long, long strand of screenshots and as you approach it coming from the future you are going back. To you then the last parts are coming first. The composite of those few camera angles captured like the ones in the shed house made into a coffee hut, they are quiet and dark in there. The ones outside show a world of white shone over in orange sherbet.

Suddenly there on the tape is her concerned boyfriend, late in the night he is there and he is looking around the Expresso stand and trying to look inside. All is at rest and quiet in there. Circling once they watched every nuance and much later: **"Law enforcement agencies release new details of abduction, slaying of Samantha Koenig" 12/4/12**

In their tapes they show the young man eventually shrugging and blinking lashes wet with cotton ball snowflakes. He drives off of the screen, which would actually be when he had pulled up, looking for her for the very last time of the night.

So eerily, only four minutes rewinding on the tape as the suspicion is building upon her boyfriend. When walking heel first and looking the wrong direction is a tall guy wearing all black and as he approaches, he just won't turn and look at the camera. The snowflakes are lifting up from the ground exactly as they had fell earlier. The dark man on the tape is instantly into the back door of the coffee stand somehow effortlessly and he appears to slide some small thing from his hand, out onto the counter and it stops there next to the empty cash register tray where it had been laying. Next there were some thin plastic sticks that ended up to be the cut off ends of some zip-ties. They seemed to appear and scatter on the floor of the warm little trailer building. A set of keys zips from his hand and are instantly still as if cast in glass, the intruder having seen them and snatched them. They were right where she had told him The Intruder then suddenly exiting the man-door. This is the first time that they could see his much too obscured face and it was only as he is walking backwards away into the static. Back to the truck where she was on the floor of the back seat, a constant assurance that this is just a ransom for money, he said. The cold air outside the bottom of the coffee shop door is creeping up in a cold whisper razor inside because at the top of the door, some tiny warm air always lulls free through the weather seal. In the rising air is the likes of exotic coffee roast and sweet syrups and the working floor of a coffee stand where pretty girls make drinks and count change through steamy little windows iced over when below freezing. There on the counter next to the empty till, the dark quiet is shattered by a phone screen now flashing light on the tapes. In a few minutes her boyfriend will receive her text she is mad and,

"Hey, I'm spending a couple of days with friends, let my dad know."

Let my dad know?

The flashing screen is him calling and texting her over and over again.

How the wallpaper of the world will have changed for her father over the next month and a few days more. The events coming out in the news, the world for him knowing that sitting in the jail down town was the murderer of his daughter. Becoming blurred in spider toxin, wild bear coming out from behind the steering wheel, clenched jaw breathing out whiskey steam into the cold night and its thick hide, cast over in blue and red flashing and the entire time so very heartbroken.

All of these strands converging again in the moment state. Instantly blinded in the monkey routines is the girl opening the little coffee stand the quiet next morning and finding the till was empty and it ends up the new girl that worked the night before had left a bit of a mess and had apparently sent another text to her boyfriend that she knew what he had done! Possibly cheated on her or something and also one text to the owner of the Coffee stand that she was going through some stuff and she needs to disappear for a while, in similar.

CHAPTER NINETEEN

2-1-2012

Alaska Airlines Flight (Anchorage Alaska to Houston, Texas)
February 2, 2012 Wednesday Morning

The arm rest is shaking, the roar is somewhere and everywhere. Hissing airs balancing in the cabin over land then over water. The vision of the beam from his wobbling head-lamp as it had splashed across the dark. The aisle seat is rattling empty. Glancing over the rolling hills and there in the light swath passing is a small belly button ring through the cleft of a young navel. She appears to be trying to roll away from him or something, fading deep into blackness.

One quarter inch of the likeness of life there across the face of his chameleon skin.
Made in the likeness of other people. Especially the ones that you knew during the long summer days of your adolescent.

At times sitting with the girls, wanting to dissolve amongst them laughing, as the tent flap yanked back!

Littlest sister for now, laughing after all of them having jumping startled, scrambling out of the tent after the little rascal! Peering out from the flap she could see that he has caught her, dropped there on the shamrock and clover. He growls coming in so close, her squealing and pinching her neck and tiny shoulders. The higher registers of her

shrill going out of range as he gobbling on the back of her tiny peach
neck.
Whatever it was we have no inclination, they were God fearing and
they were vehemently so with lower lip spittle flying, forgive us Lord
our many trespasses!

While the town's people back in Coleville sang praises to the Lord, the
little girl's tears as she would be gripping tight. Her little blood vessels
bursting fighting for one breath. The eyes of the river, maybe wild
down into hers, flashing pennies of fire as her little feet are tumbling
off from the little straps.

Or maybe it was just some terrible accident and both just some
horrible coincidence.
Sinking into greyness.

"The only person that knows about these things?
The things I'm telling you?
Is Me."
"I've been two different people for a long time' he said.

When they asked
 "How long Israel?"
he thinks about it and trails off

"14 years…,,,…"

He had boasted of his study of serial killers to them. Acknowledging
then the list of childhood statistics for the ones that "do" what he does:

 Daydreaming
 Compulsive masturbation
 Isolation
 Chronic lying
 Enuresis (bed wetting)
 Rebelliousness
 Nightmares
 Destroying property
 Fire setting

Stealing
Cruelty to children
Poor body image
Temper tantrums
Sleep problems
Assaultive to adults
Phobias
Running away
Cruelty to animals
Accident prone
Headaches
Destroying possessions
Eating problems
Convulsions
Self-mutilation

Sexual Homicide Patterns and Motives, 1995, pg 29, R. Ressler, A. Burgess, and J. Douglas

When they kept needling him for some insight into those years he said,

You know, "all the things you'd expect" and he said it flat and free of any poker face.

The forever days, ending in maple burst over cut black forest tops of grand trees in the lonesome up near Canada. Out on the fringe the Genome strand is clicking so diligently, in the mind it is taking samples from observations. Years later realizing their strong influence over your relationships and your long life-patterns.
Colville, down by the river. He said that was the age that he realized

"The things that I think are normal and ok, are not the things that other people think,
are normal and ok"

He starts laughing during the second half.

All the while the genetics' clock speed dictating by chemical hormones, dictating that it is the appropriate time to pulse the nuts and fire off the Puberty Sequence. By now the elements of the scenarios and the still photos would have had mostly been logged in already.

The archetypes that will soon drag their fingers on the walls of the
dream cave for him,
coming out of it gulping aloud and dryly. Still a boy really, his eyes
are glassy and erratic scattering around. There had been some kind of
a buildup or something right before the impact and then he appeared
again there instantly:

In the quietest, in the most serene, it must be the softest of breezes
dragging slowly through the Douglas Fir boughs out there, because the
inside of the wall tent canvas is brilliant and glowing warm
illuminated. Beautiful mid-morning light and his knees are almost at
her back. The auburn hair is gold spun and best friends they are talking
and smiling. Things of how the days are changing. Gentle rake of
fingers laying her thick braid across his palm, the tines of his hand
separating the cords in her hair. They are caring and sure. A gentle
tug-tug, periodically to perfect it.
There are things kept secret between them, becoming older as they
make conclusions together about things that they don't really speak of
in front of other people. The sun shone through on highlights of red.
It sounded as if she was clicking gum in her mouth, her looking back
over her shoulder, the deepness searching in to her brother.
His eyes coming to some conclusion, then them skinning over to the
texture of rough Slate.

He always talks about the cat story, where he took one out to the
woods. This time with his sister and his friends, all of them young
teens and he tied the cat to a rope that was tied to a tree. Watching it
develop they were surprised when he then shot it in the stomach. It ran
around the tree winding the cord until it hit the bark and started
puking. Looking across the faces of his young friends the oldest boy of
them was vomiting. After that he said that he stopped sharing those
"things" with anyone.

The abandoned farmhouse with the hole in the second floor and going
up to the roof. The transcripts said it was perfect. "Like a cannonball
had blasted straight through" Lorraine completely restrained must've
been very close in proximity to the hole to knock the camp stove down
into it, he had to immediately address it he said. Imagining her seeing
the headlamp through the hole, having seen it leave the room with her

there, it wobbling down the stairs and seeing it emerge below all from the hole in the ceiling. Seeing the light orb down there scanning over the debris in the darkness and there is her Bill. The intruder playing along and talking to Bill for stretches of time in between. As Bill being in his "part to play" how terrible it could be. The headlamp in one of the rodeo arcs of the bad man's free arm swinging back. His black eyes locking up into the blackness of that hole in the ceiling, it is her floor. How horrible the crescent of light washing across her eyes, hair plastered back with the sweat, face framed in dark curls. The Intruder washed in the dopamine when scanning the darkness. Gaping at her shock and the slapping horror she could've been his mother. Bill had "ruined it" he said. When she came down the stairs later, Lorraine was wearing nothing he said, but making a point that she was all used up. There are worm castings and muck from the soil up there in those apples now. Every family engagement, celebration, gathering he would be gliding in on a rental or airfoil and attached to the chassis or the airframe, a rattle ribbon lamprey. Nibbling and so giddy on the cold under belly, rattling in the current.

Like feeding the fish that he had caught from the ice hole in Matanuska Lake to his little daughter. A normal object placed so incidentally; it comes sizzling out into the open air. Making those strong fantasies part real, in the real world. The older him, arranging the same certain elements over again, to result of having it "feel" the way "It" felt to him back when whatever it was. Meanwhile as he is attempting to play out his fantasy scenarios invisibly, he is leaving etchings, of memories, of fascinations in the scene-work. Imagine clawing out at life as the realizations are setting in. Frantic and scratch rattling into darkness, the entire time having another person's face laid over yours in light play, only a few inches behind the intruder's ravenous threshing eyes.

In the quietest and in the most serene,
the breeze must be so gentle through the boughs of those, grand Douglas Firs.
The light it is washing in large swells of wave shimmer. Cascading across the back of the little canvas. The tent is glowing and warm and the sunlight

Fetching water together, the reflection of the water buckets looking up. They are a sloshing image of the darkness in the tall lane of trees. The deep blue ribbon of stars and beauty overhead.

Awash in peach sherbet and sparkling across her eyes. The small music box's spring advances, one click of its tiny toothed gear. The random tick of the sequence falling, to a pin strike in the peach light. While bringing the cool rag in for her and startling her from a daze, maybe the deep pools in her eyes would've splashed away. The background blurring as the pin strike falling randomly. Braiding yards of hair. In this giant storage facility, the rails were all still new and bristling back then.

Headlamp slashing across the thong and onto across the other wall inside of that horrible little toolshed. The zipping clicker of the zip-Tie locking each miniscule click. Using it to flirt with her. That same hand was upon her shoulder as he had described it. Individual clicks running as a violent zip suddenly and as it bottomed out with the other hand yanking the cord as hard as he could he said. It would've pinched her little skin. Feeling like God he said because she had been doing everything he wanted. Glimmering world made good but,
"Her Eyes", it says in the Letter.

Tug jostle, becoming oil brush stroked of shock. She cried out once at first, he said. Then she was quite for a long time. Her eyes staying open as they were slowly closing to this world. Ink spill across her eyes, the ears still hearing a little longer. He was there only as a blurry inconvenience in the background though because, when you are clawing out for life, the heartbreak is made up of Loving everything that you've ever known,

But she never made a sound, he said,

and it poisoning him like venom.

All these years later, older now, in Texas. These rails will have appeared to have slipped too close to the sun. They are worn out to splash on the corners, into the Catalogue Storage for all of the Sex stuff.

In the deep of that morning, just before he came in to wake his daughter. The bags were dutifully packed. He had went through Sam's little wallet earlier but this time he grabbed the loose change that was in there. Looking down at the coins in his hand. Freeze frames of silver edged dates or knicks or markings as they are slide settling together. He says that he came into the house, blood vessels in his eyes from the all-nighter becoming the day after.

His mind floating there in a tofu brain. The feel of being carted through the door atop a jostling mature male body:

Thud stepping up into the floor level. Those first moments back in the atmosphere of the house. He put her change very specifically with a heavy collection of others. It was there in the corner shelf of his office desk. Something you could slide around in your palm anywhere, anytime. He said the shelf from it going right: was lined with various knives, in the interview. Rolling them, warming. Imagine then the haunting crying out that one Wheat-penny might have, if it flashed briefly from behind the others. The light upon it conjuring voices even gasping in shock.

"a range of chemicals (have been) released including norepinephrine, serotonin, vasopressin, nitric oxide and prolactin.

The refractory period

~ the blood from the pelvic region is released. Contraction of tensed muscles takes place. ~ Morphine-like chemicals such as endorphins are released which can relax the body of the man. This is the reason why men tend to fall asleep more quickly (than women) after.

~ After all that energy is released, the body tries to return to a ~ stage wherein the heart rate slows down along with slower breathing.

After ~, the physical exhaustion, a chemical Oxytocin is released in the body. Oxytocin is called the "love hormone" which builds trust and closeness between partners.

He said he let hers fall onto the top of the others.

Floating down the hallway.

She opened her eyes to the world and he was there over her. Her seeing him with her ears first. The mind is half there waking almost drunk. So much more reptile then and even the child can see as an old person can. When they are passing in front of you and you can get an instinct of them.
The plasma across the child's mind is lit in the constructs that become Identities. The identity of the Patriarchal role is like God or it should be regarded as such, for the sake of the small child. Awaking to the world her eyes gasping open and she is seeing him and from what he had said, he was in an amazing mood on the plane and it made it all so sweet anytime during the cruise to lift his spirits he could think of those hours back there with her, at first.
He said that he had washed up just before. Walking out, locking up and the two of them scuffle stepping along on the ice grip. Passing right by the tool shed, now cooling in the darkness. Off to the airport for a family cruise to the Caribbean. It was right there in the driveway in front of everyone. A skip in the shuffle step.

 The landing gear clunking open and now hissing in the terrible flightpath wind. The strut lowering and locked hard into position. The blinding light shining forward.
Hanging gorilla tires - chirp to life, out behind a puff of smoke and it is wafted apart in the jet wash of the ground effect. The pilot throwing the clamshells over the back of the engines, and the throttles advancing to its greatness and then he appeared again there in the seat. The seatbelts seem to be quickening heavier into his shoulders as a crayon rolls forward and down into the seat rows. He tried to reach for it but,
        The cabin door is closed and the lights are dimmed then the cabin dings, coming to a stop the big airship last rocking. Maybe his ears might've popped just then. Something is all wrong on the deep morning flight to Texas.

Mucal and sunbaked are the clicking eyes. Awaking on the plane from deep in the utmost, waking into some other spider bite dimension. Looking around glaring across this real world up here again in the bristling atmosphere. The port window is all black and there is nothing out there. Dry tacky fish throat, looking around upon all of the things in that dead flat peer, looking at all of the God's Creation as if saying,

"You're such a fucking letdown"

THE CLOSEST CALL

CHAPTER TWENTY

CARNIVAL

After a 6-day cruise on the sea, rolling back into Texas on the **15th,** in the Kia Soul.

The latest location was known. The Church of Wells, in Wells, Texas. He had spent hours analyzing his predictions of:

if you were to hit this particular bank in that particular town, the law enforcement would most likely arrive from which overall direction?

Then calculating if from the next town the wave of red ant lights flashing over the terrain.

The first couple hundred miles on that Kia Soul he would've been replaying that deep morning over and over again always hitting the replay on loop, just before he had cleaned himself up and entered the open air of his daughter's room.

Soaring in now, coming over the small open range that he had made at a radius from his mother's new Porch, in Texas. Standing there now upon it, the compass needle hits on 3 then 4 strange points out over the dark horizon. Out over where the Skidmore Crossing is.

When they finally saw him this time after the cruise and coming in from New Orleans, there apparently seemed something was wrong. He speaks of losing the luster for life. Trying to "kick start it" with Kim on the day to day. He said it wasn't working anymore.

His plan is setting down over some parcel of land out in the sticks. There would surely be a light glow from up in the narrow lane of trees. Lines becoming too perfect along the edge of the gable or the hip of a roof, making itself known as man made in the black organic background. Crossing in front of the golden warmth, dissolving in focus as the intruder's eyes are locked onto the lamplight in there.

Soaring in, eyes across the soft glow of that interior. The pin lights
from the lighting shining across the laminate floor, a garden window,
seeing there are couches as his eyes are scanning the textures. My wife
one afternoon telling me that our youngest daughter having come
tumping feet down the stairs. Saying that she had found it! My wife
following her up into her bedroom to her little TV/VCR combo. She
had been watching the Nancy Drew tape when she saw what she had
seen! Her little fingers quickly and diligently playing the tape as the
screen is scratching along and she pauses it there. On the screen is a
man's eyes cast in dimness from outside the glass. He had been there
the whole time; she is frantic then relieved. That is what she had seen.
My wife staring at the paused screen a man looking in menacing and
wild, locked captured on pause.

Scanning in along the penlights across the new laminate and then
seeing something having been there the whole time, an apparition. The
top part of a pillow case flimsy, then beautiful little girl shadow lines,
those are curls.

Then so shockingly two magnificent black eyes locked on his
dark presence through the reflection of the glass. The pajama fabric
seemed to smear and drift behind her as she is disappearing out of the
frame of the large window. Little heels heard thumping up the stairs
through the framing. The dry gulp, snapping out of it and zipping back
into the moment state. Back in Texas. The first couple hundreds of
miles on that Rental Soul were spent with him no doubt playing these
moves over and over.

Heidi Keyes should have looked to the Creation like God had
said to. Learning from the herbs of the garden and the beasts of the
field behold my daughter, who is called for such a time as this. Are
you seriously going to look me in the face and lie to me my son?
When she pressed the point, she knew more than she had before. Her
remembering when walking along when they were there together in
the wooden path in Indiana on his way back to Alaska. Her never
knowing for certain but him just days after, killing the Curriers. In the
lane of trees looking from afar the mother her daughter and son, they
would have appeared to be as a story from the bible. The old woman is
walking with her right arm down straight along her side the other arm
is bent at the elbow coming across her lumbar and the left hand is

grabbing the right forearm. It looks like a painting on a tarot card when she does that. Part *servant* part **Master**. It is **Feminine** crossing holding *masculine*:

That is how mother walked on the tape a few years later, on a local channel in rural Texas. This young girl was a legal adult. However, it was her parents whom had been pressing the point, they were there with cameras rolling, outside of the cobbled little outdoor shelters on part of the compound of the Church of Wells. Hollering over towards the young girl dressed now from a different era. They said, it is mom and dad and we just want to say we love you and just want to see you and to look you in your eyes.

There was a hand gesture down low or a guttural bark under breath and the girl looking over at the camera crew there over the fence, to a road that is usually always empty. The girl looking back and shuffles slowly and perhaps hesitantly away, just behind the slat board corner of an outbuilding. Then the little Down Syndrome girl, Jubileea his youngest sibling, scuttles after her. Off to the side of the speechless frame, from the stillness of the brush, the old cow moose gives some old bull call. She gives a glance at the camera almost like she wants to see you see the soured milk,

and to watch you have to kneel your chin to lap it.

As she walked away smugly on the evening news, she walked away with her arm just like that.

Gods' son and daughter spinning in verted helix. It is spinning in strands of chromosomes silvery titanium in her daughter and in her son there in the wooded path back in Indiana, just at the close of the Currier trip. You can see across the dell that this has been set up from before. Pre-ordained movements as they shuffle out a little bashful at the charade of following along.

His sister, little mother wringing her fingers subconsciously, so sure in her Lord and his manifold promises. When she breathed in, he might've expected there was some great help that he could be there for them but there were so many things to be done?

There the apparent last days in Indiana on the Currier trip, walking in the grove of trees, this is where the realities and thus then the logistics that Mother and a few of the girls would be relocating. The process would be looked at and evaluated, pacing back and forth, praying and thinking, counting with her fingers, she shakes them off no and she braces her chin. She would most likely start from a point that illustrates the relationship that they have always had. Him gritting his teeth that this is out of bounds with who he is in the family! That as she interrupted him and continued, she had been a young kid back then, little mother at times. His sister could have moved on effortlessly about their early development and that after he left there were those months that he had promised he would return and retrieve her, in actuality rescue her?

That he had instead went out into the Worlds and she had in fact become stranded. Only after father, in horse whispers to God for a sured healing, dry cracked throat hissed out slowly. The old man's hand slowly opening. We could never see the color of the things that he had held onto most precious, they were now on the other side with him. Her brother had never come for her, acting nonchalant at family functions and he was there devoutly at certain ones every year. The things that deeply affected her for years the Patriarchal Figure and all, and to please let her finish! Him glancing up bitter and she continues with slow eyelids. She was almost certain that he would come now, better later than never and take his place as Prince of the Family becoming Father's stead and to give his life to the Lord again? They will all be relocating to Texas, all of them together.

She had said as she saw that he was possibly going to reject God and her too? She was diligent and reached out to him. Sensitive in the Spirit, moving through the steps, talking so honestly to her brother, little papa. Who had sparkled in her eyes. Remembering praying for him out there in the night, he was always such a bad ass, her breath cut short as he then burst forth into tears and weeping, she said. Blood curdled to vinegar in his voice and her eyes becoming wide. Her telling him that the Lord has confirmed for her that….
Him blurting out over *her* in raspy voice rattling!!

"You don't know the things that I've done!!" according to the FBI report

Holding the sybil eye gaze while he wobbled his head back and forth and she couldn't believe it when he scathed hissing "NO!"

"I have to drink to forget the things I've done!!"

The lower eyelid quivering like the slaughterhouse floor. He shared one time about his deployment in the military. The guys, he said, had found a good college aged girl who would do them, one at a time in an apartment bedroom. When it was his turn after a commotion, she came out very agitated speaking broken and quickly making hand gestures of choking and pushing around. The word in Arabic is khanq: meaning to strangle but he volunteers randomly saying that "she was a young Russian girl". Dead pan eyes he had told the one girl, something about not wanting to get his pecker bit off. She was trying too hard he said, she tried to laugh, but. He described it later in his letter: *"nervous laugh as it burst like a pulse of blood from your throat"*

To gently bite your lower lip, he says that his eyes became still and fiery in the shed and he thought about what she had said to him. It had gotten very late into that deep morning. Already flashing scatter across the walls and the ceiling and behind his eyes. Even Lorraine in the photos online. Maybe there in the morning light as their birds still fluttered under the sheets of the cages back at her house as she was coming down the old decrepit steps. He said she was so out of it "Pretty much gone". The Breaking of the Defiant, watching her eyes angry and humiliated fading to coma, watching her lose with each time, he wouldn't have missed it for the world. When he described the pulling off of Bill's very light fabric bed time shorts, he implies pulling them down and later barely being able to drag him for the slick floor. If at the moment that he was splashing the Drano onto the Curriers, the splashing no doubt upon his shins, did it fall upon fabric there or haired flesh? As he was squatting at times, tucking them both quietly under heavy black trash bags. If at that moment instead they too were awakened on the other side? Now solemn walking so carefully and looking, laying that Prophet of Nazareth in the cave, tucking the shroud of Turin over him in so much Honor. Then suddenly Israel reappearing again he is standing there in the grove of trees with his mother and sisters snapping back so suddenly. Old lube yet there in latent film spreading slowly thoroughly across his grimy crotch. For Lorraine and Bill, the carpenter of Nazareth would have rolled the massive Easter stone away yesterday morning. While he is fresh and He is risen, Bill and Lorraine were now distorted through the chemical waves, sweltering in Drano. His Mother's spittle, all his life casting from her lip as she condemning with such vengeance for the judgment day the accuser, pointing in disgust at the likes of Lorraine's filthy cigarette ash tray on the back deck, looking over the pool. Lorraine's neighbor and his dog too. When the Law Enforcement had sat the neighbor down and made inquiry, he said he knew something was wrong and so did his dog. He spoke of striking the last smoke it was getting real late, the night blindness out over the backyards as the flame's bright strike, fading away to a low brightening ember, the pupils glowing in the dark. The scent of smoke lingering yet in the air floating stretching across fences as the man had finally gone in for the night. Israel said that he had been in the garage already for some time. Both of them describing the same events from across the hedgerow and the two lawns. At one point Israel retreating in, passing by the little air compressor, the smell of the fluids from the Saturn and stuff in the dark. From inside their kitchen through the exterior glass door to the garage just in the darkness, there he is standing looking in. His eyes they are locked on the lamplight in there.

On the return leg from Essex Junction and the recent caught fresh lake fish, had been by his recollection melting under the Drano and he said that they were then tarped over with the large trash bags to help keep it wet. To keep the goo going so to speak. This is one of the parts of the tapes where his loved ones would report getting sick to their stomach there as the tape rolled. So casually that voice they knew so well speaking of putrid corruptions to, then of, the flesh, as if discussing the qualities of top end sour cream. Clouded over periodically in the swamp gas belching from under the horrible black plastic bags in the corner. The stench and the things that creepeth upon the earth, they would have been praising The Intruder for his abundance. The Bible speaking so clearly of a Couch of Worms reserved for him.

Maybe jostling weight to another foot as to adjust his crotch. He is bitterly in front of them there in the wooded lane. Loraine standing flat feet in the slick blood down in the farmhouse.

She could've been his mother and yet she too is looking upon him there now.

The victims' terror slicing like incense smoke, stinging his eyeball as it had passed over. The front of him looking nearly flawless to them but over the edge of the perfected sight lines, it is lifeless, crossing over the shady tree contractor's skin.

Israel remembering waiting for hours by the Curriers pool for the neighbor to stop peering out over the darkness and smoking his cigarettes. The man from Colbert St.'s dog whimpered for hours into the night. When Israel had described to them, hanging out by the pool then lingering in the dimness of the garage. He made it very clear that he was speaking of surveillance around the Currier's house, so that he would feel more "comfortable" and he starts using that catty bitch lispy lispiano on the S's in the story right before he busts the glass to the door in their garage. He seems to be relieved that he caught it and perhaps because the story was framing up nicely without those parts. Evading the trails that lead up to the part where he has something in the form of his "mother" tied up in front of the stage in the little church. Slipping by the snare wire in the question about Lorraine's "looks". Only one of the pig's back feet held closed in the trap there is a terrible pounding, thudding, frightening banging, smearing pigshin. Then it is all silent and there is nothing but waxy crumple skin and curly hairs wet on the wobbling wire of the question. Eventually the neighbor says he had stamped out the last of too many smokes and went to bed. Israel even volunteering information that he even had a cigarillo out there simultaneously cloaking his puffs under the neighbor's cigarette across the hedge row. Continuing on even more unprovoked that it is just rolled up tobacco leaves, that there is no butt. He says that if you crush them up and smear it in it is just brown leaves and you would never be able to see it right there in the ground cover. An interesting point indeed then he starts again even that he usually gets them from a special shop in Chicago and they didn't have them, implying making a few stops before lazily heading out to Mother's in Harlan, Indiana.
And when the mid-morning was coming so soon, the breakfast traffic was already glinting on the country lane those hours wasted watching the fucking pool and he is so amped up.

Their plans of relocating from Indiana, showing themselves approved as he is there now on a Texas Sunday evening, stopping in to see his one sister as they were in the process of relocating getting nearer, down to Wells. Out here on the Grand Prairies of Texas. The nearest boulevard would be in Lufkin. Maybe he could help them tie up any loose ends as he was passing through. The brother in-law even tried to witness to him there while they had fellowship. Him eventually reviling again "You don't know the things I've done!" After the fiery evening they woke to find only a note that he had "went to bury his guns" and he was gone.

The rental car's dash lights becoming so much richer as the warm sunlight is fading, racing eyes deep in the night before.

Israel popping up over here, keeping a very tight timeline, it is part of his normal signatures. The pool and the neighbors and the adjoining streets, there is almost none of those things here this time.
Lifting off slowly moving from one spot then to another. Over the Sky Maps and back again, one of these trips was leaving the Pickup-Truck. The creature wisping jolted now and passing over the land in his mind and into the trees and into its endless leaves.

Israel's sister has been watching the clock as the sun was dropping down. Making the tree tops golden, then watching them dissolving to absolute black. Pacing about on continual counting fingers. A strange calling in the mountains scoured of Iron. Thinking now of this part Amish Church marm, her mind is thinking of New Orleans and that of the mileage thereto being 347.91 miles.

Calculating the drive time in homeschool arithmetic, her measuring over and over the sequences in minutes and distances. Blistering thoughts of these recent incidents. Her teacher all those years ago is there looking into her eyes already as she is turning. The result or the sum coming back queer and making it once again so skeptical.

If her brother had driven straight there, he would have been here hours ago. They had called and called his phone it appeared that it was not online? He came through briefly, was it the static or the wind, he had run into some problems and he was too far to drive tonight they insisted "where he was?" He told them that he was at the Cleburne Mall, in Cleburne. It is too far of a drive for tonight and that he would sleep in the rental car and that he would be there tomorrow, early then?

It really is a bit too far of a drive and it really says something that they drove there any way. Maybe in that maroon Church van, a 3-hour drive going one way if you allocate a 9-minute piss and the Part-Amish do everything the old-fashioned way.

Packing up the travel accessories at dusk and making the commitment. It seems to be lit from underneath, resounding of: suspicion. An hour or two into the drive, in the dark on the long stretch, the conversations randomly had of her brother and the evil glow of the dash light undercuts the rise of her eyebrow. The leer light indirect making gestures becoming inflections in her voice. Even recalling for hobby this list of coincidences that stacked and arranged you can see through them, the layers of still photos and inconclusions making a paper scene in a shadow box. Each time in the undercut of the leer light the cards rearranged and shuffled with all fairness and understanding, worst case scenarios accounted for and the scene is the same the big guy listening as his eyes were already on hers as she was turning towards him. Wobbling there in the alpine of her eyes. The phone was useless as they pulled into the Cleburne Mall, in Cleburne. They were relieved at first passing under the light poles. The halos of light lamps dissolving the maroon van, it appearing blood black in that kind of light. Accumulating these frightening conclusions. The odometer numbers moving slower like molasses maple as the van is creeping to a stop in the empty mall parking lots there in Cleburne. From the cold outside the motor is running. The heaters are ticking, and inside is warm and through the glass she is underlit and she is looking around the emptiness through the windows. Maybe her arranged husband offered to take her to a hotel room.

Knowing later on counting fingers that this was the same night that one Electrician guy disappeared, or was disappearing from his unfinished cabin. Just over those hills from them as they had gone over so many instances, they were approaching 20/20 and getting those flashes of hindsight.

In Texas, back to Anchorage, then back to Texas. He even still had receipts on him from the previous trip, while he was on the next one.

"James Lamar Tidwell Jr.

Details of Disappearance

> *Tidwell was last seen in Mount Enterprise, Texas on February 15, 2012. His boss last saw him at 5:30 a.m. that day, after he finished working the night shift. He had been working for an electrical company in Longview, Texas for about ten years, and he and his wife lived in a cabin they were building on a ten-acre plot in Mount Enterprise.*

> *Tidwell was supposed to come back to work in the afternoon to do some overtime, but he never showed up. When his boss called his house and spoke to his wife, she said he was asleep and refused to wake him.*

> *On February 20, Tidwell's boss became concerned about his uncharacteristic absence from work and asked the police to do a welfare check, but no one was able to find him. On February 28, the authorities tried again and still couldn't find Tidwell, and his boss filed a missing persons report. His wife gave inconsistent statements as to when or where she last saw him.*

> *On February 29, Tidwell's white 1979 Ford F100 pickup truck was found abandoned at the intersection of FM 95 and State Highway 315, about five miles from his home. A photo of the truck is posted with this case summary. It had been parked at the roadside for at least a day, and possibly since the day his boss last saw him. His glasses were lying on the seat of the truck, but his cellular phone, wallet and keys were missing. There was no sign of him at the scene.*

> *Tidwell's sister does not believe her brother left of his own accord; she thinks foul play was involved in his disappearance. His case remains unsolved."*

Bitter, part Amish morning. Waking stiff and part cold in a fucking mall parking lot! and lo and behold the White Kia is somehow there now all of a sudden and covered in mud? Her brother is coming out and he is looking at them in shaking head disbelief?! She is coming out of the van 40 years older creaking from the seat cushion not having time to really wash the look off of your face. Her voice in free form when she had him repeat that he? Couldn't believe that they would drive all the way out here? and that he had been right over where!? all night! and that all that they would've had to do was drive around to the other side. Standing there looking at her in the face.

There is something giddy in him though. Something in there out of place in this setting, what is it? The upper outside of his eyes raising and they are flashing excitement. Scouring a split second of gold fever, the searching look in his eye: Wondering, did she let him fuck her in the van last night?

They said, that morning when he had arrived, that he stunk terribly and that he was wild looking. Driving home her chin would've been up, just like in the funeral photo. Out the window in a deep gaze and if her arranged husband had reached over and touched her shoulder then as she turned to him, he would've saw sweet little rascal looking up at him and she is worried for her big brother. Her eyes could've been covered in glossy star speckle almost bursting and in the heater air blowing, suddenly somehow the atmosphere smelling of the old tent house. Her eyes coming around already meeting his and then she instantly re-appeared there again. The surface in her eyes crackled to granite and slate. At the last of it squeezed a tear from in them.

THE CLOSEST CALL

CHAPTER TWENTY-ONE

"THESE SIX THINGS DOES THE LORD HATE"

The town of Wells, Texas had become overrun with these cult members. They speak with this very cautious meter. It carrying the Amish or maybe Quaker up and down, they hold a word at mid-inflection, not to build tension my brother. It appears they are at times making sure the word of God is perfected over their lips and to be caught in blight if incorrectly you had *Uttered* it? However, the debonair young Pastor coming through this Texan town he'd stopped at the neighbor girls playing in their yard. He struck up conversation leading right into that, her, her father and mother are going to hell and that even if they always go to church, that is not what God Demands! He demands Sacrifice and you giving your life to the Lord??! Him having approached on foot dressed as a studious missionary, wearing a back pack with both the shoulder straps. There are bus routes along these rural streets out here and he is dressed like he is almost one of them. The Church of Wells had started in another town but the pioneer, "Alaskan-like" Texans ran them out after much discord. They were founded as "Street Preachers" to their good credit or at least they were when they were the "Church of Arlington" that is when they were living out of Heidi Keyes' driveway in Indiana. These two brothers, much rather the one in particular was so compelling that within a short time hence? Heidi had sold off the assets like in the good old days and Momma and the remnant sisters already have pulled up stakes and with the brothers, "we're soon heading to Wells in Texas to be His church there then. Once there the legal reports began to surface around them. They were frightening with guns bordering on brandishing the report saying possibly "Branch Davidians" the law enforcement typing each one in.

Eventually for the Federal requests becoming commandments, that they relinquish the product of our precious investments. Finding they had him in the files with almost certainty that Israel Keyes at 14 years old or so was there in the photos of the protestors. Some of their mouths click frozen yelling something or another, down with "Big Brother!" their eyes were wild and the young boys were there with no other than Chevy and Cheyne Kehoe! And that they couldn't believe their eyes that he was almost certainly one of the boys in the photos coming into the large Cities of Man. They were in caravan the Aryan People's Republic; a white supremacist organization.

At that time Israel's father wrote a letter to the local paper in Colville. When he defending his community church. He wrote:

> *"It is my understanding that the Marble Community Fellowship has very little to do with the Christian Identity Movement, but so what? Haven't we as Americans a right to exercise a belief in God and celebrate our White heritage and Christian Religion? After all, many Jews consider their race to be God's chosen people. Is this not racism at its zenith?"*

At times like this in the room with the tables Israel always tried to knife slit the throat of these years in his Story. It was gasping, silent clicking while his hand was rolling, looking for the right way to say, that stuff was "Ancient History" he says and moves on without them. They are dumfounded at their own metal contraption with tank treads and ridiculous swinging arms they had touted it as counter balance? Laughable, swinging into the room in android. The part Amish kid having hated the Federal Govt. since he was being led into darkness by Kirby Kehoe's two sons! Leaving them there abandoned, they spoke boasting in tones of the connection that they made with that one thing that the one Kehoe did for that one guy Timothy. The good kid who had been in the army? The Govt. fucked him big time so one of the Kehoe's helped him fuck them back.

The federal searchlight after years clanging back with this:

"Timothy McVeigh used thirteen barrels filled with explosives. 9 barrels contained ammonium nitrate (a common fertilizer) and nitromethane (well known as racing fuel in Top Fuel drag racing, and as an important component in the fuel). 4 barrels contained a mixture of the fertilizer and about 4-U.S.-gallons diesel fuel. Two green cannon fuses were connected to two sets of non-electric blasting caps, which, when set off initiated 350 pounds of Tovex Blastrite Gel "sausages"'" which in turn set off the configuration of barrels them becoming a messy plume of stuff. The open chemistry lab in the air now at atmospheres all the way inland in Oklahoma from over those grand mountains they have only risen 1200 feet from sea level? The inches in Mercury defining the state of the weather in the air, the drums of shit and gas everywhere it immediately oxidizes in the heat and the utmost stripping of being invincible it starts to bleed off everything it held close. The air compressing in a type of pyroclastic expansion of available components becoming gasses the ears popping as the Hg climbs in barometry the eyes pushed in with air thumbs, the phantom thumb pressing in the belly and the chest air even everywhere under there, under wear, then it ignites like a reactor. Every stroke of pain she tried to open more for him like he is insisting! and She Is!! but he says something about more, she sees it in him run dry on the stones and he is pulling away from her. Sitting now interrupted, blush race at what was it, something she said? a name? What?! And it ruined it for him, at least that is how he made it seem. He was going to have to think sternly about what he is to do about this interruption, him saying it in breath flutter. The paper unfolded, over years working methodically for this exact moment. He says that she laughed out. The burst from her neck a bit of shame and nobility there,
coming to terms and that first beautiful flash in her eyes toward him. The haunting that
"He is such a fucking let down" you could've been anything but this.

The explosion blew the daycare out the back ass of the shins of the building when the charges magnified upon themselves. Popping through atmospheres and the tea kettle was sky high, coming down through chemical after-blast, falling to earth through a giant hot fume.

The lay of the land below, coming into view with teary burning eyes it is falling on towards roof sections, over bent pan decking and girders twisted astern, the drywall and the conduit was intermingled as cobweb and dust wrapped in and upon all of the steel millwork. The kettle tumbling down to ringing ears blown out. They got them good.

"On April 19, 1995 – exactly two years after the fiery conclusion of the botched Waco siege – McVeigh detonated explosives planted in a truck outside the Alfred P. Murrah Federal Building in Oklahoma City.

Equity from Mother's land sale in Indiana floating, unknown if it was used in part, or in whole. Perhaps becoming an offering, or a tithe, a gift perhaps, or a donation. It has been considered that if we could weigh these actions against something else, something from within those very secretive compound walls, something from within the recluse commune itself that would give us leverage for our suspicions. When they had been in the grove of the trees it was the last stretch of the Currier trip, when Israel denied the Lord back in Indiana. That is where they had laid it on him, his sister, beginning to explain that, although it is an "Arranged Marriage" and that it is not quite what she wants, per se? But the younger brother, the very stout man, he seems to yield immediate to his Pastor. Luckily, he is lacking that attribute so very strong in the other Brother's eyes. The Pastor who stood upon the absurdly tall ridge of the newly built and paid for, Amish farmhouse, it is massive. Walking from gable to gable like a rooster vain. Reading aloud, to be heard hollering out to that same neighbor that "He was going to Hell. The man recording it is heard asking him to not speak to his daughters or his family and the Rooster vain upon the roof top hollers back and continues on, the debate becoming nonsensical. The local news airing it and it was in the papers there in rural Texas.

The attribute in the Pastor's eye appears to be:
a proud look: in less than 15 minutes condemning a welcoming church in the small town for minor differences of interpreting basic scriptures. The other church was flabbergasted. Open mouths, some smiling in disbelief. The video shows the bewildered Pastor attempting to offer his hand to part as brethren but instead he is rebuked by the Rooster Vain. The Pastor nearly grinning himself, it could still be a practical joke but it was real and they had taped it.

a lying tongue: hissing to the children that they are going to hell without his specific doctrine. "Suffer the little children" the Messiah said as he held the children close and told all that ANY, that offend one of these little ones, that it were better that a millstone was cast about their neck and they were cast into the sea.

An heart that deviseth wicked imaginations, his feet swift in running towards mischief, A false witness that speaketh lies, and he that soweth discord among brethren. 6 out of seven the Young Pastor is off the charts.

THE CLOSEST CALL

CHAPTER TWENTY-TWO

BY ALL APPEARANCES

Dressed so demure, as he helped her hand.

The stout good Brother arranged as her husband was really there for her, this wife that God had given him.

It is clear in the photo.

He was attentive to her that day in particular as they were walking up across the edge of the game trail? It appears that a light snow had fallen appearing to be lingering at freezing, as her nose is red. She is walking confirmed and still hand. She appears stoic as she is getting slush grip up into the old Potter's Cemetery, the fence is meant for what. As they are leaving the frame of the photo it appears that he had been checking for the keys to the maroon Church van there in the background. The hand she often counted on while talking and praying it snatches a short movement at her husband down low and seeming almost tactical. He had been patting the lapel down on his vest, the van keys perhaps, tut tut, and he seems to scuffle up after her as she looks chin forward. She is this woman from whom God somehow cast in peach light for him. The other brother with the cunning eyes, they were stern as he had slid the dowry from the Banquet table. Wealthy in Riches, a Beggard in Spirit, once they were betrothed and were made good, he had seen it upon her face and every once in a while, this girl who knows so many secrets, she flashes and him seeing oscillations in there, becoming gravities. Looking at the star models rotating, he knows that he is a fool in this world; if it is without her.
and shouldn't it be, so?

Strange creature, creating these strange moves.
Crouched at Mother's new Compound in Wells.
Sky leap, up over those low hills, they are throwing sun shadow across the terrain,
 and then he is down in them somewhere.

Over there some tiny population mass is glistening platinum scratch like sunlight through the trees, the brambles obscuring it and the Kia Soul zips as it flies badminton, through a pass road landing just over there. The morning he arrived muddy, Soul smelling of "Feces"? This was the supposed return day. The sixth day of a 6-day round trip flight back to Anchorage on the 15th of February. He had lost track of time and blew out the schedule. His little daughter left there with Mother nearly the whole time. With all the inquiries this last year and a half, his family very slowly turning him over distant coals. That day in the grove of trees back in Indiana, coals in his eyes, his skin could've seemed to sizzle and squeal of steam making the flesh smoke.

Now of all of the times to be rolling into town, all fucked up. When he came in to Mother that evening, after a most thorough wash and fresh clothes, no doubt, him shuffling in and he is listening to her now. He is nodding and attentive and as they clasped hands maybe when he arose it was agreed that, because he was now somehow flat broke, that would she purchase a plane ticket for him and his daughter, but very distinctly for in a day or two. He absolutely must return to Anchorage; it is imperative, but he still had somethings he must do on this trip, and she did it. There so often, inlaying narrow strands of their relationship into and through his deviate plans. Making her complicit as it plays out. In the midst of "when it happens" glistening in the rodeo rocking looking over at the thing that she bought him so oblivious, or something more touched of the oil of her skin, if even only in fingerprints she is there in the room or a part of her is. There was an associated e-mail Re: Ticket Changes, that was promptly sent to Washington State. There too were eyes waiting to see niece or daughter in a passing layover just before T S A at Sea-Tac. He either drove off alone that night or so very early the next morning straight away. "He had to go bury some of his guns" they had pleaded with him to stay and to "let them do it for him later" and he was perturbed responding. His daughter watching these things, listening to the slow wind chimes soft clanging so familiar somehow. Being able to see these exchanges between her own Grandmother and the daughters, now Aunts. As they are circling around their eldest brother, her son; her father. Blinking glitter in her sharp little eyes, perhaps as the dust from <u>their</u> Kia obscured him as he went out of sight, head rocking along the headrest on towards some unknown way point.

THE CLOSEST CALL

CHAPTER TWENTY-THREE

2/16/12 HOUSE FIRE 201 EAST TERRACE COURT, ALEDO

Maybe they had an illness or something and don't make it down these parts lately, God Bless them. The kids can't bring themselves to pull the plugs on Dad's old taxidermy freezers, maybe while he had lingered on in some city on a long bed. It could've been any reason. This house and garage barn is technically abandoned however it has freezers running, buzzing over the old man's old den carpets, it could've been anything. Whatever it was it all went up in flames. The extension cords and that one freezer in the deep back it seemed to get much worse as you approached its position. It must've been the old extension cords, in the mess pile is what he said.

He said that he was there early that morning, he wavers on the wording slipping a line of something about when, he had actually found it. Then finally: is how he made it sound when he described it, freely coming through the back door of the house, he had jimmied it. Creeping in amongst the piles of boxes in corridors leading from room to room. Like a hoarder house is what he said.

Finding a planner sometime in a cluttered little human nest near the old landline phone.
"I found a planner or something" he said and as he laid the calendar paper over a month at a time, his eyes clicking across the tiles, finger slowing.

He said that he had crept through the foot trenches. A buildup of energy approaching each door no doubt. Letting his energy spread out around the corner and into the ether of the dark rooms. Fanning out in deer ear and seeing if it comes back scented in some invalid nasty old bloated thing choke snoring in a Mumu.

His eyes are slowing to the week and the previous one on the planner, they might have dilated just then. Correlating as he had said digging through the boxes for hours in there later. Digging down through the hot sealed plastic bags with the first gen Q.R. codes printed in carbon. The layers of the mounds are layers of things going down. Still elbowing in and opening proprietary cardboard boxes that a robot arm, taped and emblemed in less than a half of a second. Of all of the online purchases of stuff that they didn't need.

At 2008, it would've been just under shoulder height.

Them becoming Q.V.C shopping network boxes from the old T.V. ads. down there around the back of your calves with the first of the old bar codes on them, that was in 1991.

Down at the old carpet, there was the beginning of plastic bags and the things that had been brought in from back when you had to carry it all the way there yourself.
Swiping even those away the carpet exposed the fibers so suffocated, barely breathing out.
Crackling of vinyl from some old heavy console that had an am / fm deck and an 8-track player. The teen daughter really wanting that one thing so bad, but the thing with her friends is all up in the air and going in the blind. Needing a stiff drink or two to center yourself enough to be able to tell her no. The soft ice shake swirled in the short thick glass as she stomp turned and ran to her room, in truth just not wanting to show her tears. Those straight edged impressions of it are forever hard pressed there into the old shag carpet like if you had branded a muppet.

Breaking the dimension of the still frame,
the intruder crossing tactical into the sight line of the next-door frame.

In the house at first creeping slowly but then it is just some old rumpus room filled with two massive freezers and stuff up to the ceiling. Right before the last chance, the millwork of the last bedroom door. It is blurred over with the vision of something of a massive leg, appearing to be made of various cheeses, pulled up and out with a webbing strap, yanking on the inadequate ankle. The chocolate raspberry of rumple texture on the hot hidden inside of the daydream's 12-gallon thighs opening for him like a large moist cooler.

Pausing maybe before breaching each room, noticing at some point he says, that down the halls of the years of shopping binge, there was a newer set of boxes. A middle-aged woman's things by now. Shipped in from somewhere having had brought her stuff into Dad's old place while she went somewhere else to get herself centered. Her having learned that it is a process, of correct choices and once they are set in order then the sequence following. Scheduled, to then come and face the whole thing head on. Every limb and every bough of the Family tree does wind chime periodically in the breeze. Even distant chiming from over across or far below. Some notes simultaneous are for all matters, identical. Them sounding truly that in part They are One. Israel is crossing the last plane of the last bedroom door and there is nothing but dim storage for more empty stuff. The daughter is his mother's age now. Her schedule revealing she travels away a lot and is away now visiting her mother. She appears to be doing really good. Him almost having had a different her. There in a soundproof cave of walls made of all that stuff. Her searching for something worthwhile in this world as it would have been overtaking her. Wild scratching on the painted glass as the tumble down across the whole house is thousands of dollars of worthless shit and the sliding boxes and tipping stuff now breathing out echoes in phantasm of her mother and father nearly still there as he would've had her for hours or days. His knees sternly rocking into the layer about 2 feet off of the floor, 1996 or 97.

Instead, at least he is finally alone to hunker down in a pig's trove and turn on the old computer. Older circuits ready to process some online thing but? It has been how long? The endless data traps of expired credit cards on file and confirmation numbers sitting all this time. Tucked in somewhere with the glow of the screen on his face. Airport computers, City Libraries, these types of places are the only place that he said he would type in actual names. Back when he was smart, at home he would type into the search engine something that would bring up some article in some real newspaper but only if you knew the cipher. Was it 3 pages over to the right? Right there in the police blotter of some outlying county. Reporting the likes of:

Spokane Washington reporting for outlying rural areas and even neighboring counties.
Trailer fire at a trailer park the 29-year-old mother was found charred in the structure. Her 12-year-old daughter was last seen hours before. The flames igniting attention at 3 to 4 in the morning. The daughter was not found in the black coals. Not too far in the woods a few years later a little skeleton was found outside of a trailer home park. Decomposition and animals had deteriorated it where no identification could be made.
-Trailer Fire Fatality: Stevens County- Colville 6-1997
He would've been 18 or so back then.

You wouldn't believe the things you see in the archived margins of the old newspapers around Tupper Lake when you type in the Biblical "Deborah Feldman" into the archived newspaper like he had done. At that time there was a lady who worked in a field that had her in a regular article in the small publication that acts as the voice for all the outlying villages and forest towns there near Tupper. It ends up that her article is right there next to the police blotter every time, it is the set printing format of that very small rural publication. Month by month sliding across micro phish at times there so clearly every other couple of scans, there are a plume of arsons, hikers going missing, bank robberies, lake side burglaries, boating accidents, it goes on and on especially at that time period that he was frequenting the area. Just like back in Stevens County, back when they lived in Coleville, but the larger paper back then was down in Spokane. The arson that his dad had paid for, and the breaking and entering stealing the neighbor's guns and dad smoothed that one over too somehow. All of those fires and burglaries and the accidental missings.

After all of this time though and trying to look them up passively and invisibly pouring over photos and articles of them, like he had said, he would've forsaken any of that old stuff now though.

At that particular time the Google search engine reports that in the Houston Region Area on those specified days, someone in Texas singularly typed in the name [Samantha Koenig] into the data complex. Watching in amazement as the pages scroll of all of these photos of her. The flood of euphoric rushing upon him in the junk pile of stuff. The law enforcement wasn't even looking for some slinking terror in Anchorage though, unbelievably the cops were eyeballing her father. Implying that it was so very suspicious how the money was stacking up from the donations that all of the people were pouring in for Samantha. On Israel's phone, of all the photos of computer screens, there were a number of photos of her that he had stalked and kept. He said that he then spread clothes all along in the goat paths of the stuff into every room, opened the attic door he said and doused it all with diesel from the Jerry Jug he had selected out of the big barn out there and then he torched the house off.

He said he went to the un-attached garage it was more like a barn set far from the main house. He said later he had spent time in there at first mostly and that he popped its attic door as well for the airflow looking over the ransack one last time a farewell and he lit it all up also now that he was leaving for good.

He says that he had stored up some jewelry that he had found and there was a stack of furs that he had laid by the door he said, laughing. He said he left the furs by the door then forgetting and never grabbing them.

Him discussing doing the arson but then shutting them out and he left the rest hanging and he courteously stonewalled them around the table in the room. The red ants came crawling over the landscape. What was in there? or was it just a distraction for:

2/16/12 National Bank of Texas robbery - Azle

Floating over to Azle, Texas and slowly landing. Dissolving the money from inside the drawers from all of the tellers at this very particular hayseed bank down in this lichen town, growing over there, part starving and the small blue lights blinking they arrive crawling all over the area. Moving just under the sinister filtered sky. There was a sighting placing Israel Keyes in a disguise getting fuel at the gas station. He was very clear on that point. Casually waiting, for the cops to arrive at the bank. This would be the biggest thing they'd ever been part of and they'd have to playback a few movies in their head of how to do it right. The town diner has sent out a tray of coffee for the responding officers, waving at Dale and his wife in there. In the blurry background dressed in disguise he could've used a right on red or the suicide lane it didn't matter. The seemingly lulled organism slips up and away in a violent instant. Returning to Mothers house,

They had each questioned him regarding these strange coincidences, for instance coming back and immediately reimbursing his mother for the ticket changes in cash?

These exchanges being seen from below.
His little daughter looking left then to the right. Up through the newly printed boarding passes and the wad of paper money as he doled it out to Mother. The little one hearing and contemplating the slow wind chime, coming from down in herself now. Part surprised as it laid out the slow cards before her, contemplating things like, that her teacher had begun to call the house lately. She has been trying to get him on the phone to set up another teacher parent conference for the three of them to sit down together. They had missed 2 already. The teacher had been giddy at first but now a stern and concerned eye brow troubling, because this thing was supposed to be a big surprise! Knowing that when she would've started the meeting with the same opener about,
 "If she could clone her, she would",
that you are not supposed to have a "favorite student" but....

smiling at her so honestly. What it must be like to be of Eve, to be an entrance point of life into this world. Them caught standing between two such places, this one and the other. At times us seeing them giving in, to some beautiful thing, it must be sweet whispering from the other side. Us only seeing them having to wave it off, away from them nearing their ear here in the real world. The reveal over the school table was that his daughter has been accepted into the Gifted program! Learning to monitor the emotions of her maturity the teacher excited but serious when saying something about these: critical next steps of his wonderful daughter's Success Path-cutting it short, for a part dry gulp glittering as she shakes her lifted hand waving off some invisible thing there at shoulder height, caught herself barely, smiling twinkle so honestly.

Just before returning the rental SUV with all of those miles that he had put on it, while nearing the walls and the fences around the runways of the airport heading home now, days overdue. He says that he began to see in his mind something troubling.
The bank robbery had gone very well however all of these lower denominations, he said people freak out when they see large amounts of small bills. So, he wrapped them at the last minute in a loose plastic bag and found an area secluded just off of the edge of the Airport and buried the small load of folding money, just before they boarded to the return flight to Anchorage and there had been such a strange vibe from whoever was there in the car.

(Thrifty) 2011 Vehicle rental;
Texas license plate CN8M857;
- Houston, Texas. February 2-17, 2012
Carnival Cruise Port of Call; New Orleans to Houston 347.91 miles.

What was he doing all of that time out there?

2011 Kia Soul return (Thrifty) mileage driven:
Rolling in with **2,847** miles on the receipt.

CHAPTER TWENTY-FOUR

SAGGING EYELIDS

It is easy to sleep having driven 2800 miles. The sagging eyelids having closed but for one glassy slit. The giant pupil in there, that has seen in the cast of that headlamp. The armrest is shaking and he said that after the stupor of the return flight dragging into Kim's empty house on Spurr Lane, an early night my love. The little girl hearing him floating down the hall he is giddy and can barely contain himself. She could've heard the clicking on of that doomed laptop. Not much later he came by her door from his impromptu blow-up mattress in the common room now. Passing by, a cursory peek in to check in on her and make sure that she is out like a light. Her breath tiny puffs under her sheet, eyelashes blinking. Hearing him with a skip in his step going out of the exterior door. Then the wisps of that cold air swooshing into the room as the scent of the dirt and the old rain is alive again in the room's warmth, mostly washing and refreshening the large room once the door closing quietly. Hearing him move directly out to his shed, he says that very quickly he had her there in a way that if you opened the shed door, she was right there exposed for him.

There as the sun had been changing in the heavens, the old radio and the hum of the heater fan in there. Eyes are frantic hearing only for himself her sweet muffled voice. The fantasy overlaid now over the real world, amazed at it in slow closing eyes becoming morbid and there was a rap on the metal door! Glistening, looking back so suddenly to hiss!

Her warm cooing voice snapped out of it there and scurrying away. The groans of the organs of the cathedral clanging doom instantly and collapsing beads of sweat. Eyes scattering for any loose blade or blunt instrument. Them all tucked neatly under the maroon tarp and sheet plastic for now though. Breathing in sharply, sweat and gasping eyes the voice is still there though, still sweet but all muffled? Unable to gather your bearings as the needle keeps swinging, when you are half in one world and half in another.

The little girl can be seen in the photo next to his truck he is wearing black military pants with a wallet chain. The little girl, she appears to be kicking a leg up in sing song next to her father there with the tailgate down. It has her just outside the door and he cannot even hear for the heartbeat pounding in his ears. She had waited so long that she eventually came out to his shed it says in the report, and his eyes gasped then flared of frustration. It was late mid-morning already? Breathing in sharp the last of it touched of breath flutter. Holding his breath back, he loosely implied that it was so difficult, speaking like a human from the other side. Telling her through the door to "(breath heave), to go inside and get ready (breath heave) and that he would be right there" his eyes then surely looking about wildly and drenched in sweat and searching to assess the terribly horrible scene.

He says that when he first opened the door returning from Texas nearly that last time, he saw some blood coming from the edge of the cabinet! He cleaned it up and brought her out and got the little heater going for her. He said that he was very surprised at the amount of blood that had overflowed the shallow Rubbermaid basin.

The early light hours becoming late morning and then the noons each fading to dusk light. How long had the heater been on this time? It all blurred as moments. He got himself cleaned up and he said that when he walked into the room and prepared the breakfast with his daughter here in the real world, that it was falling apart and him having just been spread out with the ransack. Feeling the meter as he dropped her off at school, he was anxious and blurting out too giddy as she got out for the sake of the bell, maybe: her looking back,
How the wallpaper of the world would change for him over the next month less a few days. Her alone being able to recall that one evening that he came in and they sat down for dinner, he had been off in his own world for days. Seeing now the attempts at doing C P R on relationships, alas they are showing fatigue. Smiling and gliding the

fresh fish, cooked to a steaming hot out into the open air and the dinner shared by them then saturating the house. The smell lingering for hours.

But for now, yet the sun glinting across the hood and the shadow arcing under the truck as he turned back from the school and headed towards home. The immediate path pulling in. Fumbling at the lock trying not to look hurried in the driveway on this quiet neighborhood street, all the while stuff settling down somewhere else into swaths of blackening plum. Music haze now muffling and after a little bit of time the music stops and there is shuffling from inside. They are in there together *and some soft voice nudging from within*. At 6 a.m. that morning it hit a low of 12 degrees. The church folk would drive to Church with steam from the tail pipes and from the pipes on the rooftops. Frost fingers slowly coming clear where the old heater fans are blowing up on the frozen glass. By noon there was a high of 28 degrees. Pickle fingering the lock,

They asked him around the table if he had to choose one of the others, the people that do "things" like the things he does.
To have your own dungeon he clarifies "to keep them indefinitely" he told them.

Along the lowest parts of the shed door, out in the frigid, the air is floating by. Any vapors within it are a bristling glitter twinkle. Along the siding of the shed, if the re-used metal roofing made shed door, would have swung open in the photos, the vacuum inside would then suck in the brisk frigid air. Sucking it into the room tumbling in at ankle height. Moistures from the wild wetlands, wafting in the faintest scent of dirt as it warms, but mostly it is that crisp, clean sharpness of frigid air entering, freshening and recharging the smallest of abodes in the far north winter because, the top of the door opening being the apex. The air having had become swollen and warm, staggering by at the top of the door there is a mustiness, there is a putridness strengthening as it would have swung open. The humid thickness bloated and sucked out into the bitter night.

The hot air rolls gushing up over the small eave of the small roof. Sending it hot, and pluming up curling and being stripped of its degrees in a frenzy as it rises.
Ice pepper crystals, collecting in shards on any hanging splinter.

Within the shed the vapors becoming stronger and blacker, just staring inward and through the wall. Never needing any engagement from the other side. Sweat and poofs of air rocking as he is closing the door again and the steam let out there. It crackles and sprinkles down in ruin glitter. He skid slides getting grip and goes into the house. As he is scanning Kim's cosmetics fuck it, he grabs as many as he likes and heads back to the shed out in the driveway right, out in front of everyone, he said.

For hours he worked on her make-up and he just couldn't get rid of that look on her face, he was so attentive and he was learning as he was going and he would look up happy and excited and she was looking down and she appeared sad and glazed over. Him trying to pull her out of it. One eye loose she looked up like
"you're such a fucking let down".

By the time it was time to pick up his daughter from school he had exhausted every make-up trick and how-to tip. It was agreed that he'd go to the stores and buy some of the accessories. Picking her up from school, getting in and he is on a mission. It quickly becoming some adventure. In the report he indicates the priorities were acquiring the supplies. They never stopped for anything like maybe, just getting ice cream. Travelling again in the Silver Xterra or the large White contractor truck he never said which, however it would've been best to keep the white truck off of the radar still. The daughter looking out the glass as they are pulling in and approaching the Target. Jumping out onto the cold asphalt his door is closing. He is on task and moving directly towards the light of the main opening it was a vision of massive walls of stone directing all paths up to the thresholds of these large clear panels funneling smaller and smaller. There are people passing back and forth through the doors. Entering the realm of the store, the ears maybe popping while walking through to the sporting goods department. He is there as two different people, that is the only reason why he can still do it. Scanning quickly over the Snoopy and the Little Mermaid fishing poles they are just her size and there is a little plastic weight that she can practice casting the rod in the yard. Her little imaginations becoming tiny feathers maybe, floating up but it was something about the line it was very thin, the smallest of pound test he was very discriminating on the quality and boink, boinking the line between his gripped hands and he put it back on the shelf. He grabbed one lone plastic spool of line instead. The little girl could've never been in a position to value the one, over the new little fishing kit. The amazing thing was that they had assembled all the accessories! and it is left swinging. Her following the rocking belt chain, as he is moving through the departments passing all semblances of the things that make up a life of, Good Living, or Better Living even.

Eventually when the law enforcement shrugging shoulders had by now walked into the Home Depot on Tudor and asked to see the videos of the parking lot. The associates no doubt hurrying in a sense of urgency, ready to rewind: this morning? Last night? A blush of humility that it was actually quite a ways back. Eventually then reeling all the way back to that night that "it happened" and they saw the white contractor's truck there on the tape pull up, as it was leaving. They had narrowed the search numbers down to there being roughly 1 of 750 trucks in the area that it could've been. The most pressing point is that the one in the video had no ladder racks mounted on to the truck. Tracking each registration on the list, Israel said he was never questioned, meaning that they had come upon the truck somewhere him never knowing. Their report indicating that they had located the next vehicle on the long list of plates and they would take a quick inspection on the low.

Passing by all of the little luxuries, he walked with the little girl quizzically behind him. When he found the little sewing kit in the crafts section it had a hooped needle in the tiny arrangement. The tailored kit had all the accessories. He became so much more stable then. His vibe had been anxious and suspicious and scattering, suddenly he is more relaxed as they click stepping over towards the home electronics and the girl no doubt her eyes becoming wide and elated as he pulled down from the shelf amidst all the others the special smaller Polaroid camera! On the box they knew it was a retro product it had pink and blue pastel marketing making it evident that it is basically a kid's toy! Boy OR girl who maybe had been good

listeners especially on the Carnival cruise and spending days without
him at grandma's new complex in Texas last week, keeping herself
busy with daydreams and these inconsistencies though, while he
periodically went God Knows where. She would've heard them in
hushed tones. Them speaking about him in both of their supposed
absences. He pulled it down from the shelf and the products are in
hand and they are making their way out to the truck. They are coming
across the asphalt in reflection and shadow and as a clicking cadence.
Behind the wheel again and he is opening the box in a way that makes
it impossible to return it to the counter. The little girl washed over
excited as the box tore away! Her little eyes wanting to laugh out a
jealous burst to maybe be in the light of life with the Patriarchal figure
and all. After the Polaroid in hand the smell of acrylic plastic and he is
staring off.
The pressure in the cab of the truck was off of the charts,
"Dad?"

The sound of her voice wavering, the poor thing. Breaking him
out of it and his skin face looking over at her and it is not quite perfect.
He scrambles in the bottom of the box once again peering through the
clear pedantic bags for the film "not included" those two words were
there on the torn honey moon cardboard. They are shuffling out of the
vehicle again and his giddiness is returning now. Again, in the store
the small bit of frustration squeaks clear as the water from ice grip of
the winter slick is deep in the heated Big Box Store again. Rounding
the corner, the sales person seeing the two of them back again even
though he said he was trying to fly under the radar. The sales associate
looking over quizzically as well. The little girl in tow behind,
watching him lick his lips as he was scanning the little hooks for the
refills it should say "Polaroid" and they were looking for the pink and
blue pastel but the marketing was for that specific brand and as the
small tag over the wire holder, in the tiny black text revealing in such
bland and sarcastic plainness that the rack was empty. The little hand-
held scanner, the associate is typing it in diligently. This device
knowing the entire back warehouses in this day and age. It knowing
that there are none and of course "sorry for the inconvenience" but
they have the inventory "in-stock"! At the store in the valley; His eyes
flicking slow deck of cards as the realities struck home. There is a
search on the internet recorded in Kim's computer. It was to Target

and it was checking online for confirmation of: Stock Available for that exact film cartridge.

On this day the sun rising in Texas at 6:56 in the morning. In Anchorage seeing it happening for them as a glow on the horizon at 7:37 coming maybe from the south called Civil Twilight. The sun not rising until 8:21. Imagine savoring all of the colors that shy so swiftly by, in your moving sunrise? If laying its petals slowly over, one,
at a
time.
The inspection of the hardware made most likely with clicking flashlights on and swiftly eyeing the ladder racks now sturdy. Light clover, making short searches over metal and fasteners, how is the foot of it mounted to the cargo bed boxes?

Later these transactions of his with these large Boulevard stores, they were printed in sun ink. The actual receipt degrading and dissolving to a sheen, long after the pulsing waves of electrons came chattering down the wire in a frightening milli pulse, pausing as they passing by the point of sale. They knew that it was locked and archived already for later. Israel and the juvenile occupant are in the vehicle and they are driving off from the Target. They are heading home.

The receipts coming back to life, it shows him hedging back to the house. It had been a very shitty afternoon, becoming evening so he dropped her off after such a letdown of an outing really. To get some rest and go to bed early he says. He waited until she was asleep until firing up the still warm engine and heading out the 44 miles to the Valley. That highway corridor makes a crapshoot of certain times of the day for each of the big three: the Anchorage Police Department, the Alaska State Troopers and the Matsu guys. They've never needed a softball league of their own, because from those ends of the Old Glenn Highway, the shortstop is snapping grounders to the three of them. The old grey owl snatching over in dead lock eyes upon you.

The truck within, which she had rode, it has fallen beneath their gaze and they checked it off of the list.

The meticulous report showing back, a mostly penciled in comment that:

all clear "the racks appeared to be welded on"

Driving home, and already in the night. Grin sliding off as he is turning. Underlit in the leer light of the dash and coming back from somewhere more real and he dilates out again and you can see that he is playing the tapes back in his mind for a minute. It looks like he is scanning for damage control or something.

He was talking about this one story like it is a warning about some other guy, but his eyes had dulled, touched of honey when he had said those one parts. The dropping off, as a blur, and the drive, and here he is sheepishly standing now in line near the pharmacy with the grey hairs and the fakers. That big yawn on the tapes he fits right in. Not a thought in the world for all of the cameras and for each sun stroked log-in for each and every cashier. He walked up and grabbed the film and drove back with it in the car. This weekend not ending up how they planned, the argument in the air. He is passing the old junction there where you can turn left, right up towards Palmer.

In the dark this time of year, the cover surface of hard roof ice is structurally over the black cider water of little Matanuska Lake. You can see it anytime you want as you pass by that very main junction of highway points. The little Lake has a finger of land that goes out over the water from the shore like an Indian mound's boardwalk. The finger of land naturally directing the attention out to a spot about 40' in depth. There are gravel flats nearing the roads' side shores and a place to pull off from the highway and tighten your load if need be. All with a decent little view of the water and that unique finger of land that from above looks as if it is directing at something so blatantly. A convenient spot enough they have brought in of all things a little Expresso stand out there with a generator and their own potable and waste water tanks. An old music box clogged of hair pinging once from back under the seat somewhere and any time when nearing the jostling lake on the horizon.

Once getting home the child often will having been being bored or relaxed or excited upon hearing the car pull up, they will often shriek and run and turn off the lights laughing under the sheets to feign as if they had been dead asleep. It is a universal in our development and it is so fun, hopefully there aren't ever any misunderstandings. Hearing him pull up, without his lights on. Pulling in with impunity and hearing him do a cursory of the house and then giggling under the blankets hearing him head straight to that shed of his again? Her eyes glassy from sprite giggle maybe now perched and maybe even staring at the shed through the glare on the window. How farfetched do the stars crinkle up there, in the cold and in the grip crust under her little slippers. Part skid crunching out here in the blackness yet lit. Her skin looking vampire in that din, breathing little steam puffs crossing arms listening closer as the heaters are warming in there, as he had promised. There is soft nudging and he is pickle fingering the tin lid off of the thing for her little craft supplies. He had worked the make-up far enough that he knew two things for certain, that she looked good enough that they could pull it off for real and that he needed the sewing kit because he had tried it with super glue first. That's why it was so frustrating. He was "meticulous". He was the "you don't know how much planning" guy? and he had been driving to the valley in Kim's vehicle again giving the truck the shadow of being off of the road as much as possible for now just in case. Coming into the shed again much later, the steam pluming up as the top of the door belched out bloated in complex carbons and pentanes and the putrescene going away unnoticed only to come raining down as shit glitter later. Down upon the blue-black world frozen and waiting in the darkness.

Slowing it down but there begins to be a point of appearing to be buoyant. Atop the crinkling visqueen, setting her there to get comfortable straddling her chest a bit as he is so studiously doing her bidding. Tugging so gently on the fine suture knot, the fishing line tugged into position and it slipped into her skin there! Snapping look to her eyes, gritting teeth. He looks up at her and her one eyebrow is up and she has a smirk at him he is so ingenious.

As he loosened the piano wire of line her eye fell to sadness and that dumb look of shame realizing that Kim had been out of town and she was due back tomorrow! By then the whole Romeo and Juliet play act would be gone and sterile. The shed closed for the season and that could you be a Hon? And pick me and (redacted) up at the airport? There is the big Brown Jug by the new Dairy Queen, maybe grab a bottle of this and that. The receipt list being familiar to him. Maybe it was only his perception but him perhaps remembering staring off at that same foil label years back. The one friend said that at this time, they were

"Split up" but still "together?" kind of.

This recipe of shopping list having a more metro influence though. At one point him having had up turned their place. The daughter finding the house in disarray the giant knife was stuck into the coffee table. The little girl coming up from the archives, her earnest fingers are pushing the buttons on the other side. The phone back then the loud beep, beep, of her dialing it was so real for her back then. Her voice confirming that, she is doing good and she is taking care of him but in breath flutter that she is scared and he is passed out and he smells and the place is all messed up maybe someone broke in and he fought them off or something because, over there near the big scary knife, it has shredded the curtains too! It was recorded as a very open and interpretive capital "F - K" on the big mirror in make-up or something.

The loosening of the brilliant little tug line and her eyes becoming downcast and dumb looking. His hand on her shoulder he gently braided her hair and did the last of the touch ups with Kim's cosmetics and a few from the Target store. He knew it was some of their last moments and he stood over her there, his hand extended out not in a position of strength necessarily but in support for her. He set the timer on the really cool Polaroid. It was new and it was nostalgic but it was in that balmy air as the timer clicked and just for the briefest of moments, it exposing the mushroom film and it caught her looking off in to the ceiling. The daily newspaper was across her like a man's silk scarf, out in trail dust and horseman's musk the Genghis flash of the camera bulb in the din, it showed every nuance, in her eyes. There were debates held fair and square if she was alive or not but they never told the public that until much later.

CHAPTER TWENTY-FIVE

IN THE HAUNT

The ocean lays there warm barely moving, but she holds her heat mathematically in increment degrees. You can make charts and plot out your projections of Time and Temperature, it becomes a wire frame of curving truths. He had the clock down on the dethaw, that wasn't the problem. Leaving the heater on a little longer there in the shed, he wanted to be with no other. If there was a time when he couldn't quite remember how long the heater had been on this time? Passing over the marks in his mind chart, floating over calculated curved lines forming an orthographic funnel in a wire projection of heat and time and the liabilities trailing off, they can be mediated.

Playing along as an accomplice then, as he had to go on a liquor run for Kim and shrugging at the necessity of it. What is the Date?! Waking from a dream state, having been out too long! While he locked the shed and his blood paste quickening from frog skin, him trying to mediate the interruptions. Heading back to the shed again, he appears to brace himself just before he goes in that last time maybe? To break the news and finally do it. He will! Bracing himself sucking in, holding it as he quickly breaches the door. Wave slither pulse of air as it opening and him closing it quickly behind him. Down in him a nagging but afraid to strike a match for the off gassing in the darkness down in there.

Nearing a month now, the Solon is standing in there waiting for Israel. Bringing tears to his eyes, sneaking quickly in to her what it must've been like in that sweltering black air. The rustle of the blue tarp again. Awestruck, almost to the point when he looked at them in the interrogation room candidly. As he spoke, she saw it there in him and heard it in his voice for the first time. He had told himself and then again telling them at the table that he was thinking that he could extend the time with her a little bit more. If he actually put her, in the snow berm this time. It could be just outside the shed, cautiously moving her out and back in again would be the chore, definitely briefer this time. Limp arms becoming "real floppy" by now, he had described such a great contrast over that very same ground. This vision unexpected of that first night and there she is. Her feet shodding across the ice grip. Her there, as a phantasm in the plasma of his mind and she was so full of the light of life again. She was afraid, that was very clear and the air was so cool and fresh. It had been holding at 27 degrees all night and it was during those wonderful warm mid mornings that had disappeared away so quickly into the paradise of the heater. The thermometer watching the hours passing by, a slow-motion tidal wave pulsing slowly up and down 5 degrees or so. Lingering above freezing for just a gasp of air at mid-day before the sleepy whale's slick thick skin again sinking under. Slowly to return again tomorrow at noon. The sunlight again upon the blue-black blotching, her arm would've popped out if he tried carrying the rolled up noisy tarp. Her eyes roll over as he is trying to tuck it away frantic. She looks up as he is jostling her around, that look, on her face.

This is the part in the Mountain shaft storage facility where the rails are still pristine and untouched, going by looking in it is so haunting. The part where they start to talk to you, even from across the room. Belching now and then, lest you forget about these emotional commitments that you've made. She is staring off at the plywood grains of the makeshift table. Wherever the sequence had started, he was approaching a zero point, or had already. He despised thinking of it, becoming disrupted from everything, something was appearing on the horizon. Glowing so dark and powerful and invisible here in the real world. Counting down at some point, wanting to make it all go away. Only for a moment, so terribly horrible. When he says that, he says it like we would say the word "delicious".

The potty bucket he had removed and cleaned thoroughly. He did not want to do it but he had to! He kept mentioning that some neighbor would've soon noticed but his daughter never once saying anything in coincident about a nasty smell or 'you have something on your pants there' touching it as a child might. Kim had been in town for going on day two by now! That was it, he never should've let it go this far! And he buckled himself down after that and he says plainly that he finally did it. He was so sincere as he reached around for her bra strap, would he fumble with the click and the circle back? Her arm falls gently off, caught of the visqueen. They say that your mouth becomes starched in hunger.

CHAPTER TWENTY-SIX

12-4-8

In those latter days, coming so close for him by then. Squinting his eyes at Bill Currier just that previous summer, as he had started firing through and ruining his #1 gun as fast as he could he said, until it was empty; because he "wasn't taking him serious" and it really "pissed" him off.

Snapped out of it all at once, four years before that deep morning and those first moments of touching down in Anchorage after Hawaii and it begins to pour over the ledge inside that he is finally alone in town. On a very tight timeline 3 days to touch and go. No one in any of the circles will have cause for alarm or suspicion of what have you been doing these extended stretches of time again?

4 years before all of that is where you see outlined in the details within the FBI's "Keyes's Timeline": a blank space. It is in between some empty cells in the tall column of their data table, Kim had that one thing going. It was on and along December 4, 2008. The very nature of Kim's job now was that every time that she was working, she was going out of town. There are these Federal & State oversights that require certain Professional Safeguards, once satisfied, them then the pouring out of money upon some wealthy ones who are in the know. It starting with "minimum of Bachelor's Degree in associated field" to oversee things, maybe to observe the fundamentals, which absolutely must be adhered to by Federal mandates.

The business owners eventually having had secured their own bunkhouse for all the biology graduates that they would employ. The

Bunkhouse used to be a conventional 6 plex. The one garage having been made into a part common area. The part utility, part hang-out was sheltering two laundry machines from a half year of the bitter cold. Maybe it was because the Federal eyeball seeing the Criteria met on the certain adherences and it checked it all off the list. Them never seeing the "Minimum of Bachelor" person, Kim acting as a pocket Criterion. The rent absorbed and Uncle Sam is blinking to see around some fuzzy cataract floating by. On this instance he sees nothing.

Kim was out of town again on another blip, flying into somewhere and many times, when she is away on the clock, he was there in Anchorage alone for 10 day stretches at a time. However, he would be receiving custody of his daughter soon from Washington State. That obscure little place was so convenient it suddenly becoming though, too "Little".

In December of 2008, acknowledging that Kim's new address on Spurr Lane wouldn't commence until into 2009. Kim and her boyfriend had received mail at a short list of a few quaint places that they had rented. So of course, when it comes time for making the smooth transition, ideally you are not holding on to two sets of front door keys for very long. One set usually has a security deposit attached to it. The trip to Hawaii could definitely eat up some of that slack of time. Part of the family unit having just came back from Hawaii.

For us we must see it looking back. In the returning photos there is one of Kim's boyfriend looking down warmly at something, a child? He had on a multicolored lei made of cheap synthetic rainbowed flowers.

Trying to get away for a length of time, the cliche trip to paradise still warm on the memory. Wanting those moments of respite hopefully to have been refreshing and invigorating in the relationships all a new. Kim and her boyfriend looking forward to making love after days of discovering these deeper connections again with each other.

Returning then between Hawaii and Cancun it was three months into the dead middle of our winter in Anchortown. The temperatures had been lingering up above freezing for just a few hours in the late mid-morning. The sun glowing for only a few hours and anything in its gaze, illuminated golden as the night whale's steam plume breath blasts, just before dropping again. Losing 5 more degrees slowly under the ice until noon tomorrow.

One time the one guy in the room with the table was frustrated, and that could be understood. He had yet to have tasted that sweet ball, it had been a very elusive morning. Coming right out with blazing pink eyelids

"Come on Israel, you got to give me something! Ummmm… something not relevant"

his eyes moving over every texture flinching at opportunities, groveling in despers. Caught up in the action, he talked right over the young man at the table. The one with that creepy old Cabin in Constable, New York. Israel had mumbled something into his chest it appearing in angst teenager. What was that, Israel? The temperature seeming to drop to the cold steam breadth of those lone forests, the breath it curls up like smoke as you speak, puffing at the punctuations,

"They are all, relevant"
the last part coming much softer, the steam breath huffed before it was gone in the fluorescent room again.

When Israel had stopped at his motel with the Currier's in their own Saturn, it was just through the trees from their house. The one with the big pool in the backyard. He says that he pulled up next to his car and getting out, jostling they would've heard him as he was changing out his bag from the successful "Abduction kit" and him reconfiguring that bag then to the giddy "Need for Nothing satchel", for during his favorite part coming up. The time beginning to race by for him.

There is a set of business emails, one incoming stream is from an experimental and seemingly lucrative company that processes certain Federal adherences. In the emails you hear the business tone coaxing me that, they have plenty of money, they want this done, they need this done, at one point her reply of assurance was "we are good, do the thing "Just bill me". Kim no longer working for those gals that count fish. Not knowing then that this was the guy, the boyfriend of Kim's. Maybe he wanted to meet up on questions about his fledgling construction company again. My sister had mentioned it in between breaths long ago I remembered and I wasn't interested. She looked at me funny because "you help everyone" she said almost appalled. Much later she was there again catching breaths and her eyes went stale for a moment in the recent story as she was speaking of her friend and her friend's Boyfriend. Recalling how Kim had called him her "Boy Toy" in front of the other girls the other night. Leaning in closer, letting her hand fall as she retold it, her hand falling warmly onto the unexpecting arm of the couch. It looks a lot like the leg of a man as the laughter came down in the room. Rebuilding the scene, she is seeing it all around her in her mind. There was a deep pause in the processor coursing the bumping ticker tape back behind her eyes as she was putting it together that this is the guy, she had mentioned to me before! She drops the other story completely and breathes in she is more excited! Oh yeah, she says with a cocked eyebrow and lips. His business is doing great! He has contracts already all over the place, even in Juneau! "They are going on another Cruise can you believe it? Cancun? A few days in Hawaii, then back here for 3 days then flying into Louisiana or something, waving her hand back and forth at the nuisance of the particulars. It is the "Port of call for the cruise".

I hadn't wanted anything to do with this whole situation since she had first brought it up for some reason and it was out of character for me and she became dumbfounded and frustrated at it. Later my wife eventually bringing it up sometime, asking inquisitively, what is it about this guy, you have never even met with him? Even wondering for the sake of the strangeness that, you help everybody.

In the old days to be trapped in a boiler room meant it would have been balmy and hot and that you would've needed drinking water, but not these days in Anchorage, Alaska. The stack for the water heater and the boiler, blowing poison steam up into the blackness up from off of the cold rooftops. By Municipal Mechanical code, in the days of the Home Depot overpowered range hood, in winter the dog farts and they would run the big fan and it sucks the air from every crack and crevice in the house, the poison monoxide of carbons sucked back down the chimney pipe and back into the home!

Flowing in tugged towels becoming polluted silk sheets racing under the door slit. Racing across the Kirkland Signature Berber carpet in the family room on their way to the kitchen.

So, they made us cut absurd holes in the exterior walls of the boiler rooms. Adherences dictating of how many inches of open "Combustion Air" must be provided per each BTU. Fresh cold air pouring in like molasses over copper water pipes and the deep chill pooling across the boiler room floor getting deeper, in years after that, they had cut phone book Styrofoam shapes sliding in and out firmly of the wall like a hidden book panel and you could cut holes into it, only a portion of the universal code's size.

So, when it comes to something like a commercial boiler for a 6 plex, functioning as a Bunkhouse, the code requires it in square inches. It is nice to have too much air at your disposal. Once you dial it back to a whistle hush of frigid air pouring in all night through a hole in the large foam insert, the size of a softball. It is ever steadily flowing into the room temperature of the Mechanical room. A lonely place mostly unseen, these utility closets are often like a submarine within the building. Hearing people coming home, you are just on the backside of their pantry drywall. Plumbing stuff, heating pipes and tiny low voltage wires, them coming together like bomb pieces cranking warmth to everywhere and everyone in slow motion. Creaking pipes and often there beyond some old coffee cup long forgotten and past the dried-out pen on a shelf there will be there in the studs very likely an orchestra of larger heavier wires converging uniformly and from the top and the bottom like air traffic, right into the pre punched port holes safely into some Electric Breaker Panel Box. In the room with only the large ticking boiler it is humming too with parts that can scald to the touch. Across the room below the blueboard book thing with a hole cut in it, there is a small river of air from outer space and it is flowing like razor in whistling hush all through the bitterest of nights. The things he could do with those.

Kim was an educator now. When returning from paradise with the golden smile lines the sunglass' pale shadow still there, Kim had continued on to her scheduled "Educator" duties. Her checking through to some other airport in the lower 48. Iz and the little girl

continuing on home to Anchorage. Having to hit the ground
running. His daughter, she was still in school and afterward she will
go on a plane dutifully. He will see her off and then, he was there now
in Anchorage, alone these few precious days.
Invisible to the world before he meets Kim again in Cancun. A relief
really that it is still yet four years before the deep morning of that
flight to Texas. And he would almost assuredly be looking to "go for
it" now.

CHAPTER TWENTY-SEVEN

YOU NEVER KNOW THESE DAYS

There is a set of emails that lead up to the first part of December, when I would've been walking up to that apartment building in Anchorage. Its garage had been made into a permanent: utility & part common area. Everything mostly segregated and organized and mostly forgotten. There was an old couch on a rug that made a hangout of the one corner of the big room. The man door was swung in and open and it was a beautiful mid-morning, approaching melting temperature soon.

The forensics finding that he had turned on his cell phone, it is assumed to make the necessary contacts to confirm that apparently, she is on the plane, and that he had dropped off into a period of true *"Cell phone blackout"*

The old dust particles free floating in golden sunlight down at a banner angle there in the doom trap. Maybe the waves of ultraviolet flowing in magnetic lines over the earth, were there for me.

Over back on the side of the laundry machines is there the faintest of a warm hum ticker? creaking in slow motion. The silence was broken by a tumble thudding down from the top of those stairs. His shoes came into view at my eyeball height so instantly and already up on tempo from the first. I felt part enclosed already.

The aggression in the room, it felt so familiar to me,
like the rocking sound of train tracks would've, for him.

He is moving towards me and so hurried and he is there on the other side of the couch from me already.
I do not remember seeing him as he had passed before me crossing the floor.

"You never play another man's game"
Never acknowledging him spatially, or his actions, or his expression. Side stepping, a leaning tip-toe, to gaze up across the platform of that short hallway that he had just manifested down from.

Back into the moment state. There were no other ankles up there. Absorbing the freeze frame. A disturbing down in there clanging just below my breath.

Turning back towards him I brought my eyes onto his chest at panel height. With a disdain and annoyance, he said "I'd better get my bag!" hands already there though. It sounded rash and barely out of place. The look from his face was something menacing and gritting. There was an energy in the air it was so pressing.

When I came up his chest and to his neck, the inside of my torso was blooming and opening. Slowing at the flat plateau beneath his eyes and held it there.

Grease smearing on the lenses of the background,
Becoming purer and unhindered of all of the monkey rules for the people.

Hearing the breaths, after seeing their chest move.
The mind is residing in the eyes now.

Seeing him with his bag all pulled up in front of him there with the couch between us. It had all come out of nowhere all at once. His one hand was still, and it is in there high in the bag. Gazing into cheekbones, remembering so clearly the old lessons "every move you make, is a commitment."

He would have heard me announce myself then from the glowing doorway.

He would've been waiting at the top of the stairs, feeling me from an elevated position while I was turning.

As my eyes would've been glowing down into the room, my pupils would've been opening slightly more. While his would've been playing back the scene as fast as it could, trying to craft an answer from the bright light. What was it exactly that he had seen in the flash across the floor? Standing invisible in the shadow of that glowing door, burning me there into his mind.

The inflection inside my words? Letting the things inside me speak for themselves.
In and off to the side never changing the tempo of my stride.
Coming back from a leaning look over and up those stairs again where he had just come down from. The gravity of the situation felt like it was at the bottom of an abyss trench.

Sliding him an assurance
"Don't worry about it, it's not like that"

Flat tone and almost instantly, he responded

"You never know these days"

His hand was still,
        and still there in the bag.

I turned partly away from him to scan the room, one last look in the charade and one gaze over there at those stairs. Never knowing, as he later wrote in his letter,

"Talk is over, words are cheap unless you back it with action or it all comes off cheap"

Letting the feelings, speak for themselves.

.

Lifting my chin to look over there up and at the lay of the scene, it was so dark and heavy. Stretching my neck out for him. If he were going to make a move, he would have done it already.

"Yeah, yeah, yeah" I said, and I swiped my hand back across his position, and across his energy.

The vent stack was going up the wall out there. Remembering walking all the way around the long building and up to the warm pipe, standing on crust snow touching the siding just on the other side of the wall into the boiler room and it must be right up there at the end of that short-hidden hallway at the top of those blind stairs.

It felt so desolate, that the room seemed to echo. At one point later we would be informed informally that he had become the "go to handyman" for that building. He knew where the mechanical room was, he had just come down from it.

Looking at the door again up there, the edge of the vision seemed to, beginning to smear-spin. I wanted to depart immediately and he began again in an "aw shucks" type of opening "This bag is really special…" but I spoke right over him as he continued. My tone was curt, "I'll come back later" giving the inclination that I'd wait until the riff raff clears out, mirroring now his first agitated flash at me.

When I turned my back and walked away from him, life was appearing in charade. I felt I was behind some thick curtain, looking out. Ignoring anything else then, driving straight out of Anchorage. Later pulling up the gravel drive way, my wife coming out to the truck. The door was propped open. Her saying that she had seen me through the glass and that she knew something had happened in town.

His clothes were dinghy and he looked equally slept in and unslept. His hair was held back if it was in a tight head band or a slim hat, maybe a hoody but the hair seemed wet and clumped together like it was carved out of wet comic books. I assumed maybe the damp of a recent shower, putting the old clothes back on blinking in the late mid-morning sun.

The FBI timeline shows in an empty cell and through some milky cataract that a young woman from Soldotna, goes missing, never seen from again.

The last official reporting of a young woman named Sierra Raye Roberts, her maiden name was Mullins. When she went missing, NAMUS lists her last date of contact as March 04, 2008.

Alaska State Troopers Missing Persons Clearinghouse lists September 14, 2008, over 7 months later

She had run away from her small community years earlier. On the streets of the big city, she had tried to stay high all the time. Sierra had accumulated a few soliciting/prostitution charges but after a rock bottom and a close call she was turning her life around. Sierra was taking classes down at Trendsetters to learn how to do hair. Her own hair was dark auburn and curly.

She used to shop at the Carrs Quality Center on Northern Lights Blvd. It was the Buy-Low store back when Robert Hansen had possibly abducted Beth Van Zanten from the same parking lot, however that was on the 22nd of the month and back in 1971. The Tobacco Cache, in the corner of that parking lot was an excellent tobacco shop back then, much like the specialty shop that he insisted driving around Chicago for, there was barely enough time to make it to Bloomington from O'Hare on time if he left straight away, there is no way it could've been him. That one brand of filter less loose leaf. The lady that worked at the store there in Anchorage said Israel would come in often enough that she would always have a treat or a sucker handy for his wonderful daughter. If he came in alone, there was one in the bag for the girl before he was out the door.

Sierra was last seen by an APD traffic stop.
The Anchorage Police Department gave Sierra Roberts a seatbelt citation.
Dec 04, 2008.

The plane to Honolulu then departing on December 5, 2008, the very next morning. The temperatures lingering up 5 degrees around freezing in the noon time, well after the Wizard departed on turbine & airfoil. His head seeming to wobble like the rotting dead in those plush seats as he went up into the clouds. The sound rumbled away it was both somewhere and everywhere.

I was standing across from him, across from the couch, in a narrow three-day window in between his vacations in Hawaii and Mexico
.

He had the door propped open to the laundry, in the cold air at mid-morning, doing something up those stairs, in that mechanical room that has never been explored for clues. He looked slept in, and unslept, but that was 4 years ago.
There was a spot in there where apparently, he thought it was all over anyway, but in the hangover and in the coming out of such strong emotions, remembering himself in those hours that he gave into it. But the deafening stench and Kim coming back to town: time stamps of grease stain receipt paper the data complex showing his recorded sets of objectives playing out just as he said it did. He slipped by Connor's Bog Park. Pulling into the parking lot, the typical timber signage and boundary points of the Anchorage Municipal Park and Recreation. He too was so familiar with them as he had been the "Parks and Rec" Director for Neah Bay. At times being almost law enforcement himself, there on the Federal Native Reservation in Washington State.

Nearly a month now and a text came in on Samantha's long silent phone. There was rejoicing and tears holding breath as they read the message. At the top it said in header data 7:45p.m. it was the 24th for God's sakes. The text in such everyday font said shattering "Conners park sign under pic of albert, aint she purty"

Returning to Spurr Lane, the mission complete he did it at his own risk even driving by later to see that there were officers on the down low in the park taking pictures and stuff. The late afternoon supplies purchased at the ANCH store on the 27th.

CHAPTER TWENTY-EIGHT

PAPER COME MOULDY

There was a car but it wasn't a car, it was an SUV kind of a thing. It would be seen leaving the road in front of our house. Appearing swiftly, as we approached the end of our driveway. Frequently enough, we always lived on a dead-end street. The Google Earth car drove by one day to laminate once more their latest street view. It caught me with my children playing with toys under our tree boughs there: as they had caught him and his little girl in theirs. You can see him still, there, standing at the back of his work truck. In the photo, she is doing something, looking at him while he is straight faced looking forward: on the job. In mine, I am sitting up and looking straight into the camera as they drove by looking agitated, rising from my chair.

I remember one of those days so vividly, brighter and summerish. Pulling up our driveway and seeing the beautiful day and the world reflecting in the glass. They were no longer transparent at mid-day. Wallpapered in the bright scene, then that flashing glare crossing swiftly behind me across the spruce and the part cedar fence. The children's toys were intermingled and integrated into the beautiful rustic forest yard.

Settling into our place now for a third of a year or more and our youngest would never want to go out in the yard or even down the gravel driveway. She would say "it is the eyes" herself looking so earnestly and all so relieved when we would turn to head back towards the house. Concerned, mama asked her all the casual ways of what are "the eyes"? One random day, the sunshine angling in across the Rainbow vacuum cleaner's humming jet whir, my wife popping out of her thoughts as the little one is excited that she had found it! The machine is whirring down as she is tudding up the steps, pulling mom to her room to show her and by the time they were coming through their door into the warm princess room that the two girls shared, the lower half of the walls were eggshell baby blue, however a beautiful white chair rail moulding was at door knob height and the top of the room was painted the perfect soft pink. From down on the ground outside of the first floor looking up you would never be able to see the chair rail wood trim, the color appearing to glow a soft aura in the darkness. Until so suddenly the warm glowing windows blacked over. If the curtains at some time would've been disturbed, upon noticing, immediately the curtain would tug, tug, from the small child. Pressing the curtain's edges closed so as not to see from the inside those black mirrors of glass looking out. She was adamant.

My wife recalling being curious as the child had her little VCR queued on pause.

I remember it was a beautiful day in the deep Spring, when I had received a message that my father in-law had notified that there was an order at Home Depot, all ready, and it was paid for. It was two new security screen doors, nearly the exact same ones that the Currier's had installed in their garage man door, to hush that waxing feeling. Israel Keyes loved Home Depot; they have those damn displays for God's sakes. Just needing to stop by the big D so bad and while walking militant terse vigilante style through the tools department, daydreaming now, he fake palms a flat bar from the wire basket, jaw tight like in the photo where it caught his two faces.

So innocuous he is walking up to the display of what you would think would be called a "Security, Screen Door with Glass" walking up glad you found it. The label would say surprisingly that it is only a "Full View Storm Door" and finding that same slip bump of the crowbar as it is over the polished metal, it is exactly the same each time as the lock pops free, there in front of everyone. Standing as it's ghostly glass shadow wobbles while swinging slowly over the floor of the aisle. An aisle comprised of nearly one of every other front door installed across the nation. The nuances between; possibly even, or probably even: one just like yours.

Looking back now after the news breaks and eventually the arrest, us still never knowing that the guy on national news was The Boyfriend. Our front door swinging open, hitting the low shining sun in the south-west. Behind me, a racing light glares off of the glass of the "security screen door" that ends up was only a storm door. It was installed on our front door, that we rarely used compared to the one in our garage so conveniently right into our dining room / kitchen. Coming into the house to my wife and she was playing the 1940's farmhouse mom routine. Just finishing up some impromptu dishes and wiping then a drip run to her elbow or something as she cocked an eyebrow out the garden window before turning to me with excited eyes! Coming over and saying that, "a Federal Agent came by the house today"

"ughhhh"

It was a lady by herself, it was very comfortable and they actually ended up laughing through part of the opener together. Some of the things that we had thought we had seen and pondered? They apparently had seen some things as well and by the agent only describing the sequences, describing hushed minuscules of confidential and exclusive information. Her and my wife realizing as the one would talk and then the other, becoming hushed at times, that they were both describing the same instances but from over the hedgerow.

The thought of those large warm glowing panes of glass out in Chugiak, framed in deep black blue and the silhouette of spruce. Seeing the glowing windows through the trees. Our youngest daughter said she was afraid to look out of them at night, especially that there were eyes looking back. The lay of the land, we had chosen a great location. There were a few angles that could be had of us, but you'd have to be a risk taker to get them. The older woman, the one born with the Caul over her face, one time after dog sitting for 2 weeks, she had asked if we had felt that someone was watching you out here? We told her about the child and the other people who had also said the same of the house, unprovoked. We lived that way, accepting some lurking feeling of, something like doom creeping closer at shoulder height nearing the ear. Thinking of the Agent lady about to be pulling out of our gravel driveway out onto our dead-end street, her looking at the lay of the land, looking off for a few long seconds, it appears that she reaches down and disciplines something out in shorthand there on a notepad or planner on the passenger seat, then dip bumping over a bridge and as she drove away. The next time my wife went there on to the Streetview of our house, the trees, all of it was blurred out and it had a description of some code which authorized it.

Remembering how the world had felt darker and heavier just before and then suddenly the town was a fire and we had all been looking for this missing girl, if only in prayers and hoping that she was ok, every time it came to mind and everywhere was her Missing Poster. The news was firing, they started to run on the hour about Samantha. Coming out in the real world and it was so instantly and unbelievably alive across the splay of the television screen. He says he got carried away, going online and commenting on her missing notification page. Speaking down of her character and that she might've got what she deserved for saying she was one type of person, but totally being another and the I.P address is just a sequence of numbers but the username was Israel! There online in the data complex it was waiting. Later as they came scouring and they are still now sifting the sentinel marching across everything over and over.

Alice Mae's is over on the old Glen Highway. The small rural road used to be the only way through once upon a time. Robert Hansen, no doubt having passed that lonely intersection himself many times with a girl onboard a time or two. My wife was running up to the corner store there in the parking as the littlest one was coming out of the car. Mother's hand low across the parking lot, her baby becoming a little girl and she looked up wrapped in gear. Her beautiful little curls draping down around those magnificent black eyes they were sad for the troubling.

"Momma what is that?" The sun glint over the Chugach Mountains is magnificent. The shine off of the glass from the truck camper there, then behind it the paper said Missing: and it was the girl we had all heard about. And the little girl who would never want to see the black windows day or night, Momma told her briefly that this really special girl was missing and it sounds like someone has hurt her. Thinking to herself that, she has probably passed by us on the road out there and that it feels like the missing girl is probably no longer in Anchorage.

Out in the belly of where skyscrapers of ice once stood, brilliant and blue going up and to each side scanning from eye to eye, the Matanuska Glacier once was.

Windblown there now is only a giant basin of long rippling foot hills, forests and drainages. Later realizing that horizon scene, is upon a massive bed of gravel, and it is covered with gnarly acidic ventures, each one sifting endless empty sands and pebbles. Shivering cold and wet only finally, excited looking up then down, at one precious twinkle of sun photons, of what is now their gold.

Right there at a junction serving more area than twice the size of Texas. A convergence of three roads that on a scale that big, they really are the only roads that we've got.

A line of questions around the table had arisen or suppositions about Keyes' finances in Alaska. Citing that perhaps once having moved there, because of the remoteness of the state, farther travels, shorter working seasons; that the elements of reality would've began to create their own scene. It would be a different kind of a plan, to take someone. Finding quickly that the grand features in the magnificent background of Anchorage is the Chugach Mountain Range. Each facet of that wall of mountains may be 15 miles in rounding its belly, looking up at them from down on the tiny highway at its massive foot hills.

From in the shed in the driveway, if he clicking his watch and began to drive out of town, at 46 minutes he could be standing over a few black strewn trash bags in the thick brush near Eagle River. Beneath the black plastic is his shovel and two one-gallon jugs of Drano, right where he had said they were.

"Real deep"

"Real fast"

That shovel in the dirt near the river, was 20 minutes from my driveway and my side door made front door inside of our attached garage. There was an extra door opener that you could grab on your way out just like in the crime scene photos for the Curriers.

Hearing the Glen Highway sporadic traffic faintly passing in the dark of our bedroom window at times through the trees. Just on the other side of that highway passing is the Old Glen. The old road making a bypass of sorts of the big one. It follows along at 45 M P H in there somewhere, teasing in and out of those trees. It pops out in Eagle River right by the Fred Meyer ironically. The other side goes to just about at Eklutna where Robert Hansen left the little Jane Doe: Eklutna

Annie, all those years ago. That spot today is about 18 minutes from the gravel pull off of that little heart shaped Matanuska Lake.

"It's a sweetheart deal"

These places that we know that he chose, they begin to make the cipher.

Hearing these very specific characteristics aligning and coordinating so perfectly. Hearing then these places described by the only people who use them like he did. A normal object placed so incidentally, the laptop screen glowing upon his face right there in front of everyone, even with a child's head resting on you. Just reading some article there on the couch, watching then as he dives in reading every, single, word. His index finger then slow rolling on the mouse's little cursor wheel, it feels like the top of a wishbone that is not separated. The little spongy thing on the mouse becoming swollen and aroused as the screen moves up off the monitor. Seduced by some invisible thing there of such Intensity. On slick brochures originally now becoming websites of: outfitters, river rafting charters, hiking guides, even dive shops. His eyes so diligent to the last of the HTML prose, it apparently entrancing. Stopping at the last stanza. The convergence is opening at his touch, parting its entendre for him. From there in his eyes, it looks like it must feel like forever. Us knowing now, oblivious back then, his eyes were upon her. Seeing those beautiful shadows moving like sonar, of tiger stripe slow rippling. Over every curve as they are describing it, for him.

His roller scrolling a click, click, then,

DiveAlaska @ Divealaska.net

"WHERE:

Matanuska Lake is part of the greater Kepler-Bradley State Recreation area in Palmer, Alaska.

HOW:

Matanuska Lake is a quick 40-minute drive from the shop in Anchorage. Heading out of town, you'll drive and take the Palmer exit on the Glenn Highway, and the parking lot is almost immediately on your left (it sneaks up on you, so watch for the sign).

Parking is $7 p/day, or if you have a State Parks Pass, you're all good. It's not a bad idea to have cash, as the **caretakers may not be immediately present.**

Once there, you'll want to park as close as possible to the picnic area/**bathrooms**, as the walk down to the entry point is a bit of a walk.

There are no motors allowed on the lake, so the only thing to worry about is the occasional kayak or fishing hook.

WHY:

Matanuska Lake represents the closest (and cheapest) dive site for Anchorage scuba diving. Home to arctic char, rainbow trout, and fresh-water sponges, Matanuska Lake is clean, fresh, and easy. There isn't as much to see, and the bottom is composed entirely of a fine glacial silt that builds up quickly the deeper you get, but if you just need to go diving after a long day at work, Matanuska Lake is your ticket.

It goes without saying, but being that Matanuska Lake is a lake, in Alaska, it's un-divable in the winter. This isn't due to the ice buildup (because we love ourselves some ice diving!), it's because the park itself is gated and shut down.

The max depth of the lake is **~95 ft, with a wicked thermocline around 25 ft.** Most of what's worth seeing is **30 ft. and above.**

If you're diving on a sunny day, do yourself a favor, and flip over while diving
and look up at the sun filtering through the trees and the tree-falls. "
from underneath

It was on the first of the month, her debit card marked with the numbers he had scratched into it, is inside of an Anchorage A T M and the beep, beep, beeping of the correct P I N number clears and there is a withdrawal of some ransom money supposedly to help pay for her own way.

That very same date, the scales counting every grain of refuse by dry weight, it shows that he drove out to Eagle River to Hiland landfill.

Down in there the massive machine is idling. The electrons watching from inside the rattling mirror. The giant metal wheels start at once crushing by and over a wretched old couch, Israel's face is shaking, so is the mirror and even the breath in your lungs. The big guy in the big machine waves him off "get outta here!"

The machine steams crunching through where his computer and those other things were just thrown, he said. His own smaller tires are click driving away. He needed some time alone once he had completely dismantled the shed from the inside.   They got him burning shit in their fireplace on Spurr Lane. Maybe it was a vigil for their house dog or something? Did it die over there later? Burnt hair smell coming up out from the heat stack of the wood stove. It looked like he must've took it hard.

Then he needed some time to break down maybe, now that the shed was suddenly gone, he would go ice fishing for a few days and drag out the ice shanty. It is a little pop-up house to ice-fish while you stare off down into the blackening water.

Bringing later over to the table while his daughter waiting there, he had prepared fresh caught fish, it cracks steam into the air.

Alaska Airlines flight (Anchorage to Las Vegas). March 6, 2012

They got on a plane to Texas; the glistening rivets the lights are flashing erratically the armrest is shaking. He could have the stewardess and the pilot in the bathroom. That little hat and his little Captain's pants. He could have her splayed out over him there, here, there, he said there was a "very specific way" he wants things done. When he said it, he sounded catty bitch and flamboyant as if, shock waking! suddenly with the haze of red bloodshot eyes in his mind. He has read about this part before.

Landing later in Texas dropping through the layers of atmosphere. Coming down his ears maybe not popping until after he had picked up the rental from the annex this time? White Ford Focus 2012 driving with the little girl along for the ride. Did she have a new polaroid bumping in her lap? Or was that camera too with the Eagle River computer now?

The tiny Focus was rented in mainland Texas. The arteries are pumping. The little dot is pulsing among intersections then moving again through the sprawl of the airport. The pulse beat of them stopping off to the side of the road and the capsule made up of similar crystalline structures, we know the states of metal and the other of glass. From the capsule a hatch on the driver's side opens. There is a little girl in the car and some free agent moving across the open ground at midday. It snatches something held safe by an enchanted root bramble or a soil traducer, them giving it up to him as he chanted the antidoc. Snatching it free from the collector of debts and then the bundle of small cash is back in his cloaking hand, the small bills that he said the gnomes and the towns folk gasp away from. They are so afraid to let themselves get a taste of life. Are they not dead and marked out already?

Over the waves from the other side of our prayers, wishes and nightmares and worst fears the beep, beep, beep, of her pin number being punched in somewhere. Maybe it is Sam's precious little finger. She is 18, just a kid really.

Withdrawing the ransom now along the way to the border crossing that he has been staging in his mind. There was a trace on her debit card and as the ATM would be connecting online in clicks and clitters expecting to verify some other balance again before dispensing cash. When the sleepy little cash machine pings far, all the way out to some Credit Union in: Alaska.

Was there a short blip in the transmission? The machine receives the all clear and dispenses the cash blinking "Thank You". However silently it is sending out flashing alarms. They are initiating a location lock, local time, nearest Road or Highway system. Inside of every CCTV camera anywhere remotely in the area, inside them there is their firm little data chips and they are becoming swollen as the mother ship is now coming over the horizon.

Federal Electronic Device Access Fraud of a missing girl's stolen debit card. 10:00 in the evening there. The information is coming in clicking and from all the way down in Arizona!

The realities instantly swirling around that one line on the ransom note, the one with that Polaroid photo which he had left at Conner's Bog Park 6 days ago under the picture of Albert. It had said

"She almost got away from me in the desert"

The date is now 3/6. Phone calls were still connecting like lightning tracks an hour and a half into it. When 70 some miles later an ATM starts going off out in the lonesome. Eyes sliding along to connect the dots on the map they would cross over the state line there and be 23 miles into the little boot heel of New Mexico. Wondering if she is there in the car with him as the Velcro gear is ratcheting under the tactical communique of the raiders. By now they have had enough time scanning the kelp forests in flashing pulses and they have seen in the various neighborhood security cams and webcams, CCTV videos playing back, a small white car leaving first then approaching the vicinity of withdrawal sites.

The thing is though at that last one? It was a Failed Withdrawal Attempt of $400.00. Over the daily limit, just half of an hour before midnight.

The fingers Beep, Beeping in again of that dark spirit on the other side and it asked for a balance on the account: 3598.91 and then it punches in a withdrawal of 80 dollars and the machine prints out the money. All of it going silent again. The radios and the guns and the phones click crackling into these now rabid, dark morning hours.

Waiting.

Measuring over and over the sequences in minutes and distances. Blistering thoughts of that second ATM. Some tiny little bird shit town in the middle of nowhere, where a young Billy the Kid had washed dishes at the Hotel and the Restaurant.

The guy who gunned him down in the back? Years later in that same spot his blind daughter Elizabeth Garret wrote the New Mexico State Song in 1915.

A little yellow plane would come tracking its racing fleck shadow across tumble thickets and the dry scrub brush, watching it descend and land in grainy black and white. It was Charles Lindbergh refueling his "Spirit of St. Louis" in 1927!

Finding things to talk about. The blood beginning to cool as the hours then starting to stack up together like vertebrae. Never appearing again that evening. It should've popped up by pattern here on the map! The search in the night cooling into the late hours. The portal hanging quiet and sloppy. Perhaps there was a Binding spell in threes, he could only withdraw the cash as he would have his way in, "Wilcox" and he would have loved the sting of it, barely coming out into his hands in the, "LordsBurgh"

That was it for the night of the seventh, law enforcement sitting seething and greasy on their seats. Packing it in and watching the blinking lights all turning off now. Some still crawling all over the area.

948 miles then to Mother's porch. At 80 miles short, he stopped again in Shepherd, making another withdrawal. An hour and 18 minutes or so later he was arriving at Mother's, safely deep into Texas. Part Amish, part White supremacist cult and the little girl looking up as one of the last of the peoples. Maybe seeing as an old person can, inside the white man's schools, they called her "gifted".

Getting so intwined within the cycle of coincidences arranging.

All was quiet on the day of the 8th, but slipping away always some inconvenient coincidence and he is immediately off. 118 miles south of Mother's new compound down nearer to the coast of the Gulf of Mexico. There the large platinum and silicone shining, it is so called Galveston and Houston. They are there just before the salt water. A probing, down nearer the shore, the buttons made a beep, beep, withdrawing. It being completed by someone on the other side at some A.T.M. a half of an hour before midnight 483, the 3 dollars would've been a fee there in: Humble, Texas. They said that the girl had been abducted in Alaska?

The tenth day coming and going silently.

Him later giving a description of it to the FBI or the State Troopers or one of the APD or was it one of the Attorneys, who knows anymore, the chain of custody no longer linear. The different law enforcement Cathedrals they are spread out all across that devil city and they are massive. When he set it up with the tempo, waiting your turn in the interrogation room and they are all around you. In the line of apprentice barber stations, you can see clearly there are different types of cops, when it comes to working for tips,

and the young woman was nodding and attentive.

There was at one point, a stage in the interrogation room on the tapes where it feels like you are in the backroom of a hotel card game, late into the night. The game having wound down to lingering conversations. The gravelly voiced guy and the others, one passed out on the couch or the other pissing, wobbling somewhere. They might had even been there in the room it didn't matter. Jolene was there in the cone of light making bed sheet tent drape behind her eyes. Sounding back, listening to him finally getting to tell the intense parts.

He said that she was a little Russian girl.

His words rolling slick around something like a butterscotch candy as he said it.

Implying an inference towards the prostitute, cast into that scene that he had set when he was in the US Army, in the Infantry: Middle East Theatre

Jolene Goeden asked him about that list of escort services that they had found during his arrest. Each escort service had notes next to their name and a point system scribbled out in his stakeout codes. Jolene was exceptionally aware with missing sex workers. One of her largest cases, second only to this one now. A girl that was meant to testify, before she up and disappeared.

She had broke out from a pimp: Jerry Starr. Jerry had ten to fifteen thousands of dollars a month going out in full page Escort Service ads back then, in those huge bulky yellow pages. Jerry had a system of having multiple listings to satisfy the different appetites. A customer thumbing through the full-page ads each containing only the telephone numbers, a few select words and then some abstract drawing or picture of partial nudity or overt sexuality. The caller only need to read between the lines, starting at the top, Jerry had some girls in a clean house for the discriminating and well-heeled customers:

"American Beauties"

There were numerous houses with cool names as well. The workers too knowing that it can go both ways just before breaching the frame of the hotel room door. Knowing in there waiting with pyramid fingers on the swivel chair is someone who dialed in the number for "Tickle your Fancy". It was brilliant.

Even at the bottom of the barrel there is bargains to be made. Dinner and a show kind of, for the dregs calling in for the likes of Jerry's "Foxy's Roxies" service with a little "substance". It is technically a mule job.

Goeden, Special Agent in the FBI noted the evidence, his little scribbled list on the card paper jacket that he had yanked out of one of the two opened Porno DVDs from the car ride in Texas. Her eyes sliding along between these coincidences.

Sierra Roberts worked for Jerry.

Auburn Hair, she came from a tiny religious "community" down in a place called Naptowne.

 A Bahai faith kid fed up with the commune that "punk rock saved my life" and she is there on the big city streets of Anchorage tapping her gum to Nelly.

That horrible blue house on "ThunderBird".

How long could you throw darts at Jerry's ads and not hit on Sierra, but that was more than 4 years ago.

Jolene asked him if he saw prostitutes in Anchorage. His whole energy changed and after a thoughtful pause he said, "well, yeah",

and then he wriggled away off into the shadows again.

The A T M withdrawal money, was stacking up now. Tucking it away as he was rolling up to his sister's place. Israel was there with his headlamp on reaching deep, up and over the cold plumbing pipes, squinting to see something very small.

3/10/2012 Home Depot receipt 2:42 p.m. the purchase of a water heating element. Lufkin, Texas.

It had gone well, however later they said there had been direct confrontation about God, morals and beliefs. He "stood his ground" on his atheism, they said. Leaving their house in good standing, cordial parting as the water heater is ticking up to temperature. Grit teeth in the passing rearview mirror, pulling out onto the lone evening road.

It was on the 11th at 13 minutes before midnight, sublime as the blood money finally came out of the machine again into the real world there in, "Shepherd" Texas, for the last time. Suffer the little children.

The morning of the 12th, he would have awoken to the wedding day of his sister. In the terms and conditions of the vows and the lengthy wall drip sermon there were these obvious little jabs, and needle points in between the verses. The guy up there says a real doozy that he had been building up to and he raises his eyebrow and looks around after he says it. You can see Obadiah sitting in front of you's person inside, trying to turn around and look while not trying turn around and look. The rooster vain Pastor wasn't even there for his own brother's wedding. Later him speaking from what they had told him second-hand,

"Even at the wedding the Lord pled with him and pled with him and in the midst of it he wept and broke down weeping, balling, even wailing, but he would not repent"

To the Pastor who was there, "Israel said, "Not everyone has your morals" with an undertone of hate and murder in his heart"

At that, her son, is off again pointing out towards alcoholic beverages and a new shirt for sake of the snot and the slobber. Driving away from the paparazzi with the dying heave breath from crying earlier.

3/12/2012 Wal-Mart receipt

21:36 CT -9:36 Monday night

beer and wine

a black warm up Jerzee brand sweat pants, size M

Eyeglasses in black case.

Out under the Texas stars, the boys have all pissed, measured and they are pretty sure of the make of the car. Even the computer program spitting chaw and nodding along almost with certainty, that it will be a white Ford Focus and they were all waiting for it to raise up again from falling off of the face of the earth.

The divining sticks pointing down at your crotch in the darkness, this most diligent officer having spent so much time out under those stars. Being seen of no one but God and his creation, wandering along in the part desert like Moses in a cruiser. He heard through the wire that all the way down Houston, they are signaling out to all the little cow towns. The port lights glittering, grass and rock wash down there. It was a Be On the Look Out for this white car, feverish. All of this washing over him as he had just shuffled in to his shift there that morning. His coffee swash buckled up to the rim it almost sloshed. Everyone is sure it will be a Ford Focus and everyone has "shared" "what they know". They are looking at him, catching breath.

Gauging from the inches of mercury in his eyes, 169 miles from the shoreline, it is still only 312 feet above the salt water, all the way up here, and he is nodding yes then blinking real big to clear his eyes as he was rolling through some foggy window hotel in his cruiser. Scouring over the mile twain out in the obscure and the out of the way hotel parking lots, scanning and scanning, out here. Do you see how that D pillar comes down the back window of that car that is parked deep in the spot? It's gills must be hanging over the curb. The lines of the shape of the car is about to slip out from behind bulkier cars parked around it as the blood rush then tingles the ear tops and then he sees the car!

It is just a white car, a rental, one of the most popular by JD Power and associates from the briefing this morning. It could be any one of a million but he knew in his gut from the second that he laid his eyes on it. When the back corner first coming into view, passing skin cold to touch driving by the ear tightens to the eyebrow trying to see more without being obvious, confirmed while crackling slowly by: Ford Focus.

It ends up that Israel had returned the white Ford Focus for a fresh car and the rental company had signed him out the exact same model, make and even the color. Watching the replacement car roll up he must've almost grimaced a growl at the stupid gnome clicking the keys on the computer. Law enforcement had never gotten a lock on the license plate from the cameras though. Perhaps it would be too suspicious for him to request another color. So, he got in the fresh Focus and drove off. The car, it was clean at least.

Others could've been sleeping with their handle in their hand. The doughnut glaze across their shirt, snoring now behind the billboard, he can't believe he's making the call. That you are pretty sure that you have located the BOLO car. In the earliest of grey hours well before dawn the bugs are quieting away as everything is covering in microdot chilled water. There in the parking lot already is Texas Ranger Steven Rayburn and sitting next to him now behind tinted glass is no other than FBI agent Deborah Gannoway. There are people in the room sleeping, by all indications. The room with the corner of the curtain over the black windows. He swears he saw it moving but it was the air conditioner flapping it softly. From in the blackness there were in fact eyes back there, just out of the plane of the light. Looking out he had said later

"You mean the car I saw in my hotel parking lot last night?"

They had seen him with family members, having a good time as he left them there at the hotel balcony. Then he had skipped slid directly down to the BOLO car. When he pulled out of the dip bump from the parking lot it was grey light and they were hiding in the blinds speaking short tactical bursts as the small white Focus was becoming isolated.

Leaving Wells due south towards Houston the two ATM's were both at 79.4 and 188.5 miles from Mother's Porch. Leaving Wells south by Southwest off to the right a bit more, it heads towards Waco. On that road at 134 miles is the headquarters of the Texas Rangers and he had hit the withdrawal sites for the money up by their ear on one and down around their ankles on the other. He is just the next road over from them on the big maps and when they were ready, they gave the green light to the road cop. They were all tappin' boot leather. Getting updates, don't fuck this one up! Thank you, Texas. Then Israel broke the speed limit, not even above the Texas friendly 5 miles over for a tip of the hat but the moment he breached it, making any legal infraction, the Attorneys familiarizing themselves in the dynamics that will surely unfold: Probable Cause of failure to maintain posted speed. They have him pulled over and before the road cop gets out, they are telling him over the radio that this is what he has lived for, hell trained for! That this was a big moment and ok now! Go up there and see who it is!

The Corporal comes up to the little white car on the tape. He appears jumpy and at one-point tips his hand back across the handle of his pistol then takes it off as he is trying to play it cool. This is just a routine traffic stop that is flooding in adrenaline. There are numerous undercover officers in unmarked vehicles spread out in a widow trap all around somewhere.

Black silhouettes behind black climate-controlled glass, all lurking around the Quality Inn Suites off the highway there in the big parking lot. The Corporal looks nervous on the tape. There is a felony stop which this will become as soon as they see his identification but maybe it is nothing. Melting away as approaching from the back, the vibe was off of the charts and the guy inside the little car has a big nose and he is sleeveless. It is a muscle shirt. He is perturbed and his hair is rattling like a corpse in there over the fine new upholstery.

As the window had come down, those pristine gasses pluming up in warm air as the man's window coming down. The biomes of horsemen's musk, but he showered last night at the Quality Inn. They said it was a cool morning still and as the man in the white car with the muscle shirt on and the big nose lifts his fingers up to the edge of the rounded glass of his window with his I.D. The Corporal instantly draped in the cold skin as he flipped it in his own fingers and the Driver's License said ALASKA.

Others are arriving in plainclothes now. They said the Intruder's skin was touched of the brisk morning air and still it had become dotted in perspiration. The more they laid their eyes upon him, the drier their mouths became, becoming ravenous though, playing it calm.

It began to flash before them, as the probable cause? Him waiting to be released for want of a speeding ticket but the Attorneys in council in Houston in the spires of its evil skyline, they have nodded to go ahead, that they are good to kill for.

Put the radio down, go over there and arrest him somehow. You have carte blanche, but it must be by the book. The officer approaching the small white Ford Focus, feeling his sidearm there on his side. They get him out as the shutter is flying, catching him those first moments or last moments of flight in daylight. They search the car and find her card with the number scratched into it. The one making its supposed way towards some desert border crossing. He had said that she had nearly got away in the desert, at a time when she was still in Alaska. Here he is now and there is a pair of sneakers that he kept right behind his seat hidden incidentally in plain sight. With his daughter's bag, now made complicit, was Samantha's debit card and phone still glowing in the halo light of that other life. There is a travel DVD player with two of the opened DVDs of the several.

Putting him in cuffs there is a car cam that had been recording. It shows him watching as they popped the trunk of the small white rental. The suspect in custody is no doubt cataloging the contents of the car in his mind over and over and the also probability of them finding the hidden components.

Next to his ID in his wallet was an out of date Temporary 2-day Fishing License for the State of Vermont. It was 279 days expired. It had only been good for the day when "it happened" to Bill and Lorraine and the day after. A normal object, placed incidentally. A memento to have on hand right in front of anyone.

Just like he had said about for years "that's how I get my kicks". He could take it out and play with it anytime, anywhere. In the trunk of the car was a Ricardo brand brown duffle bag. In it was extra clothes and that Grey Hooded Sweatshirt that had those strange things around it and in its pockets. Under that was the "Hard Plastic Black Case". It contained only:

Taurus .22 caliber pistol- Black Blue Steel- cowboy revolver with 9 shots

Smith & Wesson .40 caliber automatic pistol

2 magazines: 15 rounds in each

1 old Wal-Mart receipt from the previous trip 2/17/2012 Jacksonville, Texas.

The purchase was: two days after Jimmy Tidwell, the electrician disappeared on that night at the Cleburne Mall and only one day after a man in a construction disguise had walked into that hayseed bank in Azle, Texas dressed in his work clothes, dusk mask and hard hat with strands of hair taped into it, as he had told them.

The next day that old receipt printed out real in the real world. Here it was still, on this trip in the box with the guns and the three items on the receipt were:

shovel, lube and air freshener spray

He was agitated and acting uncomfortable they reported and it was captured on the dashcam. Ready to give answer for any odd items in transit.

The print out was in there, the F B I calling it a "Computer Generated Hotel Reservation for the Riviera Hotel & Casino showing the: arriving 3 - 6 departing 3 - 7. The reservation showing it was made on the first. Below that was the Computer-Generated Car Rental Reservation. Pick-up and Drop off: Las Vegas, Avis. It would be rented from March 7th-21st.

Below that was the Alaska Airlines Flight Confirmation. Leaving Anchorage 3 / 6 at 1 in the morning. The large hanging tires chirp down on the tarmac at SEA-TAC just 39 minutes before the sun rising. The next flight wasn't until 3 o'clock that afternoon. When they took off, they wouldn't touch down until Las Vegas. Arriving 9 minutes before sunrise in the desert.

Pick-up the car, check out the Hotel Room at the Riviera. In the car was his Riviera Club SELECT gambling card from the casino that they would catalogue and photograph. When he hit the ATM that night at around 10 in the evening, he would've had to leave Las Vegas at around 2:30 in the afternoon, roughly 500 miles at 7 and a half hours to drive it. Then he had crossed over the state line down there into the boot heel and that was when the ATM pinged back empty for him in Lord'sBurgh, New Mexico right before midnight.

Mother's Porch on the 8th.

On March 10th at his one sister's place, the Home Depot receipt still there in the truck.

Home Depot: water heater element.
Maybe that is where the ¼" drill came from.

The 11th another withdrawal

After the wedding though on the 12th, yesterday wailing and balling. Last night the last withdrawal in Shepard. He had said after that "I wasn't planning on coming back to Texas".

EVIDENCE LIST MARCH 06, 2012

Green and Grey Eagle Brand Backpack

Colored Photo of black female with numbers   written on the back (removed from   DVD case)

Two DVD's "Combat Zone" and Exquisite Productions: Ultimate T Girl Full   Service

      Transexuals Volume 2" (removed from DVD case)

Brinkman Headlamp

Passport: Israel Keyes

Grey Fruit of the loom T-Shirt 2XL with one   sleeve cut off strangely

Gray Hooded Sweatshirt size 3XL

Pockets: Gray and Black Gloves Demarini   Brand

The sleeve from the grey T-Shirt

Yellow tint Winchester shooting glasses

Ziploc bag: RadioShack Police Scanner

Black and Decker cordless drill w/ a drill bit (the width of a pencil)

Wal-Mart Receipt 2/17/2012 Jacksonville, Texas: Shovel, Lube and Air Freshener Spray (removed from inside hard plastic black box)

Three rolls of Currency:

1 dollar bills: 143

5 dollar bills: 65   (325)

10 dollar bills: 55   (550)

      Paper money "emitted a strong   musty odor and was slightly damp   and mildewed"

ATM receipt (Debit not Available)

Taurus .22 caliber pistol- Black Blue Steel-   cowboy
revolver with 9 shots

Smith & Wesson .40 caliber automatic pistol   with 2
magazines with 15 rounds in   each

    2 - day Vermont Fishing License issued 6-8-2011 (expired for
    279 days)

Address on the Driver's License: 3705   Arctic
Blvd. Anchorage: The Mail   Cache- Private Postal
Service and   Telephone Messaging Service

Pantech Flip Phone

    The crashing realization of having only moments ago left her there with his brother at the hotel, and everything else, for the last time.

Being transported over the stratos in a pressurized cabin. Feeling like a mastermind in bondage, he must've loved it or parts of it. And when they spoke of these things, there was a time when the men at the table and the noble young women, they settled in that they would have a functioning relationship, clearly defined and each side helping each other flesh out the pre-agreed upon requirements as "giving them another body" as he would only have it said.

    It was when the one guy insisted that he had to have had an accomplice. That no one man could remove that type of steel truck racks with the boxes, off of, much less putting them back on. Lining up the holes without blowing his back out or crushing himself? Israel saying later that he had indeed made a wood stick to brace across it and standing up balancing at the perfect center he could skid walk the rack like Dr. Frankenstein's monster, up and down the centerline of the truck, off onto the ground then breathing out, crouching the legs, finally coming down. The truck behind him in the background now appearing nude and so very different.

To try and get the young man to "make contact with the accomplice? We want Samantha back we will pay you and where is she? The look in his eye it was part fuck you, but it was also part, fuck me. The coordinates clicking as the satellites passing over by slide rule, verifying with nuclear precision the spot on the earth. They are crunch walking across the ice, blinding white squinting at where they say the coordinates converged and there the little black ants looking down at the smoothed over scar lathe marks in the ice. Out beyond the end of that mound finger, boardwalk. In the summer they would be standing over 40 feet of lake water. Squinting at the homeowner chainsaw marks at their feet. He had said he had made them there. Cutting holes into the structural ice for the open toed floor of the fish shanty. Cutting with a recently maintained chainsaw. Scoring out upon the hard track ice, a full-size truck could have delivered their payload.

Then driving just far enough away as the black dots on a field of brilliant light mark out a mathematical triangle on the ice and sinking in those tax payer's no expense spared chainsaws. The roar of the exhaust, the operator's dark glasses glancing before repositioning the feet for grip. A scan if there is someone in the danger zone, and collecting bearings. The highway, the trucks, the forensic privacy tents, just off shore from that finger peninsula coming out into this heart shaped lake it is pointing at his feet and directly at them out there. They lit the rooster tail as they sunk that saw down into it and hit water in seconds, gushing out the spillway back there and lifting the bar out of the kerf at times, as the trigger goes full bore and the white spray is coming up at angles. The angles allowing the blocks of ice to be held and plucked out. The triangle pieces removed, there now a portal. It is man made and black, down into the cider water of the million-year drainages seeping the blackest of maple water under ice for its half-life. The corners of the triangle being tactical. It is much easier to crawl up and out of the portal. The Sacred Geometry a rosary prayer allowing safe travel hopefully too. They charge up the tanks and they regulate everything. A nod and a tap on the shoulder.

Watching him go down into the cold water the older man, his body is part like a junkie. Breathing and blood pressures changing with the second hand of his wrist watch's face on instinct alone, even if standing on the placebo ground. They flew in the baddest federal dive team around. There is a waiting list for guys like these, but hearing the school program crying out, just before it was midnight. This rescue was classified as a child and there is a wall back in California where these guys retreat to their own aqua cave. In there, on a wall are the photos of the artwork of only the babies or the children. The plane wrecks tumbling into the sea. They had retrieved a baby, later and he had been asked by some uncouth what had it looked like?

 So, he responded "bathed in fire".

They are on the wall to help the poor guys associate these beautiful pictures with that of those, the nightmare, hellish flashes and sliding textures of wax over a dead shin, any haunt behind their eyes of the things that they have handled in the deep murky that they are descending now into blackness. The blackness rising as he would have crossed 25 feet, a wicked thermocline months away in the heat of summer.

It would have appeared as a layer of "crinkled glass" below you and as you would go down through it, your ears would go down like a cat, your eyesight would become frightenly clear and your nuts would slip up inside your body, the area plumping where they went up into.

Topping out at the depth in which a very expensive sonar had said, exactly where it would be. Pinging off of something under the old ice scars 30 some feet above them, she is right below their dangling feet. If this had been the late summer, the sun at that angle would've been shining down into open water, it would shine down through the trees and the tree-falls. Making a dancing tiger stripe across you as you looking up. It is so desolate there now that it echoes.

Below the glowing portal above now, the heavy breather has come down through the cone of light and this is where he sees the things listed on the forms. Federal requests becoming mandates, the papers saying that it was Biological evidence and that they had been weighted down into the long haul never to return. Reducing down in decades to coffee stained soupbone, as her legacy of great-great-great grandchildren would have been wiped from the earth. One of the 5 pieces of evidence, the largest one, having a belly button ring and thong style underwear, the logo strangely said Harley Davidson. The other 4 were also weighted down and nightmarish approaching the surface, but part of her in Spirit, breaking the water, eyes gasping out looking around so grateful. She had been through so much and they came for her.

The chain of custody report must be filled out so strictly as she starts to remember it. Instantly and simultaneously forever only in bar smoke and there so unbelievably, in Eden, to whoever said there will be no tears in heaven. Go Fuck Yourself

CHAPTER TWENTY-NINE

BRILLIANT FLASHES

There was once a young man having had watched all of the people in the worlds he saw, moving about and across the earth. He had noticed by then staring down at these well-worn little shrew trails for the first time. Slick corners where body butter has polished the contact points to translucent. Older then, watching the people moving like slow rivers, he can see their bigger moves overlaid over the to and fro, allowing light into the texture now. Walking through that world the young man had assurances, from somewhere within him he knew for a certainty that whatever went down he would face it squarely. Life feels so sure in your hands once you've laid it down for something.

It seemed there were those brilliant flashes, it must've been a cold start for something like a tiny little sun. Belch carbon pop, singe crackling up to its blinding hum but only the first flashes and then it was gone, or rather it appeared to be. Looking back the young man glid through the world, it caught him unawares, the bear. From in the dim of that cool stone cavern, the brilliant light is shining in the leaves having changed a color as they appear to be changing. The scene bursting in slow motion. Creatures that lived off of the light of the world, they somehow creasing the photons slipping each into fixed corridors down into and through each leaf, absorbing the light. As it comes down to it for them it is so clear the parts they held on to.

The Verdant of all of those long summer days, they too setting into maple bursts across them, the last things that they let loose of, becoming awash then in the most deepest of reds. Fading to plum and blue, the ultra-violets still accumulating out from their slow opening hands.   He had sensed it, crunching the old fire bones in the damp darkness, eyes looking out at the passing of the Zenith. While heaving large clods of earth in the dimness he caught a notion of some, very real thing. But it was still only just some unknown and then on August 30, 1993, the world was still and slow rolling in a sleepwalk. When it burst over the creation of God in streaks of golden fire. It raced across the ceiling of clouds coursing elaborate, teasing and playful of its own power. The lights are glowing upon his face he is looking up at them.

Walking into the room, she is right over there and as he is approaching her, there is a click grunting down in the warm of the blankets, swaddled firmly. Having just fallen to earth, the sky had been a fire in his eyes. As he pulled slowly the little rumple blanket to catch a glimpse, swiftly from behind the clouds and the black mountain, him imagining maybe the beauty of the full moon, when it then blazed out across the blackness. Him staring at midday into the most brilliant light he had never dreamed of, and that it would somehow get to be him standing like that in the light of the world. The hot tear stinging down, not wanting to look away from her for a moment.

Breathing in sharp, the last of it touched of breath flutter. He had always had this thing, *invincible*?
His eyes are wild and cautious. Standing there now, mortal. Them both breathing in again, for the first time together.

He would've burst forth in shaking hide, rattling like thunder if any dared towards her. His eyes coming down almost upon it in a bloodshot and reckless angle threatening to shear his own tooth off at the collision, if a mere threat dared nearing her. Waking with eyes in bloodshot, across the room he had nodded off. He had heard of SIDs before and it sounded so sinister. So he would sit and watch over her as she slept. Listening to her little breaths, in the dim. Eventually, the little girl having lived with Dad on the sea, free all of her days from Mother's earth shores, knowing no other world, she reaches up to grab a sure hand as if in the rigging and pulling, she steps up over the crevasse of the couch cushions and she is hanging there like a little sailor, feet and a hand hanging loose as she swings back and forth so gently, then she remembers it! He can feel her tiny hand hooking up over the slab of the crook of his neck and his massive shoulder. The little monkey paw stiffens as she spins and wobbles, her little ankle getting grip as she big stepping to the other side of the couch.

Describing the thing and all of its accessories, she has been day dreaming about it. Swinging about the yard arm coming as second nature, crawling about all over him as she goes on in sing song describing how they could go to the stores and get all the stuff. Her little top wobbled back, her eyes rolled open whoa! She almost fell, throwing her arm out toward him and she didn't see his big hands reach out for her, floating back so suddenly, the background blurred her falling into the giant arms already there behind her. Her eyes were afraid for an instant and he winced as it shot urchin needles into him there. She is smiling bouncing cradling in. Big fingers coming down tickle pinching under her little butter ribs. He growls coming in so close, her squealing and pinching her neck and little shoulders.   Everyone would've known it and seen the little life they had made, but mostly it was just the two of them.

To be at home on the sea, there is a strange shore approaching, but it is moving like a ship and the charts show they should be squish, glitting across nothing but blue on all horizons but the Mother Earth, she is wicked or at least that's how it feels when she is standing on your shore clutching the hard-won titles. Justice being so blind they made her grab some of her little things. The custody coming in, shattering their little life. Out on the waves, the side slip down in the big swell, bottoming in the well then so suddenly the deck is lifting up out of the slithering trench of water to a sky of starn beauty. On the deck he is standing holding the rail, up to the top of the lift. The foam spray nuisance it clears and he can see. Over rolling sheets of ocean, it is all sliding in wind drift and in dusk light. He can see a glimpse of the land and he is looking for any glow in some safe little valley maybe over there and there is nothing. Down into the trough falling, allowing the body to go loose. Tensing the legs and the stomach and the hips under the stacked tea cups of the spine, as it lifts so swiftly again. The steep walls give way to star and beauty the air seems to gasp like a night flower releasing his prayers and hopes for her safety again. The foam nuisance clearing and he can see over the chin of the waves for a moment for anything and it is all cold and dim and all of it appearing to be; in the wilds over there for her.

She was older afterward and there was a blackness that could creep out under her eyes once in a while from it, but that part was over and she was a young woman wiser for the world. There is a photo of him and her, in it their eyes are laughing, they are close and happy.

Behind them the refrigerator door nearly covered with photos of the two of them, held on by little magnets and such, nary a spot for many more and in each they are on some adventure, or a small mission, or just getting ice cream. A life living off of the light of the world and for so brief of instances each time that the shutter had flown open for them, the humming bird slow jiving like honey. In javelin clusters of light splashing the image of them both into the small black cave of the camera and upon that mushroom paper. It instantly sizzling changed forever waiting in the palette of negative. Melting and swirling then freezing in plum tan and blood violet as the shutter is closing, the humming bird blinking the second, pump of his wings. Each one a promise.

When she knew she would be graduating high school, it was an accomplishment for her because when you hear the name of the one high school, to others it would pass without meaning. However, her diploma would've part rightly, come in from a school that tells you that the student there had some type of influence in their high school career that had at one point interrupted her success path. It is a school made specifically for the kids who are Wiser for the World usually. There is always some faculty member who asks about the girl who usually sits over there and when they find out she is out in the wind they try and set it up. Make contact with the little bird out there zipping back and forth in the howling, wobbling so recklessly. There hollering to her that she can still graduate. There are a few steps and from in the dead of the night the little bird arcing across the howl of the sky, came fluttering unexpected into and under the big overhang. Under a special program school made to wait with blinking lights on up until the last days. What a great way to get to heaven as part of a retirement package option.

It is no fun remembering the ones that never came back from the darkness. She could do it, her eyes glittering and as she was going to hear it aloud, there is the smile her father spoke of and the laughter he says of her and you would never have doubted her, but seeing her be proud of herself and excited as she remembered it! That she really won't miss a beat either because of the special program. It really does mean a lot or at least you can see it there so clearly when you've been an outcast of the Anchorage School District before. The entire town of kids still on track in school and you are a ragamuffin. Sure, it is cool but you can see it in their eyes when they will be graduating basically on time and if you didn't know any better on paper, you'd say that she was an any old, run of the mill average kid.

The program's most beautiful move is dissolving away as the little bird rejoins the rivers of others. She had her job at the Harley-Davidson Shop but looking out across that town when you are that age seeing now all of the people in the worlds moving about and across the Anchorage bowl. She could stare down at these well-worn little shrew trails for the first time. Slick corners where body butter has polished the contact points to translucent. Watching the people moving like slow rivers, she was so untouched by it still though. She believes in herself enough to know that whatever comes against her, she will face it head on, plus her dad has her back. Hanging loose from some top of that fridge like a little sailor. Her feet and a hand rigid all else hanging loose as she swings back and forth so gently, she wants to make her own money and that rascal's smile and eyebrows, she was so cute and funny.

Working at the shop on the clock was ridiculous for her and she was so astute, she knew she was valuable. In that town as in most, any vigorous young man can go out into the trades and whence equipped he can tackle all the half rotten repairs and half undone burdensome problems that the bigger companies know better and have stayed away from. There is a world of rodeo rides out there, cowboy.

In that town it's the same for the young womenfolk as well. The gentler gender supposedly, they get their feathers rustled so easily. Their social decorum is so complex they are in constant need of young girls to dye, cut, perm and wash the face of this pig in short heels. No one wants to deal with her anymore. In that town when the news spreads around that a small church has just split, people "in the know" immediately cross reference their red code book that contains their hair appointments. Maybe calling to reschedule, there may be some serious fallout as the factions often settle their own scores. There is always a need for fresh reinforcements and they flow steadily clopping out from upstairs at the Salon / Beauty school program, onto the parking lot off of Northern Lights Blvd. A licensed beautician in that town is the equivalent of a 19-year-old roofer with a truck and some tools. They both have the ability to make pretty good money of their own coming right out of the gate. In the meantime, she applied for a job that is still on the hour but she can make killer on the tips.

At the corner of Tudor and the Old Seward Highway there is a large complex with some commercial office spaces and utility pads but mostly it is Big Box stores, then they brought in the new Dairy Queen in town. In the old days, the young ladies of Soldotna, Alaska too, would get summer jobs there as people pulled into the parking lot 3 hours in the ride. The children peeling out ravenous and randomly leaping like little goats, a part twirl in there landing on sprite legs momma low hand watching the parking lot before, but now it is right there on the front of Tudor Road. At times the intersection is loaded across all those lanes, like a big river. The Dairy Queen finally absorbing part of that very deep new sprawling parking lot. It makes its own hangout while waiting for fries to come out.

Across the busy major thoroughfare there are businesses with almost no foot traffic. The backside of Auto Dealerships, any eyes scanning out back toward you from around the glass front, looking away in their evaluation. The windowless bulwark of the Alaska Club Gym. They pile snow back there where they can, and as the months pass in the far north the snow becoming concrete hard and taller and taller in the one dead corner right on the front of the street, you are looking at their backsides. If you donned gear and scaled up the monolith of dirty ice and stood atop of it, there in the parking lot behind you obscured in the tall winter pile is a little expresso stand. It is down in this trough but they painted the little thing light blue. The color of the bright winter sky in the mid-morning. The commuter's river there, it is efficient and at times echoes empty, across it. Breath pluming in steam, the brief hot fog glowing bright red, haloing the bright new Dairy Queen frontage against a sky of black and those orange clouds opening to stars in the late afternoon and they dissolve together in peach light occupying the whole of the background, coming into view coming up from across the deep parking lot back there shrinking to a bright orange font it said *"the Home Depot"*

She nailed the interview at the coffee stand, and after the tutorials quickly she was running the machines, and the till, and she can close up the shop on her own. After the flow of commuters dying down, she used her cell phone, the screen lighting the indiglo of her father's number. He was still working and couldn't bring her dinner tonight; they would miss each other only by an hour or so. Her boyfriend would be picking her up soon in his truck, it had been having some maintenance issues though. He never made it.

Fortunately, when her father called the owner of the Common Grounds coffee shack that something wasn't right, the guy down in Oregon somewhere said he would look into it. Looking into the remote viewing of the glass from afar, by 12:39 just after midnight the A P D had received the notification of what had happened on the tapes.

When her boyfriend, hours later opened the front door of their home to see some intruder was there. In the night-blind of the darkness, the intruder had already retrieved the debit card and her ID from inside the truck that just wasn't reliable when it gets this cold out. It all had been exactly where she had told him they would be, he said. Printing the street address up on MapQuest.com from Kim's computer. Opening the shed door, it is him with a piece of copy paper in his hand. A bird's-eye view of their house and its surroundings, and made her identify the porch, the truck, and the location of everything else. Before leaving, he had set up a make shift potty bucket for her if she needed it. He is so brazenly there black and cold staring predator, shockingly at 2:30 in the morning by then? He had said that the plan was to grab her, then grab her ride. He would only do it if "they" had a good running vehicle. He was only supposed to use his truck to get within walking distance. Using their car instead for everything else. He said that the other one "had a part to play".

The stars seem to crinkle against the blackness in the cold air, becoming frighteningly clear, just like outer space at moments like those. Crinkling out of the endless cold above him somewhere is the Pleiades, and the young man had run inside from the cold at the sight of an intruder crouched by their truck in their own driveway. Israel saying that he stared at the young man, it seemed like a long time before Duane had turned and had gone real fast. Heels thudding inside. The intruder gripping stance readying. He had gloated about earlier how she didn't try to escape each different time that he left and came back. It was the assurances of his police scanner that he brought down and slid the little swollen ear bud, pushing it into her ear so she could hear, if he heard any activity about anything…letting silence be the answer.

All the while he had disclosed that, at the time she was safe and warm in the shed.

Edging himself out there again, when body rocking with the momentum stilled to ice. The APD has known for two hours already that she was abducted. In night ears, the monster knew maybe sensing it, that a cruiser has appeared in the vicinity of their house. Tilting the hearing part, into the night breeze. Gripping stance, thinking of her there so trusting and warm. All set up and he is having to deal with this, steeling his jaw when the voice crackled again in his ear and his thoughts are circling the water: by numbers alone he was now in their, vicinity and he departed back to Kim's house.

He was frustrated that he had wasted that whole part of it because he had only been able to wrangle the one of the two. By the time he came up into the landing of the shed, a black lake lowering and soft edged ice swirling in thick glass on his breath and in his eyes, he said and he leveled off.

The door immediately opening and she asked, "Did you talk to my Dad?"

he said

There was a snow forming to falling fragments as the stars disappeared all but gone so suddenly, falling softly out there lingering just 5 degrees below the temperature water freezes at. In the video from an elevated corner seeing her in her warm sweater making two big drinks to take home very soon, the hissing steam from the little spindle and then from that little sliding window, appeared one last customer, just on the other side of the glass, and as she opened it the warm air, part her own soft breath vapors rising quickly up and out to the world alongside the smell of Espresso bean and sweet syrups. The vinyl window sliding open the inside of the little blue coffee shack becoming crackled in brown and blood and sizzled violet cast forever and instantly on mushroom paper.

The videos outside unbelievably show them walking out across the peach light.

The clanging truth of remembering those golden bright days when the lawyer at the table on first impressions and building report had told Israel that because of the proceedings and because the District

Attorney was sitting in on the "meetings" for some reason, that the Judge has said, bending the rules, that "we can talk about anything you want, but we cannot, talk, about Samantha", agreed?

And Israel was courteous and understanding he slid grin when he said,

"I'm only going to give you what I know you already have"

He had said he had fastened their feet on the bed with the zip ties in the first story, but then later in the retelling, no. Mumbling off that they had snapped off in the car. Her ribs were racking as he had grabbed her hard from off of the ground and put his shoulder around her and he walked Lorraine wobbling hair shuffling, like a friend helping a friend after a doozy of an office party. They are shuffling up to the old farmhouse and they are crossing into the shadow of the door frame.

Firing up the blue rush flame of the heater stove across his eyes in the story.

The knot is cinching, over the potty toilet there. Tied to a wall in a very small building.

By the time I brought her down, he said
she was basically" like a zombie"

Applying sales techniques nearing the end and he had stopped giving them anything anymore and they said chuckling to give up a body, even for the sake of "bringing closure to a family or a mother or a father even?"

He sounded genuine when he said scoff chuckling back, asking which is better: to know their loved one disappeared and could maybe still be alive and maybe doing okay? or knowing that something terribly horrible happened to them.

The tape outside of the Common Grounds Expresso stand recording, forever now, then seeing it played back, in real time. The two forms are moving away from the camera, her hands are bound, there nearly out of sight, and so unbelievably.

How absurd the notion that the plan was to be savoring robbing 3 banks all in a line.
Coming out of it at the table, a slow blinking…what? the candy was nice and then something like in a dream state. Remembering about the first story where the guy who got away, it felt tongue in cheek when the car was Ted Bundy's car. Then the story about the couple in the car where when the one cop, then the second showed up.
This time when they asked, he was certain of the make.

In Greek mythology, the Pleiades were the seven daughters of the Titan Atlas. He was forced to hold up the sky for eternity, and was therefore unable to protect his daughters. To save the sisters from being raped by the hunter Orion, Zeus transformed them into stars.

"It was a Subaru" he said

Whatever it was, suddenly she is running. Having broken away and she was on her pounding feet, there on the tape. Her hands are bound, you sure can't turn your head back to look behind you like that. You can see her get taken down onto the hard snow pavement, and he said he held her close under his arm and jammed the pistol into her ribs and walked her like a boyfriend helping his drunk girlfriend or drunk coworker out of the frame. She had made two drinks one for her, leaving such an emptiness now. The snow falling, like ashes.

If you had been watching from across Tudor, the report filled in from loved ones, going over recollections of who was where that week, rebuilding the scene. Blurry fog window swiped clear. Optics lens bouncing after hours, there she is. Hop skipping, then the rascal slide foot, with the big drinks she is about to get in. The dome light showing when the door opened. On the nights leading up to that week, the recollection that it was her father that had been picking her up, and they were smiling in the light of the world in there before the door closed again and the lens went to black.

The one early evening that my sister had been standing at the door years before she was excited because she had a few new responsibilities through her work. She would also now be orchestrating any routine maintenance on an apartment building. About to drive home after a large dinner, heading back into Anchorage as she began in again something else reminded her just before she left. She remembered at the last that her new acquaintance / new friend's boyfriend is new in town. Saying as an afterthought that he is starting a small construction company. She waved her hand again waving away the logistics. She popped the gear in her shiny SUV and it lurched. Crackling gravel out of the driveway her head went back as it started to roll down out onto the asphalt as she turned back, she waved and we all smiled like kids playing as adults. Her red tail lights are going into the darkness, long sweeping arc following the quick winding curves of Peters Creek, from my front glass the red candle flash over there in the trees. The red lights dim again the orb of bright light in the nothingness it is slide passing the small wooden bridge in the green glow dot of the trees, away in curves through the Birch woods before it all goes black in the night down in there.

Perhaps it was the very next engagement and the spooling in the latest story ending suddenly like heavy pouring phonebooks to a stop.

The papers were not to be smudged. Each one a skull of its own upon the dark cell walls. Hours and hours until the sun will blaze onto the world in light. It was still the deep morning as racing images crashing passed, that one girl's eyes still beautiful, even scattered wild and frantic.

The jail sheet is twisting tighter as the lights are fading from the screen behind his eyes. Creaking, pulling up more now cinching upon his cooling neck. The largest skull of the paintings, across its bottom it says in shaking finger swiping,
"We are One"

Bathed in the sun of the Chugach high over the mountains, the little child looking up to her mother and they both somehow felt like it was completed somehow, walking down the driveway so freely so suddenly. Them after coming back up the gravel. In the tall birch tops sliding past each other, the edge of a gable or the hip of a roof making too straight a line revealing it is man made in the leaves. From then on, she was no longer afraid of the windows uncovered anymore, these strange coincidences unfolding that in hindsight they reveal an echo calling of a closeness more than you'd ever want.

In the poor ship's wreckage, tumbling into the blackness down there by now. Where even prayers must singe, knowing they keep pinging back empty. When her Father in flashing lights was arrested for DUI, the man waiting at his home was Clinton Reeves' father. Clinton was a young airman who had also gone missing violently. The reports saying James Koenig was helping the family of this young man.

From within the depthless black, a cursor blinking: S.A.M Seeking Alaska's Missing. A website in her name to act as a connecting point for the families, loved ones of anyone who goes missing.

A tiny wavering light from down in the wreckage, echoing blurry through the dark.

DEPARTMENT OF CORRECTIONS

"Where will you go, you clever little worm, if you bleed your host dry?

Back in your ride, the night is still young, streetlights push back the black neat rows. Off to the right a graveyard appears, lines of stones, bodies molder below. Turn away quick, bob your head to the seat, as straight through that stop sign you roll loaded truck with lights off slams into you broadside, your flesh smashed as metal explodes.

You may have been free, you loved living your lie, fate had its own scheme crushed like a bug you still die.

Soon, now, you'll join those ranks of dead or your ashes the wind will soon blow. Family and friends will shed a few tears, pretend it's off to heaven you go. But the reality is you were just bones and meat, and with your brain died also your soul.

Send the dying to wait for their death in the comfort of retirement homes, quietly/quickly say "it's for the best" it's best for you so their fate you'll not know. Turn a blind eye back to the screen, soak in your reality shows. Stand in front of your mirror and you preen, in a plastic castle you call home.

Land of the free, land of the lie, land of scheme Americanize! Consume what you don't need, stars you idolize, pursue what you admit is a dream, then it's American die.

Get in your big car, so you can get to work fast, on roads made of dinosaur bones. Punch in on the clock and sit on your ass, playing stupid ass games on your phone. Paper on your wall, says you got smarts. The test that you took told you so, but you would still crawl like the vermin you are, once your precious power grids blown.

Land of the free, land of the lie, land of the scheme, Americanize.

Now that I have you held tight I will tell you a story, speak soft in your ear so you know that it's true. You're my love at first sight and though you're scared to be near me, my words penetrate your thoughts now in an intimate prelude.

I looked in your eyes, they were so dark, warm and trusting, as though you had not a worry or care. The more guileless [sic] the game the better potential to fill up those pools with your fear.

Your face framed in dark curls like a portrait, the sun shone through highlights of red. What color I wonder, and how straight will it turn plastered back with the sweat of your blood.

Your wet lips were a promise of a secret unspoken, nervous laugh as it burst like a pulse of blood from your throat. There will be no more laughter here.

I feel your body tense up, my hand now on your shoulder, your eyes…Forget the lady called luck she does not abide near me for her powers don't extend to those who are dead.

[illegible words] would that I could keep you, let you be the master of your own fate...knowing full well what's at stake? My pretty captive butterfly colorful wings my hand smears...I somehow repaint them with punishment and tears.

Violent metamorphosis, emerge my dark moth princess, I would come often and worship on the altar of your flesh…You shudder with revulstion [sic] and try to shrink far from me. I'll have you tied down and begging to become my Stockholm sweetie.

Okay, talk is over, words are placid and weak. Back it with action or it all comes off cheap. Watch close while I work now, feel the electric shock of my touch, open my trembling flower, or your petals I'll crush."

THE CLOSEST CALL

RESOURCES

FBI. (2020, July 21). *Israel Keyes*. FBI. Retrieved March 3, 2020, from https://vault.fbi.gov/israel-keyes

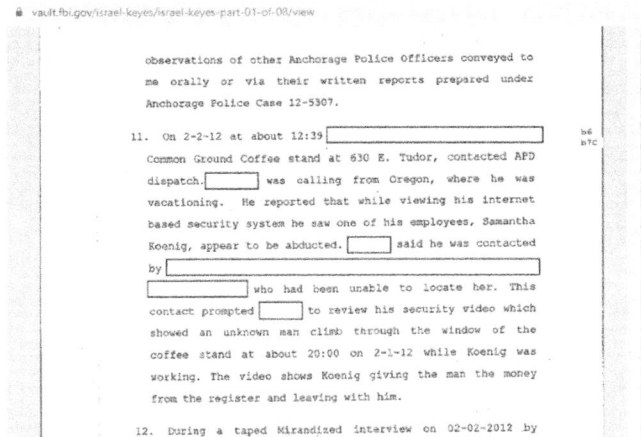

vault.fbi.gov/israel-keyes/israel-keyes-part-01-of-08/view

observations of other Anchorage Police Officers conveyed to me orally or via their written reports prepared under Anchorage Police Case 12-5307.

11. On 2-2-12 at about 12:39 [   ]   b6 b7C
Common Ground Coffee stand at 630 E. Tudor, contacted APD dispatch. [   ] was calling from Oregon, where he was vacationing. He reported that while viewing his internet based security system he saw one of his employees, Samantha Koenig, appear to be abducted. [   ] said he was contacted by [   ] who had been unable to locate her. This contact prompted [   ] to review his security video which showed an unknown man climb through the window of the coffee stand at about 20:00 on 2-1-12 while Koenig was working. The video shows Koenig giving the man the money from the register and leaving with him.

12. During a taped Mirandized interview on 02-02-2012 by

49, True. *Joe Millionaire*. Independently Published, 2022.

Hunter, J. T. (2016). *Devil in the darkness: The true story of serial killer Israel Keyes*. RJ Parker Publishing Inc.

"TopNotchDocumentaries." *YouTube*, YouTube, https://www.youtube.com/@TopNotchDocumentaries.

The Charley Project, formerly posted Currier file, https://charleyproject.org/

ktuu. "FBI Interviews with Israel Keyes." *SoundCloud*, 1 Apr. 2019, soundcloud.com/alaska-news-ktuu/sets/fbi-interviews-with-israel Accessed 4 Mar. 2020.

Valdes, Ana M. "5 Years Later, Police Still Searching for Killers of Mother, Daughter Outside Town Center Mall." *The Palm Beach Post*, 13 Dec. 2012, www.palmbeachpost.com/story/news/crime/2012/12/12/5-years-later-police-still/7260325007/.

Sawyer, D. (2014, April 4). *Church of Wells has parents asking questions*. YouTube. https://www.youtube.com/watch?v=Hx3bMdz1XOk

Smith, S. (2014, January 10). *Sinners in the hands*. Texas Monthly. https://www.texasmonthly.com/articles/sinners-in-the-hands/

Demer, L. (2009, April 9). Prostitution kingpin ordered to pay $3.6 million. *Anchorage Daily News*.

Grove, C. (2012, March 22). Details emerge about man in Koenig case. *Anchorage Daily News*.

The Mob Reporter. (2018). Israel Keyes 5 — FBI interrogation [Video]. In *YouTube*. https://www.youtube.com/watch?v=9bZtXcz_ues&t=229s

What Happens to a Man after Sex? | Metromale Clinic & Fertility Center. 5 Jan. 2023, https://metromaleclinic.com/what-happens-to-a-man-after-sex/.

Ancestry®. (n.d.). Family Tree, Genealogy & Family History Records. Retrieved March 3, 2023, from https://www.ancestry.com/

Reclaim The Records. (1998). *New Jersey marriage index (brides) - 1998 - surnames A-H*. https://archive.org/details/NJ_Marriage_Index_Brides_1998_A -H/mode/1up

Staff Reporter, Free Press. "Video of Bank Robbery Released." *Burlington Free Press*, 11 Nov. 2010, p. 13.

Douglas, John E., and Mark Olshaker. *Mindhunter: Inside the FBI's Elite Serial Crime Unit*. First Gallery Books trade paperback edition, Gallery Books, 2017.

THE CLOSEST CALL

.

True Crime 49 is a group of individuals who share their experiences in the Last Frontier. The most violent state in the nation has many stories to tell of betrayal, injustice, and everyday people.

Listen to the True Crime 49 Podcast

Available on most podcast platforms

Visit the blog

truecrime49.blogspot.com/

.

Printed in Great Britain
by Amazon